THE PHILIP LARKIN I KNEW

MANCHESTER
UNIVERSITY PRESS

THE
PHILIP LARKIN
I KNEW

Maeve Brennan

MANCHESTER
UNIVERSITY PRESS
Manchester and New York

distributed exclusively in the USA by Palgrave

Copyright © Maeve Brennan 2002

The right of Maeve Brennan to be identified as the author of this work has been asserted by her in accordance with the Copyright, Designs and Patent Act 1988

Published by Manchester University Press
Oxford Road, Manchester M13 9NR, UK
and Room 400, 175 Fifth Avenue, New York, NY 10010, USA
www.manchesteruniversitypress.co.uk

Distributed exclusively in the USA by
Palgrave, 175 Fifth Avenue, New York, NY 10010, USA

Distributed exclusively in Canada by
UBC Press, University of British Columbia, 2029 West Mall,
Vancouver, BC, Canada V6T 1Z2

British Library Cataloguing-in-Publication Data
A catalogue record for this book is available from the British Library

Library of Congress Cataloging-in-Publication Data applied for

ISBN 0 7190 6275 6   *hardback*
      0 7190 6276 4   *paperback*

First published 2002
10 09 08 07 06 05 04 03 02   10 9 8 7 6 5 4 3 2 1

Typeset by Carnegie Publishing, Lancaster
Printed in Great Britain
by Bookcraft (Bath) Ltd, Midsomer Norton

For James Booth and Jean Hartley
without whose encouragement and help
this memoir would not have been written

Contents

List of illustrations

The illustrations appear between p. 84 and p. 85

Acknowledgements

In the course of writing this book, I have consulted many people whom I should like to thank for their help. First of all, friends, colleagues and others who have given me information or allowed me to quote from letters, conversations and interviews. These include Jim Allcroft, Joyce Bellamy, Fr Jerome Bertram, Sally Boston, Freda Carroll, George and Tina Cole, Brian Cox, Peter Crowther, Jean Curtis, Pauline Dennison, David Gerard, Mark Hancocks, George Hartley, Anthony Hedges, Anne Holbrook, John Hooton, Patricia Hurst, Terry King, Molly and Maurice le Pape, Ann McKeown, Wendy Mann, Alan Marshall, John Merriman, Natasha Merriman, Brenda Moon, John Morris, Angela Myers, Dilys Rees, Janice Rossen, Lesley Scarr, Gillian Scott, Mary Simpson, Bob Smeaton, Patsy Stoneman, Fr Anthony Storey, Ted Tarling, Trevor Tolley, David Watson and Geoff Weston.

Secondly, I wish to record my gratitude to those who read the earlier and later versions or parts of my manuscript, and for their helpful recommendations: Ray Brett, Charles Brook, Margaret Casson, Frances Curnock-Newton, Win Dawson, Brian Dyson, John Farrell, Margaret Fowler, Audrey Hall, Pam Heath, Don Lee, Angela Leighton, Virginia Peace, Ruth Siverns and Elaine Sommerville. My thanks are also due to Anthony Thwaite and Andrew Motion, the Literary Executors of Larkin's Estate, who read the completed manuscript.

I should like to record special thanks to the following members of my family who have helped in various ways, not least with their patience: Dermot and Patricia Brennan, Claire Brennan, Edward Brennan (junior), Moira Robinson, Michael Robinson and Nellye Woolerton. I am particularly indebted to Margaret McNally who gave much appreciated advice at a sensitive time. My father, Edward Brennan, whose anecdotes provided so much of the historic information in 'My proper ground' died before I even wrote it. He was a compelling raconteur and I never tired of listening to his accounts of his student days and his early experiences in (dental) practice. Recording them is a tribute to his memory.

Jim Sutton, who in letters and conversation, contributed greatly to my understanding of Philip Larkin as a young man also unfortunately died before this memoir was completed. I am most grateful, however, to his widow, Madge, and his daughter Daphne Ingram, for giving me permission to quote from his letters to me. Thanks are due to the Society of Authors on behalf of the Estate of Philip Larkin, and to the Archives Department of the Brynmor Jones Library for permission to quote from Larkin's letters to Jim Sutton. Acknowledgement is also due to the Society of Authors on behalf of the Estate of Philip Larkin, for permission to reproduce Philip's letters to me and also photographs taken by him.

I wish to thank Faber and Faber Ltd for permission to include three letters published in *Selected Letters of Philip Larkin 1940–1985*, ed. Anthony Thwaite (1992) and the following institutions and individuals for the use of photographs: the University of Hull Photographic Service; Yorkshire Post Newspapers; Gloria Gaffney; Suzuyo Kamitani and Alan Marshall.

Thanks are due to Angela Morkos who undertook the typing of my manuscript initially, and to Ann Schultz who later took over this task and simultaneously transferred the text onto computer disk for my editor. Not only am I indebted to her for her patience in deciphering my writing and interpreting my often complicated instructions, but also for her unsolicited enthusiasm for what to me was an entirely new venture in writing.

Lastly, my deepest gratitude is reserved for the members of the Sub-Committee on Publications of the Philip Larkin Society, James Booth, Jean Hartley and John Osborne without whose guidance this memoir would not have taken its present form. In addition, James Booth undertook the task of editing my text and skilfully welded its different elements into a harmonious whole. I am immensely grateful to him, not only for voluntarily assuming this chore, but also for his unfailing encouragement of a somewhat reluctant writer. Likewise, my debt to Jean Hartley, whose constant guidance and reading of my manuscript have spurred me on, is enormous.

Introduction

This memoir is a candid account of my friendship with Philip Larkin. Inevitably, it will be criticised as biased but I have tried to record events and feelings as accurately as he himself defined his emotions on the copy of 'The Dance' he gave me, 'long afterwards, with undimmed memories'.

It has not been my intention to make any special claim about my relationship with Philip Larkin. The fact that I saw it as romantic and idealistic does not mean that I believe his other affairs lacked these, or equally valid, qualities. On the contrary, I recognise that each liaison was unique, and therefore important to Philip, and that I played no more nor less a part in his life (with the exception of Monica Jones, his companion of nearly 40 years) than other close women friends. It is, however, only *my* association with him that this memoir attempts to describe and analyse, without presuming to draw comparisons or make egocentric claims.

What I have tried to show is that Larkin's life contained a good deal more happiness and enjoyment than is generally supposed, and that he himself was considerably more compassionate, generous and warm-hearted than autobiographical, biographical and critical works published since his death have revealed. The most effective way I could demonstrate this, as I ultimately learned, was to describe my relationship with him openly, chronicling both its frustrations and its fulfilments.

But this has not been easy, realising, as I did after several false starts, that in order to portray the Philip Larkin I knew, I was obliged to overcome a lifetime habit of reserve and reticence. I intended initially to write only an objective analysis of Larkin's letters to Sutton, which would enable me to circumvent reference to my own close friendship with Larkin, since the letters pre-dated the Hull years. Larkin scholar, Dr James Booth's comment on reading this account was: 'The best contribution you could make to Larkin scholarship would be to reveal what *you* knew of Larkin, something no-one else can do.' The idea was anathema to me. Later Dr John Osborne, editor of *Bête Noire* magazine and authority on Hull poets, observed: 'This book is crying out for a detailed account of the Hull years from all aspects, and you are the obvious person to write it.' Professor Brian Cox, formerly of Hull, advised: 'If you write a memoir, you really need to be willing to give maximum information about your relationship with Philip. You might not wish to do this' (27.i.97).

Of these suggestions, Osborne's struck me as reasonable and appealing for I felt I could write up the Hull years objectively and still remain detached. But of course the narrative did not come to life until I was able to write unselfconsciously. Thus, very gradually, it became easier to record experiences and emotions without obfuscation or embarrassment, until eventually it seemed natural to write with a frankness which at one time I should have considered inconceivable and undesirable.

Philip himself was reticent about love and never spoke in public of his female friendships. In the closing years of his life he was occasionally accompanied at public events by Monica Jones, and there was no attempt to conceal the fact that she was living with him at the end of his life. Apart from that, however, only the love poems hint at other women in his life. He probably would not approve of this account of our friendship but without telling it, I could not have portrayed the Philip Larkin I knew.

The day before he died, a woman I did not know asked me how he was, adding that she was sorry he was so ill, although neither of us suspected his death was so imminent. She told me she worked in the University bookshop and recognised me as a member of the Library staff as well as a friend of Larkin's. She went on to say, somewhat apologetically, how much she and the other counter staff in the bookshop disliked him, finding him arrogant, boorish and bad-tempered. I was astonished and felt affronted by this as I, who knew him well, had always found him gentle, courteous, generous and witty.

In the years since Philip's death, I have come to realise that neither of us had the true measure of his personality. But it was not until I read his letters to his school friend, Jim Sutton, that I began to have some appreciation of Larkin's extraordinary complexity and chameleon-like characteristics. In fact I learnt a very great deal from them which had been hidden from me in his lifetime: his predilection for bad language; his self-obsession; his tight-fistedness; his contempt for the Establishment. All these are revealed in his letters, as well as the characteristics I knew: the idealism, the lyricism and the romanticism; the wit and the *joie de vivre*. In these letters, written by a youthful Philip whom I never knew, the philistine and the cynic war with the romantic and the perfectionist, clearly showing the youth as father to the man.

My own acquaintance with Jim Sutton began when, in 1987, I was researching Philip Larkin's early life for the biographical sketch which I had been asked to write for *The Modern Academic Library* (1989). Philip had often spoken of his youthful friendship with Sutton and the stimulating correspondence which followed their schooldays. My contact with Jim was fruitful from the beginning as he skilfully gave me, in answer to my enquiries, an insight into the content of the letters and their importance in tracing Larkin's early literary development. In May 1988 he suggested coming to Hull, partly because of the re-awakened interest in his *rôle* in Larkin's life – the letters had already excited the interest of biographers and editors – and partly to meet me who had revived his affection for his former friend. As he was about to depart, I enquired casually what he intended doing with the letters, conceitedly imagining that I might nudge him into leaving them to Hull, and having no idea of their market value. To my consternation, he replied that they were to be sold at auction in six weeks' time. He explained that he had been advised that the University of Hull had no spare cash for extravagant purchases – the reserve price I had by now learnt was £30,000 – consequently he had not approached the obvious repository for such a rich Larkin archive.

By chance, within half an hour of seeing Sutton off, I was due at a committee meeting of the newly formed Friends of the Brynmor Jones Library. Raising funds for purchases outside the scope of the library's budget was its *raison d'être*, but this was a very ambitious undertaking. Nevertheless, the committee eagerly supported the decisive strategy of the Librarian, Ian Mowat, for launching an appeal whereby whatever sum was raised by the Friends would be increased proportionately by such grant-giving bodies as the Victoria and Albert Museum, the National Heritage Memorial Fund and others. Mowat, with assistance from the archivist, Brian Dyson, and me, promoted the appeal with such zeal and success that by 22 June 1988, the date of the auction, the Friends had secured pledges – from all sources – of more than £80,000, a sum considerably in excess of the sale price of almost £36,000 (including commission). But without the advance information I had so fortuitously obtained, it would not have been possible to organise the fund-raising in time. My meeting with Sutton could not have been more opportune. Happily it also led to a rewarding friendship which continued until Alzheimer's disease undermined Jim's health. He died in November 1997.

Thus I came to read the Sutton letters, written before Philip came to Hull, in the very library in which he and I had worked together for three decades. Christie's had described the 'Sutton letters' in their sale catalogue for Wednesday 22 June 1988 as 'A unique twentieth century statement of the growth of a poet's mind'. Anthony Thwaite, in his introduction to the *Selected Letters* writes of these particular letters: 'They are very much a portrait of the artist as a young man.' Larkin himself facetiously used variations of this description when reporting his literary endeavours to Sutton. As I read the letters, with their vivid narrative of Larkin's interests and preoccupations from 1938 to 1952, I found much that was new and unfamiliar to me, though much, also, which recalled the Philip I had known. Inevitably I found myself struggling to reconcile the youth who comes to life in this correspondence with the mature man I knew in the second half of his life. And it was this struggle which precipitated the writing of the memoir which follows.

As Philip had invariably presented his 'better' side to me, I had been unaware of his darker traits, or failed to recognise them. Although, quite early in our friendship, he struck me as the most egocentric person I have ever known, it was not in a ruthless, selfish sense. On the contrary, he was regretfully aware that this defect prevented him from making an ultimate personal commitment. In order to write, he would explain, he needed to be completely untrammelled by emotional and temporal involvement with others. As he put it to Sutton, 'It's not much of a talent that can be overthrown by deeper contacts with other people'.[1] He made the same point to me less bluntly 20 years later, and it was obvious that it was something to which he had given serious thought from an early age. The need to be alone, to reserve so much of himself, he explained, would make him a very unsatisfactory husband, no matter how attractive marriage might at times appear. Larkin was in fact aware of his limitations, and far from condemning him I found his frankness endearing, honest and acceptable, if a high price to pay for genius.

Similarly, I was incredulous the first time I heard the charge of meanness levelled against him as I had always found him excessively generous. He never went on holiday without bringing me back a present. Once, he went to Leeds on business for the afternoon and returned with a silk scarf (in those days a most expensive luxury). Whenever I hosted a party or a dinner, he would turn up with a more extravagant gift than the token chocolates or wine, or he would order a lavish bouquet of flowers to be delivered.

[1] *Selected Letters of Philip Larkin 1940–1985*, ed. Anthony Thwaite (London: Faber, 1992), 116. Subsequent references (*SL*) are bracketed in the text.

As for offensive language, I never heard Larkin use it. In fact, so surprised was I to learn from the letters to Sutton that its use was commonplace in their school (an independent day school in the 1930s) that I drew Jim's attention to it. He explained that the use of four-letter words was the *lingua franca* of the peer group to which he and Larkin belonged, and an essential qualification for membership. It was a means of releasing the pent-up frustration he felt in the midst of his family, something he found all the more repressive once he had gone up to Oxford. By his first vacation, the air raids on Coventry had forced Larkin's parents to seek refuge in Lichfield with relatives whom he found even more exasperating than his immediate family. He told Sutton he longed 'to return to Oxford just to get into the company of people under the age of 40. People I can swear to' (20.xii.[40]).[2] In the meantime he could only vent his irritation in letters to Sutton: 'My tooth still aches. Balls & anus! I feel shat upon' (9.xii.40).

I had been on the Library staff two years when Larkin took up his post at the University of Hull in March 1955. From 1960 we became close friends, and for the next eighteen years we spent a great deal of leisure time together. While we shared many interests in addition to professional concerns, one notable difference, which could be expected to drive us poles apart, was my religion – Roman Catholicism. Paradoxically, it created a singular affinity between us. Again I was fascinated to find the same spiritual Larkin I had known, in more youthful, ingenuous guise in the letters to his schoolfriend. One letter in particular, the self-styled 'Moment of Ecstasy' letter (17.viii.43), seemed to make explicit so much which had been implicit in our relationship. Since this letter is not included in Anthony Thwaite's edition of the *Selected Letters* I have reproduced it in full following Chapter 5.

The 'Moment of Ecstasy' letter shows Larkin in an unusual light. It is full of idealism, raises ethical issues and is sharply critical of contemporary values. It is thought-provoking and is expressed in very lyrical language with all the fervour of a moralist. It would be easy to dismiss it as a typical essay in youthful exhibitionism which any twenty-one-year-old might dash off on the spur of the moment. But in both style and subject matter it is quite untypical of the Larkin who, at nineteen, had written an obscene parody of 'La Belle Dame Sans Merci', which he described to Sutton as 'the latest work of the brilliant new Post-Masturbationist Poet,

---

[2] 20.xii.[40]. Henceforward, where letters (or passages in letters) to Sutton or to me, are not included in the *Selected Letters*, the date is given bracketed in the text.

Shaggerybox McPhallus. This new book of verse, "The Escaped Cock", deals almost exclusively with problems of intense spiritual value' he explained (4.xii.[41]). It is difficult to visualise the author of the 'Moment of Ecstasy' letter and the young lout who helped a fellow-student to wreck another student's room as the same person (7.iii.[42]). Its substance has nothing in common with the man who denounced his female contemporaries at Oxford as 'stupid, silly, and ineffectual ... inferior to men in particulars and in a queer general way which robs them of "sparkle", of style, of clarity of character' (28.vii.43). Most of all, it was uncharacteristic of Larkin to proclaim his finer sentiments in such detail. On the contrary, fearful of being ridiculed, or of uncovering a weakness in himself, he invariably belittled his deeper feelings except in the company of very close – often women – friends.

I therefore had no difficulty in recognising the 'Moment of Ecstasy' letter as entirely characteristic of the Larkin I knew. Nevertheless, in 1989 I was still astonished to read in this letter the same idealistic views on love and marriage which he had voiced to me in the 1960s, and penned twenty years earlier still – a time span of 46 years. It still strikes me as a remarkable consistency. The observations about divorce are particularly poignant because Larkin was always genuinely distressed when friends' marriages broke up. I found the letter reassuring, especially after recognising how oversimplified my judgement of him had been: it restored my faith in him. At the same time, it enabled me to put into perspective some bewildering aspects of our relationship which I sensed, but was reluctant to probe, at the time.

Reading these letters, I could almost hear Larkin's soft, low voice, suppressing a chuckle or openly chortling with laughter as he unfolded jokes or enlivened his narratives with witty asides. For humour, throughout his life, was the antidote to his endemic pessimism. It was what made him such an amiable companion. It transmuted all his darker thoughts and transformed malice to goodwill. It was often gentle; sometimes acerbic; often narrative; always funny: more often than not it was turned against himself. It was a natural gift but one which he also cultivated and expected his friends to appreciate.

Larkin's self-disclosures in this correspondence – and in general – have done him a disservice, focusing as he did on his negative traits. When I first read the letters to Sutton, my reaction was one of confusion and distaste: there seemed little in them to redeem his now tarnished image. However, when I read them a second time and penetrated below the surface, I discovered finer qualities – those which had made him attractive to me. Then I remembered the inscription in my copy of *The Whitsun Weddings*: 'To Maeve, who can read between the lines. 1 February 1964.' This, I realise, is what I did thirty years later with the Sutton letters. Perhaps this portrait will encourage others to read between the lines also, and to discover the more humane face of Larkin, not just the 'foul-mouthed bigot', 'sexually-disappointed Eeyore' and 'lyricist of wretchedness' projected by the media since the re-appraisal of Larkin's reputation in the 1990s.

1

My proper ground

My father was born in 1899 and spent his childhood and schooldays in the historic town of Kilkenny in the south-east of Ireland. Before his seventeenth birthday he went up to University College, Dublin, a constituent college of the National University of Ireland, to study dentistry. His student days, 1916 to 1921, corresponded with the most formative period of modern Irish history and many of his contemporaries became founder members of the Irish Free State after 1921. Like most of his fellow students, my father was inevitably drawn into nationalist politics and joined the Irish Volunteers in 1917. Initially formed in 1913 as a moderate citizen army whose aims were defensive and protective, in 1919 it became the Army of the Irish Republic, more popularly known as the Irish Republican Army and subsequently as the IRA. By 1919, my father had ceased to be a volunteer and so was never a member of the IRA. My astonishment was considerable therefore, when shortly after first meeting him, Philip Larkin, with uncanny perception, observed what a strong resemblance my father bore to an IRA man. I explained the tenuous connection but had to admit that even at 60 my father, in the off-white trench coat which he usually wore, together with his brisk walk, had a distinct military bearing. Philip undoubtedly intended no affront as in 1960 the IRA had not yet acquired its subsequent infamous reputation. Nevertheless as a result of his years in Belfast, his natural sympathies, I realised later, were with the Unionists.

Although the Easter Rising had taken place six months before my father went up to Dublin, the city seethed with military activity throughout his student years. Eamon de Valera, Michael Collins, Constance Markievicz and others who had taken prominent parts in the Rising, were familiar figures in the streets of the capital. House-searches were commonplace. One of the lodgings in which my father was living was raided in the small hours by the military police who frisked all the occupants and ordered them to line up against the wall while the house was ransacked for incriminating evidence. Their suspect was the landlady's daughter, a member of the Cumann na mBann (League of Women), an organisation whose principal role was first aid, ambulance driving and catering, but whose members were also trained to handle firearms. On another occasion my father himself was on a list of suspects: his company commanding-officer's notebook, in which details of all his men appeared, had been found. The police called at the address listed for my father which he had fortunately left, the landlady nobly denying all knowledge of his subsequent whereabouts.

There were frequent gun battles in the streets, especially in the narrow alley ways in the slum districts. One main thoroughfare near the city centre, where the road suddenly narrowed, overshadowed by tall buildings, was a notorious lair for snipers and was known locally as the Dardanelles. On 21 November 1920 my father and a friend were innocently caught up in the first 'Bloody Sunday' when the Black and Tans, an army of ruthless recruits sent over from England to assist the Royal Irish Constabulary in their combat against the IRA, shot dead twelve spectators at a Gaelic football match. This act was in reprisal for the IRA assassination, that morning, of eleven British Army intelligence agents living under cover in the city. My father and his friend had just left a late morning Mass and were walking along a main road when they heard the all-too-familiar sound of shots being fired at random from a convoy of approaching Crossley tenders, the transport used by the Black and Tans. In the nick of time, my father and his friend leapt over the counter of a nearby news vendor's booth and crouched under cover till the tenders had passed, still firing indiscriminately. When they later learned of the Black and Tans' mission, and that in addition to the twelve dead, sixty more spectators had been injured, they realised how easily they too could have been numbered amongst the casualties.

In the early years of the century not only was Dublin lively politically, it was also very stimulating culturally. Two of its leading poets, Padraig Pearse and James Connolly, immortalised by Yeats in 'Easter 1916' and 'Sixteen Dead Men', were executed for their part in the Easter Rebellion. These were the years of fruition of the late nineteenth-century Irish Literary Revival, inspired by Lady Gregory and the writers she brought together, Synge, Wilde, Shaw, A. E. and Yeats. The Abbey Theatre, which she and Yeats were instrumental in setting up, was a vibrant vehicle of nationalist and republican feeling which found its most realistic expression in O'Casey's trilogy of plays highlighting the tragic impact which the fight for independence had on the lives of the Dublin poor.[3]

[3] *The Shadow of a Gunman* (1923), *Juno and the Paycock* (1924) and *The Plough and the Stars* (1926).

Yeats, and his friend Maud Gonne, were familiar figures in the Dublin of those days. They were an impressive pair; both were tall and eccentric in their dress. He wore a long black cloak and soft wide hat; she invariably wore widow's weeds (her husband, John MacBride, had also been executed by the British Government for his role in the Rebellion and is commemorated in 'Easter 1916'), was always escorted by her pet Great Dane, and even though then in her fifties was strikingly good-looking. Forty-five years later when Philip Larkin likened me to Maud Gonne, my father retorted: '*You* like Maud Gonne? Don't be ridiculous. *She* was very beautiful, even in middle age!' Yeats had pursued her unsuccessfully from 1889 to 1917 (when he married), and even afterwards: 'I was twenty-three years old when the troubling of my life began' he wrote of her in his *Memoirs*.

Not only was Maud a society beauty, she was also a militant feminist and, although not Irish by birth, a fervent nationalist. She was imprisoned in Holloway for her seditious activities, like her close friend, Constance Markievicz, who suffered a similar fate. Constance, née Gore-Booth, came of a prominent Anglo-Irish ascendancy family, married a Polish count, and was even more militant in nationalist politics than Maud Gonne. She had fought in the Easter Rising for which she was sentenced to hard labour in Aylesbury Jail: it is doubtful if many countesses have scrubbed floors in an English prison in the twentieth century. On her release my father was amongst the crowds who lined the streets of Dublin to give her a heroine's welcome home. After her death in 1927, Yeats recalled his first meeting with her and her poet sister in 1894 at their home, Lissadell, in Sligo, in the poem 'In Memory of Eva Gore-Booth and Constance Markiewicz': 'Two girls in silk kimonos, both / Beautiful, one a gazelle.' Philip first drew my attention to this poem when he visited Lissadell in the late 1960s; he was captivated by the area on account of its dramatic scenery, its associations with Yeats (who is buried in nearby Drumcliff), and the fact that Queen Maeve is reputed to be buried on one of the mountains dominating Sligo Bay!

At the time, my father did not consider the historic and cultural backcloth to his undergraduate years as romantic. He took it for granted as all part of the stimulation of student life. Furthermore he had too little money for such indulgent thoughts. In the days before student grants were readily available, his father paid his accommodation and tuition fees directly, but *my* father's personal allowance was one shilling a week in the first year and rose to five shillings in the fifth year! The intention was that shortage of money would keep him out of mischief, which it did, although he did find ways of augmenting his income a little. One was to order on account, which my grandfather paid for, more sheet gold, used for fillings, than he needed and to sell the surplus to a pawnbroker, in those days, the student's closest ally. Those who lived at home had easier access to pawnable goods; one of his friends regularly removed a painting from the wall or a piece of cut glass or silver from the sideboard when he needed cash. By and large he replaced what he appropriated, but questions were never asked if the gaps remained permanent, for his was a well-to-do family. Thus, it was not until thirty years later, when I became fascinated with my father's matter-of-fact accounts of his student days that he realised, in spite of the hardships, how privileged he had been to witness the political and intellectual re-birth of his country.

Neither was his early professional life without colourful incident. In the autumn of 1921, unable to find work in Ireland, his first post was as an assistant in a practice in Barnstaple, Devon. However in August 1922, unable to settle there, he secured another assistant's post in Hull where he immediately felt at home, especially after the kindly intervention of a senior colleague resolved an unexpected dilemma. My father had been offered, and foolishly accepted, the job without an interview, only to discover on arrival that his would-be employer was unqualified, a not uncommon situation at that time. The 1921 Dental Act, in an attempt to regulate the profession, permitted dentists without professional qualifications to continue in practice on condition that they revealed their limitations. The dentist in question had failed to do just this in preliminary negotiations and on discovering the deception, my father refused the job which seemed to leave him no alternative but to return to Dublin, ticketless and penniless. However, a local doctor whose advice he sought, referred him to the senior dental surgeon in the city, Charles Charter, who fortuitously knew of a neighbouring colleague in need of an assistant. An interview was arranged and my father was engaged on the spot. He never forgot the man whose altruistic intervention brought about this happy conclusion: he became his patient, and remained with the practice of Charter and Wilkinson until it closed forty years later.

After a year or so, my father obtained the temporary post of manager of an adjacent practice which he ran for two years at the end of which he had either to look for another assistant's post or set up in practice on his own. He rashly took the second option even though his prospects were very precarious. He needed premises, instruments and equipment but had no money, and no patients; and banks, in those days, were

11

unwilling to lend to youthful would-be borrowers who had no guaranteed income. With considerable faith, my maternal grandfather (before my parents were married) put down the deposit for some modest premises in Newland Avenue, Hull, while my father used a small legacy to buy basic equipment. For the rest, he and an equally impecunious colleague who had just inherited his father's run-down practice, agreed to buy and share apparatus jointly, as they could afford it. Neither of them drove so they exchanged and delivered equipment by bicycle.

The contrast between today's well-equipped, hi-tech, purpose-designed surgery and the austere, rudimentary, and in my father's case, even makeshift surgery of eighty years ago is inconceivable. A similar comparison would be between the kitchen or bathroom in the 1920s household. All were drab, bare and extremely basic. Likewise, dentistry itself was crude and primitive compared with today's highly sophisticated procedures. At the Dental Hospital in Dublin, which presumably had the latest equipment when my father did his practical training, the extraction of teeth was a very crude process. The operation was performed in the basement, which resembled a dungeon with very little natural light. The patient was strapped across the chest and legs into a shaped wooden box, known, for obvious reasons, as 'the coffin'. Anaesthesia was not only primitive but dangerous. Nitrous oxide was administered in just sufficient quantity to make the patient comatose. If this failed and the patient struggled, fellow students who were awaiting their turn to operate simply held the patient down by force. It was many years in the future before research into patient trauma was undertaken. My father had a fund of horrific anecdotes of his early experiences in practice. Most had an amusing twist: in fact, without a sense of humour he would have found it very difficult to carry on. Preventive dental care was not a priority for most people between the wars, especially in the north of England – although my father always tried to insist on this – so that in the early years patients were slow to materialise and when they did were often even slower to pay their bills. Non-payment of accounts at Christmas, for instance, could mean the difference for us between a feast and a frugal meal. Even in the 1940s, before the advent of the National Health Service, when my brother, sister and I were at school, I remember my father saying at times that he did not know how he would pay the following term's school fees.

My father and mother met in 1925 through an aunt of hers with whom my father lodged for a short time before setting up in practice on his own. My mother, Gladys (*née* Moody), was born in 1902 in Beverley where she lived with her parents and two younger sisters until she married my father in 1927. The three sisters were educated at a small private school where the main emphasis was on good manners and preparation for marriage. My mother never went out to work but managed a decorating materials shop owned by my grandfather, who ran a painting and decorating business. All three sisters were strikingly good-looking but my mother in particular attracted the attention of a local artist, Fred Elwell, R.A. (1870–1958) who wanted to paint her as a young woman in her late teens.

Although not well-known nationally, Elwell exhibited 190 pictures at the Royal Academy and some of his paintings have been popularly reproduced on greetings cards. Amongst these are *The First Born* (1913) and *The Last Cab* (1931). He painted several authentic scenes of kitchen staff at work and at play in the Beverley Arms Hotel, notably *The Beverley Arms Kitchen* and *Elevenses*. He did not, however, paint my mother. Her parents forbade it, considering all artists to be of dubious reputation, even though they knew the Elwells were a highly respected Beverley family. Fred Elwell's father, a master wood-carver and cabinet-maker, designed and executed the exquisite carving of the choir screen, commissioned by Sir Gilbert Scott, in Beverley Minster.

My father was a great admirer of the artist's work and often voiced his regret that Mother was forbidden to sit for Elwell. In 1993, the Ferens Art Gallery in Hull, which owns *The First Born*, put on a major exhibition of his work. The younger of my mother's sisters, then aged 84, asked me to take her to see it. She proved a fascinating guide as she was able to identify many of the sitters and the settings in which they were painted.

Notwithstanding my mother's lack of conventional education, she was highly intelligent and articulate. Under my father's guidance, she was an avid reader and throughout her life she had a far greater ability to choose the recreational books he liked than ever I had. They used to read to one another in bed, my father usually starting the ritual, with my mother taking over until he fell asleep. They shared a love of music and were keen collectors of gramophone records with which they entertained their circle of friends, particularly in the early days of their marriage. Like all young girls of her time, my mother learned to play the piano and sang quite sweetly.

Before she married, my mother, who was brought up an Anglican, converted to Catholicism as she thought it would facilitate the upbringing of any children in my father's faith. I was born in 1929, my brother,

Dermot, in 1931 and my sister, Moira, in 1933. Before Dermot was born we moved from the poky little house where my father first set up in practice to a more suitable house on Beverley High Road where we stayed for five years before transferring to a larger, Victorian house a few doors away, very conveniently arranged for the separation of the practice from the living quarters. Philip Larkin became a frequent visitor to this house from 1960 to 1977 when my father and I left it following my mother's death. If life was a financial struggle for my parents we, as children, were unaware of it. We were well fed and neatly dressed; we had a fortnight's holiday by the sea in summer; we had bulging pillow-cases of books and toys at Christmas. Moreover up to the war we always had live-in help who looked after us, let the patients in and did the cleaning. My mother ran the house and did all the cooking.

At the outbreak of war, the maid left to work in a munitions factory which meant that my mother took over her work and acted as my father's receptionist. By June 1940, however, my brother, sister and I had been sent into the country to escape the expected bombardment of Hull. During some of the worst raids in 1941, more than once, my parents were ordered to leave our home at short notice because unexploded bombs, and once a landmine, were discovered nearby. On one such occasion, they were told to leave immediately and not to wait around for public transport: bicycles were almost the only form of private transport then. They therefore started walking towards Beverley, to seek refuge at my grandmother's, my father wheeling his cycle alongside my mother, who was carrying, of all things, a budgerigar in a cage, until a bus finally picked her up. I cannot imagine how my parents came to have a caged bird. I can only guess that my mother volunteered to house it for a neighbour who had left 'for the duration'. Anyway, it never came back to Hull and lived happily at my grandmother's until it died.[4] Dogs were a different matter. We had always had dogs until the raids started, when the Airedale we had had since I was very small had to be put to sleep as he was absolutely terrified by the sound of gunfire and falling bombs, just as he had always been of thunderstorms. Dogs resumed their place in the household after the war and succeeded one another until the last one died, much to my grief, in April 1999.

The war years were hard but challenging for my parents as the somewhat

---

[4] My brother's recollection is different. He maintains that we had the budgerigar before the war and associates it with a particular event on Easter Monday 1938. I find this surprising as none of us liked caged birds: perhaps it belonged to the maid.

nomadic life-style which circumstances often thrust upon them imparted a certain instability to their lives. My mother was less agile than my father and was already beginning to be troubled by the arthritis which later all but crippled her. But she had an indomitable spirit, was gregarious and mostly cheerful, and always gentle, warm-hearted and hospitable. Everyone liked her for she was a sympathetic listener and was always ready to pour oil on troubled waters. As a young child I *hated* Wednesday afternoons when I returned home from school, knowing Mother would not be there. From the time of her marriage until my grandmother's death in 1953 my mother visited her twice a week, on Wednesdays and Saturdays. I didn't mind Saturdays as my father took us for long walks, but on Wednesdays, there was only the maid to give us our tea, and she had no time or inclination to listen to our prattle about school as Mother did.

In common with most children of that time, we were not allowed much freedom and certainly never went anywhere without permission. For one thing we lived on a main road and furthermore we only went to friends when invited. However, my mother always kept open house and made our school friends welcome. Both my parents were good at managing our pre-war children's parties. My father devised a thrilling game called 'Daggers' which derived its name from the fact that he carried a black and silver rubber dagger. He used to go off and hide – anywhere in the house which was full of nooks and crannies and long corridors – and it was then the children's challenge to find him. Whoever found him shouted 'daggers'. This game was highly popular with the older children who clamoured for it time and again, but some of the younger ones were less confident and stayed with my mother who provided quieter forms of entertainment for them. Needless to say, she prepared splendid party food.

The war, of course, put a stop to parties of all kinds, at least in air-raid-prone cities like Hull. Even so, when my parents were not taking refuge in Beverley, or visiting us in the country, our well-built underground air-raid shelter was a focal point of hospitality in the area. Air-raid wardens, firewatchers, policemen, first-aid officers and anyone else who happened to be out-and-about during a raid, knew that tea and sandwiches would be available in the Brennans' shelter which naturally became a regular check point on their rounds. My father did regular firewatching duty and one of the men who shared his watch worked at a nearby grocer's. Whenever he could he smuggled a packet of tea, sugar or biscuits to Mother to help supplement this nightly hospitality. She also made it her business to be on good terms with the staff of the Co-operative store beside us who occasionally slipped extra butter, meat or cheese into the weekly order, but of course provisions were never lavish. Nevertheless, in spite of the rationing of practically every commodity, my mother always managed to find enough to share with strangers.

From the age of five we attended Endsleigh primary school, close to our home, which was run by the Sisters of Mercy. When the war broke out in September 1939 we went to live at my grandmother's in Beverley where we went to a smaller convent school while my parents returned to Hull each day. When France fell in June 1940 we were dispatched to the Yorkshire Wolds as part of a mass schools' evacuation programme. Plans had earlier been made for us to go to Ireland: Moira and I were to have gone as boarders to the Ursuline convent in Sligo, where cousins of ours were pupils, while Dermot had been enrolled at the Marist College in Dundalk. Our tickets had been purchased but at the eleventh hour my mother would not let us go. All my life I have had a niggling regret that I did not go to school in Sligo. Situated on the banks of the swift-flowing Garavogue, which is dominated on either side at its exit to the sea by a high, isolated mountain, Sligo is a small picturesque town, rich in Irish mythology. Knocknarea, the mountain on the south bank of the river, is reputed to be the burial place of Maeve, first century queen of Connaught. Ben Bulben on the north bank, a wild forbidding promontory, is said to be where Dermot, another folk hero, lived and died with his love, Grania. Yeats's maternal relatives, with whom he spent much time, lived in Sligo. He loved the area and is buried in the village of Drumcliff at the foot of Ben Bulben. Inishfree, the lake isle of the poem, is one of many small islands in nearby Lough Gill; Lissadell, the family home of the Gore-Booth sisters is also close by. At ten, of course, I was not aware of these facts although I was familiar with *Diarmuid and Graine*, *The Combat at the Ford* and other Celtic legends associated with this area. When I first visited Sligo many years later, I regretted even more the lost opportunity to spend my school days in such a magical place.

As it was, it was adventure enough in 1940 to leave home and parents at the age of ten, be responsible for my siblings and adapt to a completely different way of life. One Sunday in June, eighty children from our school went, along with our headmistress, Sister Mary Kieran, and three other teachers, by train and bus to Weaverthorpe, in the heart of the Yorkshire Wolds. The village had already hosted one influx of evacuees from Middlesbrough who were rather wild and disorderly. Its inhabitants were therefore not too eager to welcome another batch of undoubtedly unruly townschildren. However, when they saw how well disciplined we were, under the strict supervision of our headmistress, their fears were soon dispelled. For most of the villagers, this was their first close contact with a nun and before long we were approvingly referred to as 'Sister Mary's lot'. Initially, Moira and I were billeted together but we did not like our foster home and after a few weeks separated to go to farms two miles apart. Dermot and his friend, Peter, were happily lodged with an elderly childless couple who lavished on 'them there bairns' the affection for which they had not previously had an outlet.

We found life in the country primitive, but fun. The farmhouses, insofar as they had running water, had better amenities than the cottages in the village, but even they had no electricity or mains gas. Downstairs rooms were lighted by oil lamps or Calor gas and one took a candle to bed. Most of the villagers had to draw water from pumps in the street, which froze in the hard winters. Toilet facilities were an earth closet up the garden path. The elderly couple with whom my brother lived never knew what it was to turn on a tap or switch on a light or plug in any kind of electrical appliance. There were no refrigerators, deep freezers or washing machines and television was a phenomenon yet to come. Baths were taken in a zinc tub in front of the fire; water was heated in a hand-filled copper, also used for the weekly clothes wash, under which a fire was lighted. The multi-purpose kitchen range provided facilities for cooking, hot water, drying clothes, herbs, kindling wood, and for generating warmth. Even in summer it had to be lighted each day if only to cook food or boil a kettle. To us it was all an exciting novelty and we had no difficulty in adapting to what our elders regarded as hardship.

Our parents visited us every fortnight. Most of the children only had their mothers or grandparents to visit them as their fathers were in the forces. My father had applied to join the Army Dental Corps at the outbreak of war but was told that dentists were needed on the home front. He soon discovered that his services were badly needed in Weaverthorpe. With a once-weekly bus service to Malton only, and very few private cars on the roads, visits to the dentist were difficult to arrange, so with the appearance of one in their midst there was no shortage of patients. The schoolmaster offered his large garage, which was also used by the visiting school doctor, as a temporary surgery and very soon my father had a full appointment list on alternate Saturday mornings and Mondays. This proved a very astute move as it compensated for loss of earnings at home, and simultaneously the fortnightly breaks afforded my parents much needed relief from the frequent air raids on Hull. It meant, of course, transporting a certain amount of equipment backwards and forwards, including a foot drill which my father carried for the last five mile lap of the journey if it had to be made on foot. Sometimes a farmer returning from market would pick my parents up at Driffield. At other times the local taxi driver would meet them at Sledmere but often this was not possible as he fulfilled many other roles.

At Weaverthorpe, for instance, he was also a general carrier, coal merchant and bus driver. Each Saturday evening the coal lorry was swept, covered and fitted with seats to provide transport to take us to Mass on Sunday morning at the Sykes family's private chapel in Sledmere House, five miles away. At the foot of a particularly tricky slope, everyone had to dismount and help to push the bus up the hill. My parents made life-long friendships with the schoolmaster and his wife and a farmer's family in Weaverthorpe. My brother regularly went to see the billeting officer until his death in 1997. Each time the latter proudly produced the note book in which he had recorded the names of all the evacuees and the villagers who accommodated them in 1940. Philip Larkin, who was seventeen when the war broke out, never experienced evacuation and consequently was fascinated by my stories of our adventures. He and I frequently drove through Weaverthorpe on our excursions onto the Wolds, but by the mid-1960s most of the friends I had made there had either left or died.

All the evacuees attended the small village school where we were taught either by our own teachers or by the incumbent staff of three. Except those who were dispatched to boarding schools at an earlier age, the village children left at fourteen so there was no routine preparation for secondary education. As time passed, many evacuees' parents, including mine, had to balance further education against their children's safety, and as I approached my twelfth birthday in September 1941, my parents were very anxious that I should begin my secondary schooling. Therefore I returned home to attend St. Mary's High School for Girls in Hull by day, while sleeping at my grandmother's in Beverley. Hull was one of the most heavily bombed cities in the country although it was only ever referred to in news bulletins as a 'north east coast town'. It was believed that any information concerning damage to its efficient functioning as a port of strategic importance would have played into enemy hands.

My new school was run by the same order of nuns as the primary school I had attended and by 1941 both schools were on the same site. St. Mary's had been built on the other side of the city but had been burnt out in a heavy raid that spring. Little was salvaged from the ruins but the school was able to move into the premises of the teacher training college (also run by the nuns) whose students had been evacuated to the safety of the country for the duration of the war. At that time, convent schools, because of their emphasis on discipline and decorum (deportment was actually a section filled in by the headmistress on our term reports), were equally popular with Catholic and Protestant parents. Consequently, non-Catholics outnumbered Catholic pupils by approximately three to one. The only manifest difference our religion made, as far as we were concerned, was that we had Religious Instruction daily while the non-Catholics made a start on their homework. The headmistress was a nun, as were roughly half the teachers; the rest were all women too. My performance in the first year was abysmal, my place in class being well below half way. Knowing I was capable of doing better, my father read the riot act and threatened to withdraw me from the school – where, socially, I was very happy – if I did not improve. The threat was effective and in the following year I climbed to fourth position in form and thereafter maintained a place in the top handful.

The curriculum was conventional and, by today's standards, very limited, with almost total emphasis on arts subjects. In fact the only science subjects taught were mathematics and biology, in both of which I was weak. For several years I had extra coaching in maths, but the only advantage that gave me was an impractical flair for algebra. On the other hand, the teaching of English, French, Latin and History (which, curiously, both Philip Larkin and I studied to Higher School Certificate level) was excellent. Our English teacher, Sister Mary Cyril, was particularly outstanding and innovative in her teaching methods. She instilled into us the rules of grammar and syntax, parsing and précis which I have never forgotten. The breadth of her teaching was wider than the examination curriculum and in the sixth form at least, she endeavoured to cover the major landmarks of English Literature from *Beowulf* to Yeats. (My Early English tutor at University was very surprised that I had studied both Anglo-Saxon and Chaucer at school.) Shakespeare was brought to life by performing the plays as well as studying them in depth. Sister Mary Cyril herself staged some first-rate productions. Greatest emphasis of all, however, was placed on the Romantic writers of the nineteenth century, while scant attention was paid to the major figures of the early twentieth century: our education stopped short of Eliot, Pound and Lawrence. Looking back on my early education, I have frequently been struck by its emphasis on Romantic literature, beginning at the age of three or four, sitting on my father's knee while he read to me 'The Jackdaw

of Rheims', 'The Lady of Shalott' and Keats's ode 'To Autumn'. At school
we concentrated on the tragedies of Shakespeare, the major poets of the
nineteenth century, the novels of the Brontë sisters and the poetry and
fiction of Hardy. Little wonder, therefore, that my outlook on life, as
gleaned from literature, was idealistic, a view in turn supported by the
Church's teaching on the sanctity of marriage and chastity in love.

As a result of the course I ultimately chose, my university education
was a continuation of that which I had received at school. I had been
expected to do well in French at Higher School Certificate and take it at
honours degree level. However, I only managed a pass grade while, to
my complete surprise, I obtained a distinction in History. This deflected
me from my original intention and instead I registered in 1948 for an
honours course in History at the then University College of Hull. I quickly
realised my mistake and transferred the following year to a general degree
course, with French and English as additional subjects. Unlike my father's
time at University, mine was quite uneventful, and when I graduated in
the summer of 1951, I was anxious to finish with studying and earn my
living. The only money I had hitherto earned was during a two-month
spell one long vacation, when I worked for my father as his receptionist.

My decision to go in for librarianship was prompted more by my
determination not to be a teacher than any deep vocational desire to
be a librarian. In 1951 professional careers guidance was practically non-
existent and (like Larkin eight years previously, who similarly secured the
first library post he applied for) I simply applied for the first suitable job
I saw advertised in the local paper, a new post of Music Librarian at Hull
City Libraries. This sounds a great deal more elevated than in fact it was.
My salary (c. £240 p. a. after tax) was the same as the non-professional
assistants on the issue desk in the Lending Library, which department
was responsible for the Music Library. Admittedly, no specialist qualifi-
cations were then required for the post other than a basic knowledge of
classical music. In 1951 music libraries were a relatively new development,
especially when they provided a record lending service which Hull was
about to initiate. The work was undemanding although the issue of
records necessitated considerably more careful handling and scrutiny than
the issue of books. Friday evenings and Saturdays were hectic but during
the rest of the week there were long periods with very little to do. The
Music Library overlooked the Newspaper Reading Room whose idiosyn-
cratic habitués, the down-and-outs who came in out of the cold ostensibly
to look at the papers, occasionally disturbed the tranquillity of my do-
main. If the duty porter, who normally supervised them, was called away,

he would ask me to keep an eye on any recalcitrants whose most serious crime was to take a stealthy swig from a bottle of methylated spirits or beer concealed in an overcoat pocket. This of course contravened library regulations. I hated having to go in and remonstrate with offenders but I disliked even more penetrating the stale, fetid atmosphere of unwashed bodies which pervaded the room.

On joining the Library in August 1951, I enrolled for the classes leading to the Registration examinations of the Library Association which were run by specialist staff of the City Libraries for their employees but were also open to assistants from other libraries in the vicinity. I passed the English Literature exam in December and that in Bibliography and Assistance to Readers the following June. I subsequently made half-hearted attempts to get to grips with the remaining two papers but it was not until Philip Larkin took me in hand in 1960–61 that I completed the syllabus and qualified as a Chartered Librarian. In January 1953, I moved to a post at the University College Library which, although classified as non-professional, carried more responsibility and a higher salary than my job as Music Librarian. Almost immediately I felt I had found my niche. The College acquired independent university status in 1954, and Philip Larkin arrived in March 1955. Until 1960, however, my association with him was quite tenuous.

2

Innocent days in the Library

In the twelve years between his graduation and his appointment as Librarian at the University of Hull, Larkin had spent three years as Librarian of Wellington, a small urban authority in Shropshire (1943–46). His next post was Assistant Librarian at University College, Leicester (1946–50). There he met Monica Jones, an important influence and life-long companion. From Leicester he went to Queen's University Belfast as Sub-Librarian (1950–55). At the age of 32 he took up his next, and last appointment, at Hull, where he died in office in December 1985.

After Belfast, where Larkin had been seduced by what he, characteristically, called 'bloody society', Hull at first appeared a dull and unwelcoming place. When he took up his appointment at the University Library in March 1955, his only contacts off campus were his new publishers, George and Jean Hartley, the very young (22) proprietors of the two-year-old Marvell Press. While still in Belfast, he had contributed to their poetry magazine, *Listen*,[5] and liking his work, the Hartleys had written in 1954 to say they would be interested in publishing a collection. Larkin's response was positive. Consequently plans to publish *The Less Deceived* in the autumn were well in hand by the time he arrived in Hull. Naturally anxious to meet his new publishers, he promptly got in touch with them, and for the next thirteen years visited them frequently at their home in Hessle. As Jean recalls:

> this was a very lonely period in his life so perhaps it was partly for this reason, as well as our shared interest in literature and his desire to be involved in the production of his book that he became a regular visitor. (J. Hartley 74)

On campus, however, we, his colleagues in the Library, were the next best things to friends and anyway, apart from the Hartleys, were, in the early days, all he had. In time some of us became close friends, but such a possibility was very far from his or our minds on the March day in 1955 when his predecessor, Miss Agnes Cuming, introduced us to our new

[5] The Marvell Press: Hessle, 1954–62.

boss. We saw a very different person from the ponderous, sombrely-dressed and somewhat gloomy figure he cut thirty years later. At 32 Larkin was tall and slim, with a diffident manner and an embarrassing stammer. By contrast, his dress was unconventional by the standards of the day: sports jacket, corduroy trousers, socks in vivid plain colours, and often a pink shirt, which we considered very daring. His outfit was invariably completed by either a spotted, silk bow-tie or flashy, floral-printed knot-tie, one of which, I particularly remember, had a bold blackberry design, very reminiscent of the wallpaper he chose for the Committee room in the new Library four years later. (Only recently I spotted that he was wearing this same tie when being interviewed by John Betjeman at 32 Pearson Park for the BBC *Monitor* film.) The only other two men then on the staff wore the customary dark, pin-striped suits at work. The library assistants, nine of us and all female, invariably wore regulation pale-blue serge fitted overalls which showed off good figures to advantage! The men, the deputy librarian, and an assistant librarian, were on academic-related scales; the rest of us were on clerical grades. I, being a senior assistant, was on a higher scale than the others.

We knew very little about Larkin in March 1955 except that he had had two novels published and wrote poetry. We had never heard of the Marvell Press, nor its plans to publish *The Less Deceived* in the autumn. His spare-time activities were of little concern to us then. Naturally we were wary of him and our main preoccupation was that we should develop as good a working relationship with our new boss as we had had with Miss Cuming. It was inevitable that he would introduce changes which we hoped we would be able to absorb without too much disruption to the routine of our lives. Being young and female, most of us were attached or engaged so that our ambitions lay in the direction of marriage, rather than a career. In those pre-feminist days, before maternity leave was a legal right, the two were virtually mutually exclusive. This view was upheld by Larkin himself ten years later when contemplating marriage: 'You would have to give up work,' he said to me, 'It wouldn't do for the wife of the Librarian to work.'

To our surprise, in the early years, he seemed intrigued rather than irritated by our frivolity and soon began to display a keen interest in the ups and downs of our love lives. On Monday mornings he would ask: 'Well, any more engagements this weekend; or better still, any disengagements? That's the news I should like to hear!' Inevitably there were some of the latter: I myself experienced both states twice in his first three years! Notwithstanding the banter, he was sensitive to our distress in such circumstances. At social functions, which he attended very willingly then, he met our boyfriends or fiancés, and always enquired with interest about the weddings when they took place. On the occasion of the Assistant Librarian's marriage in September 1955, Larkin took the unprecedented step of closing the Library so that we could all, including him, attend. He had, of course, acquainted us with his views on marriage but we took little notice of his wry comments for we knew he had a girl-friend (Monica Jones) whom he saw regularly.

This familiarity did not come about immediately. Larkin took some time to overcome his natural reserve. Besides, the proprieties had to be observed: Employer/employee relations were much more formal fifty years ago than they are now. After a while he called us by our Christian names (Miss Cuming never did) but we did not reciprocate. Eventually we compromised with the mock-respectful sobriquet, 'Sir', taken from the title of a book *To Sir, with Love*,[6] a new acquisition he had recommended us to read when it was published in 1959. The epithet stuck for years and it was perhaps not until the late 1970s that I referred to him in the Library or addressed him in front of others as Philip, and then only rarely.

In spite of the *badinage*, however, Larkin was lonely during his first eighteen months, especially at the weekends: 'Lonely in Ireland, since it was not home, / Strangeness made sense ... / Here no elsewhere under-writes my existence'.[7] Apart from Ray and Kitty Brett who befriended him on his arrival, he met few people outside the Library and he sorely missed the convivial friends he had left behind in Belfast. Ray, as Chairman of the Library Committee, had been a member of the panel which appointed Philip and later he recorded his impressions of the interview:

> There was a quiet authority in the way he described, of all things, the work of the issue-desk in the library there [at Queen's]. One could hardly imagine a less promising subject to impress the committee, but he made it intensely interesting, with a wealth of detail that never approached the tedious. Above all, I remember the exact and lucid sentences formed without hesitation and the incisive mind. (Brett 101)

Later kindred spirits, however, like the Kenyons, the Garnet Reeses, the Coles and the Norton Smiths, had not yet arrived in Hull. In 1955 he felt unsettled in the Library where everything was new and strange. Worst of all, there was no opportunity to meet colleagues on the campus after

---

[6] E. R. Braithwaite, *To Sir, With Love* (1959).

[7] *Collected Poems*, ed. Anthony Thwaite (London: Faber, 1988), 104. Subsequent references (*CP*) are bracketed in the text.

working hours. At the end of the day everyone went home; Larkin had nowhere to go. Not surprisingly therefore, just as he had complained to Sutton five years earlier about the dreariness of life in Belfast, he wrote to Queen's friends in even more robust terms about Hull. 'I've just been growing more fed up & more bored & more angry & the rest of it – I suppose this is what they call settling down', he complained to the Egertons four months after his arrival. 'I wish I could think of just one nice thing to tell you about Hull – oh yes, well, it's very nice & flat for cycling: that's about the best I can say' (*SL* 246). At the same time he grumbled to Patsy Murphy (formerly Strang):

> Life here varies from dreary to scarcely-bearable ... I've no friends and no gramophone and find this address far from satisfactory. In retrospect my life at Queen's seems likely to represent the highwater mark of my life in general. (*SL* 248)

We were unaware, of course, that Larkin was quite so discontented in his new surroundings although we knew that he found his accommodation unsatisfactory. I remember walking with him once towards Cottingham, a village-cum-suburb just outside Hull. As we passed a field in which some smart new pig-styes had been erected, round aluminium huts with coolie-hat-style roofs, he commented: 'Those pigs have better accommodation than the University Librarian!' He first lived in Holtby House (Winifred Holtby's parents had lived there between the wars), a small hall of residence in Cottingham reserved for bachelor members of staff and post-graduate students. This he found intolerable. After a fortnight he moved into lodgings in the 'village' (as Cottingham is called locally). The first were so bleak that they inspired 'Mr. Bleaney'. The second were the 'far from satisfactory' digs he had complained about to Patsy Murphy. Nevertheless he stayed in them for almost a year before moving into a self-contained flat virtually next door. His next move, five or six months later, was to a University flat in Pearson Park, which he rented for the next eighteen years. This proved to be a significant turning point, both from a literary and social point of view, and we noticed a marked improvement in Larkin's spirits.

Before moving in he had to buy furniture – all his previous accommodation had been furnished – which gave him an unexpected pleasure. He discussed his furnishing plans with us, asked our advice on the best shops for his needs, and regaled us with his purchases in the weeks before he moved: a rose-pink carpet for the sitting-room, offset by bottle-green chintz arm chairs and settee, book cases, storage units for records and, last but not least, a primrose-patterned tea-service which received much use in the coming months. Once everything was in place, he invited us in twos for tea on Sunday afternoons – a series of mini-house-warmings. We admired in particular the spacious attic sitting-room, with its arched high windows at tree-top level, overlooking the park below.

The following summer his mother made the first of several annual visits, and again some of us were invited to tea to meet her. Like her son, she was tall, reserved and gracious. I suppose she must have visited Philip in Hull at least once a year from 1957 until the mid-1960s when, at 80, she could no longer manage the long flights of stairs at 32 Pearson Park. I met her several times because, as my friendship with Philip grew, I was a frequent visitor at the flat. I'm sure I reciprocated by inviting them to my home as he appreciated different places to take his mother, but I cannot recall the details. It occurs to me only as I write that it was Mrs Larkin who first introduced me to Monica Jones, in June 1960, when they were both guests at the opening of Stage I of the Library by H.M. the Queen Mother. They were sitting together when I went up to speak to Mrs Larkin, but of course at that stage I meant nothing to Monica other than that I was a colleague of Philip's. She would therefore have had no reason to register either my name or presence. I, on the other hand, was mildly interested to meet my boss's girl-friend! I did not speak to her again for another 25 years, when I drove her to see Philip in hospital after his cancer operation in June 1985.

I liked Mrs Larkin. Although initially she seemed of a somewhat nervous disposition, she was friendly and I found her easy to talk to. Philip told me she liked me – even to the extent that she hoped he would marry me. She talked a good deal about Kitty, her daughter, and Rosemary, her granddaughter, and was obviously immensely proud of Philip. She was clearly anxious to please him, and by extension, his friends and colleagues. The later image of Larkin as a morose, self-pitying misanthropist was quite the reverse of that which we, who knew him when he first came to Hull, recognised. He was genial, courteous, amusing and, once he moved into the flat in Pearson Park, expansive. In Belfast he had cursed 'bloody society' for invading his life; now, albeit tentatively, he was encouraging it to enter his life.

In the early years, Larkin encouraged us to accompany him on Saturday afternoons – we worked on Saturday mornings – to the monthly meetings of the Yorkshire branch of the University, College and Research section (U.C. & R.) of the Library Association, which were held at Leeds, Sheffield, York or Hull. Sometimes, a guest speaker would give a lecture, not necessarily on a professional topic. Richard Hoggart, who was then at Hull, gave a talk in 1957 at the Brotherton Library at Leeds University on his highly acclaimed book *The Uses of Literacy*. He was surprised to encounter so many of his audience, including Philip, on the train. I was quite fascinated by the huge tear in his overcoat which was held in place by an enormous safety pin! On another occasion F. R. Leavis, the eminent Cambridge critic and editor of the influential periodical *Scrutiny*, gave a talk at York University. At other times the purpose was to visit libraries, old and new: the Wren Library at Lincoln Cathedral, the much older foundation at York Minster, the new library at Sheffield University which opened at the same time as ours. We in turn also acted as the host library, to show off our new building. Visits to the National Lending Library (now the British Library Document Supply Collections) at Boston Spa, a wholly new concept in bibliographical provision when it started operating in 1961, were essential since all libraries in the country gradually became dependent on its services.

The U. C. & R. also organised annual outings involving a full day's scenic drive to places of literary or historic interest. I recall one particularly enjoyable excursion through Wharfdale, Wensleydale and Swaledale to Barnard Castle and Bowes Museum, almost on the Durham border. At lunch, a rather nervous junior colleague and I, to our dismay – it was before I knew Philip well – were joined by Philip, B. S. Page and J. Tolson, librarians of Leeds and Sheffield Universities respectively. Page was the doyen of University librarianship then, and together they represented an influential trio who could so easily have excluded us from the table talk. They did not: on the contrary, they were most amiable, and the conversation was relaxed and all-embracing. Philip clearly enjoyed these jaunts which enabled him to become better acquainted with us and colleagues in neighbouring libraries.

In fact by the late 1950s life was going very well for Larkin on every level of activity. As *The Less Deceived* (1955) brought him increasing national recognition, new poems, which in turn would make up the next collection, appeared regularly in the literary periodicals. The tree-top flat in Pearson Park was more truly home than anywhere else he had lived. Its lofty position safeguarded his privacy. He was one step removed from the hurly-burly of life while still an observer of it. Moreover, he was on top of his job; the new building, completed in 1959, was a great success and brought him much professional esteem. He was very popular with the still small but growing staff, especially 'the girls', as he called us. This was not because he had any intention of importuning us but because he felt at ease with us, and we in turn had achieved the good working relationship with him we had desired. Although his confidence with women was increasing, his stammer was nevertheless still pronounced and his diffidence of manner never completely left him. In fact his reserve was the key to his popularity with women – of all ages and status – making them feel protective towards him. The first time he gave me a present he was so tongue-tied it was excruciatingly painful watching him struggle for words and I longed to help him.

Personal feelings apart, he normally overcame his reticence by chaffing us, often about our love lives; then, having secured our confidence, he would often make fun of his own predicament. In 1956 or 1957, he was quite open about his infatuation with a very pretty student whom we egged him on to date. We watched him chat her up on the lawn at lunch-time but in spite of our exhortations, I don't think he made much progress. He was more in earnest about another student whom he did eventually date. She was of Amazonian build – Philip entertained a fantasy about well-proportioned women – and he named a tiny room in the new Library after her, where, the idea was, he would be able to seduce her. Needless to say, nothing came of this passion. As for the room, it was first used as a stationery store and subsequently as a broom cupboard, but the name stuck: it was always known as Miss Porter's room. He also had an eye for comely girls on the staff. But he was well aware of their allegiances and made no attempt to lure them astray. It was merely that he was still young and reacted approvingly to grace and beauty. It was a good-humoured game, the rules of which we all knew and no-one broke them – until he fell in love with me. Girls came and went, of course, but with those of us who had worked with him from the 1950s, there endured an obvious rapport and affection which was apparently the envy of later-comers. As one of them said to me some years after Larkin's death: 'Oh, but you who knew him from the early days were so privileged.'

Contrary to the popular belief that Larkin was curmudgeonly and uncaring, he was quick to show concern for any member of his staff whom he knew to be in distress. If someone was in hospital he always wrote to them, and if appropriate visited them; alternatively, if they were troubled in some other way, he offered sympathy, advice, or, if he could, practical help. If, on the other hand, he felt it would not be fitting to intervene himself, he expressed solicitude through someone close to the sufferer. However, a surprising number of people confided in him directly. When he himself was hospitalised as a result of a mystery illness in 1961, Wendy Mann, a young library assistant, simultaneously underwent prolonged investigations, followed by surgery. In letters to me from his London Hospital bed, he never failed to enquire after her, and once back in Hull he 'phoned her every week until she returned to work. Another time, when a colleague's marriage was in trouble, he was exceptionally co-operative about hours so that they fitted in with child-care arrangements: at the same time he asked me to befriend this colleague with whom I developed an enduring friendship. Ironically, Larkin, the confirmed bachelor, had unconsciously adopted a role of *paterfamilias* soon after he had arrived in 1955 when we were a staff of twelve. As numbers increased to over 100, it became harder to maintain this closeness with everyone; nevertheless he liked to be kept informed of individuals' difficulties so that he could offer sympathy or advice if appropriate. He had a rare gift, not only for showing his personal concern, but also for stimulating the solicitude of others for the victim.

Moreover, after the initial reserve had been overcome on both sides, he took an interest in our social life, and was given to acts of spontaneous generosity. Having seen and enjoyed the 1920s musical, *The Boy Friend*,[8] in London, he encouraged us to go and see it when it came to Hull. Five or six of us went together, and the following morning Philip presented each of us with a copy of the play. Mine has turned yellow with age: I wonder how many of my colleagues still have their copies. In 1957 or 1958, we began the tradition of a Christmas party. As there was nowhere we could hold a party in the old library, Mary Judd, a very gregarious young woman who had recently joined the staff, invited us all to her flat. Even with the addition of partners we were still small in number and Philip was easily persuaded to join in. Once we had moved to the new Library, where we had a kitchen and staff common room, Christmas parties were held there. For many years, until numbers grew in the 1970s to the extent that the parties had to be organised altogether on a more business-like basis, Philip supplied the drinks while the girls provided the food. Until we parted he never missed one of these parties. Like everyone else, he entered into the spirit of the competitive games, one of which one year involved knitting! Having himself successfully accomplished whatever the rules of the game required, he was astonished to discover that Brenda Moon, his deputy, who could do anything with her hands (let alone her brain) from wood-work to electrical engineering, could not knit! I had not taken part in this particular game – I was no doubt dealing

---

[8] Sandy Wilson, *The Boy Friend; a play in three acts* (Harmondsworth: Penguin Books, 1959).

with the food – and when I returned, Philip could hardly wait to tell me, with amused disbelief, that he had discovered Brenda's Achilles' heel.

Dancing was a major diversion at these parties. At first we danced to records of popular dance tunes of the time, some of which were lent by Philip. From 1962, however, as the country became gripped with Beatle-mania, we chanted and jived to 'Love Me Do', 'A Hard Day's Night' and 'I Want to Hold Your Hand'. Philip repeatedly said I was the only person he could, or dare, dance with, so the Beatles' number 'I'm Happy Just to Dance with You' took on a special significance for him. He joined in the long, extended congas through the book stacks with sheepish enthusi-asm, and as putative host he was astonishingly relaxed and good-humoured, going out of his way to put everyone, even the youngest junior, at ease. It was a wonderful time to be young, or even not so young; in fact 'life was never better' than 'Between the end of Chatterley ban / And the Beatles' first LP' (*CP* 167).

Another highlight of these parties in the 1960s was the showing of homemade films. There were three of these, masterminded clandestinely by Alan Marshall, the University Photographer, with the help of other staff, after hours. They were pure slapstick comedy, solely designed to entertain. The opening frame of the first film was a still: 'The Library staff arrive for work'; the next showed a herd of cows, their stupid, placid faces well in focus, sauntering across a meadow towards the main entrance of the Library. The impact on the audience was hilarious. In the second film, we were each asked to play a part without knowing how we fitted into the plot. Each role either exploited a known idiosyncrasy of the individual, or featured something completely out of character. One of the Library's prized assets was a complete bound set of *The Times* newspaper, from 1788 to date. Philip's part in the film was that of a helpless bystander, watching, in horrified alarm, as dozens of these huge volumes hurtled past his first-floor office windows! By means of trick photography it appeared that they were being jettisoned through a window from the floor above: flagrant sacrilege! And if *The Times* flying through the air weren't enough, Arthur Wood, deputy librarian, was seen throwing himself off the roof of the Library, while Brenda Moon, who was then chief cataloguer, was filmed at the open drawers of the catalogue, frantically tearing up spoof card entries such as *Mickey Mouse Times* and *Donald Duck Daily* as they sprang up spontaneously. The more cards she discarded, the faster the hoax entries proliferated, so that in the end she was engulfed in a snowstorm of torn cards. The organisation of bookbinding was one of my responsibilities and in the film I was presented with a boxed parchment scroll which turned out to be a luncheon assignation with a bookbinding firm's representative. There was a time when it appeared I was always having lunch with periodicals' agents or bookbinders. These films provided incalculable amusement both at their first showing, and for years to come, as they were shown to later generations of staff. They have been preserved on videotapes held in the Archives Department of the Library. They appear very dated now and probably would not have any appeal for a present-day audience, but at the time Philip enjoyed them as much as the rest of us. In the words of Alan Marshall:

> Despite his eminent position in the University and his world reputation as a poet, he was able to become a 'member of staff' when we gathered socially at ... retirement presentations or ... Christmas parties ... His laughter was as merry as anyone's when [this film] had its *première* ... The idea that he was a dour and dismal man is plainly mistaken. (AM to MMB 17.vi.96)

One post-party incident I remember vividly occurred in 1962 or 1963. It was before Philip had a car and we were walking home well after midnight while he tried, unsuccessfully, to hail a taxi. Snow had fallen unexpectedly and I was teetering uncertainly in high heels, clinging to Philip for support. Eventually, resigned to not getting a taxi, he continued nevertheless, in high spirits, to flag down passing traffic without looking round. Finally, a vehicle drew up alongside us and a voice asked if we were in trouble. To our acute embarrassment, the voice belonged to an ambulance-driver and the transport beside us was a gleaming ambulance! Assured that we were not in need of help, the vehicle drove off and we collapsed with laughter. The pathos of 'Ambulances', one of my favourite poems, is always affectionately tempered for me by the memory of that evening.

After we split up, and particularly in the last few years of his life Philip became more reclusive and stopped going to the Christmas parties. Besides, the staff now numbered over 100, plus partners, and our festive gatherings had long since outgrown the simple but more intimate parties of old. The disco, which had replaced the old long-playing records, was deafening and made conversation impossible. Philip felt out of tune with the music and with the times. In 1984, however, we agreed to go together to what was to be my last party as a member of staff as I was retiring the following September. As it happened it was also Philip's last Christmas party, for within twelve months he was dead. I am very glad we went for although he was already anxious about his health, it revived memories of happier times for us both.

In the 'swinging sixties', however, library parties were not the only ones Philip attended. The post-war expansion of the University was in full swing. Staff and student numbers increased substantially. New buildings mushroomed. Academic departments proliferated, often before permanent accommodation was available for them. When this happened they were temporarily lodged in private houses which the University had a policy of buying up on a significant scale. Altogether, the University was a very vibrant place, with a large annual intake of young and lively staff who generated an enthusiasm and excitement that has never been recaptured. Consequently, any excuse for a celebration was seized, and every time a new building was completed, or a department moved into new accommodation, whether temporary or permanent, a party was thrown. Philip was on an endless party circuit, both on and off the campus, for colleagues were not slow to give house or garden parties, invitations to which he gladly accepted. On one occasion, leaving a library hostess's about midnight, he thanked her with his usual charm and said with a broad grin: 'Now the skeleton is about to leave the feast, the real party can begin!' This, as he well knew, was not a true impression. No-one felt constrained by his presence; he was in fact a popular and courteous, though diffident guest. Many hostesses were surprised by his ready acceptance of invitations. It seemed to me, his usual partner, that one reason was that he still needed to bolster his self-confidence and overcome his stammer. Gatherings of this nature provided the right environment for perfecting social skills. Another reason was that in the 1960s, in spite of his earlier and later distaste for it, he clearly enjoyed 'bloody society'.

The only party I recall Philip giving in his own home was in honour of John Wain who had been invited by the University to give a public lecture and poetry reading. As they had been students together at Oxford, Philip wanted to offer John hospitality beyond the formal dinner and accommodation provided by the University. Consequently Jean Hartley and I were enlisted to prepare simple party fare at the flat, while Philip, John, and George Hartley, along with the other three or four guests (all male) whom Philip had invited back to the flat, dined at the University. They returned to Pearson Park some three hours later without the guest of honour, who, Philip explained with some exasperation, had been on a day-long binge for which he was at that instant paying in the park below. Wain duly surfaced, shoes covered in mud and leaves which he deposited on the thick, rose-pink carpet, much to Philip's further annoyance. Ever after Philip referred to his guest as 'that fool John'. Not that any of them had been exactly abstemious at dinner, and some of the glasses and plates I had loaned got broken as the intellectual discussions which followed became increasingly heated. It was just as well that Philip had encouraged Jean and me to sample his bourbon-on-the-rocks, which neither of us had ever drunk before, as we prepared the buffet snacks and put out the drinks and glasses. We were consequently sufficiently relaxed to overlook the evening's excesses.

Though he was prepared to cater for close women friends, Philip preferred to take other friends out for meals. He had no dining-room or dining furniture, his cooking facilities were limited, and while he provided interesting supper snacks for close friends, or a simple meal for two, his menus were somewhat restricted. However, for me it was a novel experience to have Philip cook a meal for me as most of my male friends had lived at home and were not in the habit of shopping or catering. I found the meals he provided enterprising and exotic as he served fare we did not have at home, such as haggis and smoked kedgeree. He introduced me to avocado pears and asparagus which were then only just beginning to appear in the more upmarket shops in Hull: certainly, they were not to be found, as now, at every local greengrocer's.

'Bloody society' was also to be found in the Senior Common Room which was very active in the 1960s. In 1955 it had no bar, and since Queen's had had one, Philip, supported by like-minded colleagues, agitated for the introduction of one at Hull. This came about while I was secretary of the Common Room in the early 1960s. My duties involved interviewing brewery representatives and bargaining for favourable terms for the supply of their merchandise. Unlike the booksellers' and binders' representatives, these gentlemen provided no free lunches or even samples of their wares! Ironically, I knew nothing about beer and had to rely on Philip to brief me. His favourite brew was Worthington E which he insisted should be available. For the next twenty years or more, he was a familiar figure at lunch-time at the bar which, after the demise of the Senior Common Room in the mid-1970s, became a very democratic rendezvous for professors and porters, lecturers and librarians, typists and technicians. The Common Room also organised social functions, principally a supper dance each term and a dinner-dance at Christmas. Philip attended the latter event regularly, but only once patronised a mid-term hop, an experience he found emotionally threatening and commemorated in the unfinished, bitter-sweet poem 'The Dance'. A year after his death Anthony Thwaite showed me the admission ticket, dated 10 May 1963, which he had discovered amongst Philip's work-books, 23 years later. I was astounded that he should have thought it worth preserving among his keepsakes. Had he kept it to remind him, as it now vividly reminded me, how 'It happened in the spring or early summer, April, Maeve, June'? (PAL to MMB 26.iii.64). Thereafter, Philip always referred to these months in this way.

He soon began to feel disadvantaged by not being able to drive. He had taken a few lessons in Belfast and then abandoned the attempt. This did not surprise me as he struck me when I first knew him as mechanically illiterate, as well as lacking the determination and motivation to drive. Consequently, when he said in the late autumn of 1963 that he was taking lessons again, I was astonished. Three months later, when he passed the driving test at the first attempt, I was simultaneously amazed and deeply admiring of his achievement. In spite of complaints about 'the fearful onus of *buying a car* – aren't they all ugly! and small, or else terrifyingly big!' (*SL* 366), it was with great excitement that he bought his first car on the same day as *The Whitsun Weddings* was published, 28 February 1964. Having consulted my father, who had learnt to drive even later in life, Philip emulated him and chose the same model, a Singer Gazelle. The fact that it was made in Coventry, with the Rootes group emblem, Coventry Cathedral, emblazoned in the centre of the steering wheel, was an added incentive. He became a competent driver while, at the same time, driving boosted his confidence and gave him considerable, albeit wry, pleasure.

Being mobile opened up his lifestyle. The monthly visits to the Midlands to see his mother became much easier, involving a door-to-door drive of two hours instead of the previous half-day journey by train and bus. Hitherto unreachable places for holidays or day excursions suddenly became possible. Visiting friends locally, or taking girls out, no longer involved booking taxis or being circumscribed by public transport timetables. I, in particular, who had not yet learned to drive, benefited from this new facility, for Philip's main motivation in taking up driving again – so he said – was envy at the ease with which other friends (potential rivals in his eyes) wined and dined me at places inaccessible except by car. By this time we had been close for three or four years, though how this unlikely friendship came about never ceases to surprise me.

In taking up his post at the University of Hull in March 1955, at the age of 32, Larkin made the significant leap from Sub-librarian to Librarian, thereby by-passing the grade of deputy. From the moment he arrived the job was a challenge, since the plans for Stage I of a purpose-built library had to be finalised and submitted to the University Grants Committee by Christmas. They were already at an advanced stage but they were unacceptable to Larkin whose critical eye detected several major flaws in them. Thus, in addition to grappling with the day to day running of a new organisation, he had to hastily modify and complete the plans for the new building, a task made more difficult because Hull's was one of the pioneer post-war libraries. There were no existing models and there was little professional experience or corpus of literature on which to draw. Larkin, however, went to work with characteristic determination, shutting himself away every afternoon in a monk-like cell, remote from staff and readers alike, inaccessible by 'phone, with instructions that he was not to be disturbed except on matters of extreme urgency.

By these means the plans were submitted on time and accepted by the University Grants Committee. Nevertheless, it was another two years before construction work began (January 1958) and a further twenty months before the building was ready for occupation (September 1959). In the interim Larkin was a familiar figure at weekends, clambering over bricks, rubble and scaffolding, exploring its half-built expanses. As soon as it was safe to do so he took us over the shell of the building in small groups on Sundays, so that by the time it was completed we were familiar with its layout. By contrast with our previous quarters, which were cramped and makeshift, the new library was palatial, bright, airy and colourful. It incorporated some very attractive architectural features. Coloured end panels (colour denoted subject) – Larkin's innovation – brightened the book stacks, and the committee-room wallpaper, a vivid splash of black, green and purple climbing blackberry stems, also his choice, was startling but successful. An elegant oriel window with fitted seats graced the far end of the catalogue hall where readers could leisurely examine the latest books. Alternatively, they could sit and admire the spaciousness of the reception area with its wide wrought-iron staircase and corresponding balconies on the floors above, allowing natural light to be directed from the glass roof to the ground floor. Most of these features sadly disappeared when Stage II was added.

The move was planned by Larkin with meticulous precision during the summer of 1959; it marked a very rewarding period in his life. Indeed for all of us who worked with him in those early years it symbolised a culmination of achievement which stands out as one of the happiest and most memorable phases in the Library's history. The transfer of stock took place in the first half of September. The sense of occasion and the glorious weather which held throughout, created a holiday atmosphere, and although the work was physically exhausting – one girl was actually discovered asleep on a pile of bound volumes of *The Times*! – everyone, not least Larkin, worked with a will. Half way through the operation, he showed his appreciation by inviting all twelve or so junior staff (all female!) out to dinner at the best hotel in Beverley. It was an exhilarating time in the Library's development and we were proud to be part of it.

Our pride was increased the following June when the Library was officially opened by Her Majesty, the Queen Mother, and we were able to show off its features to a large invited gathering of civic dignitaries, visiting librarians, relations and friends. It was a sparkling occasion; the hospitality was lavish (a formal lunch, then afternoon tea), and the abundant floral displays in the Library were changed between the morning and afternoon receptions. Everyone looked their best in formal dress: female guests and staff who were invited to the lunch had to wear hats, gloves and long sleeves. I wore an elegant chocolate and coffee-coloured dress of satinised cotton with cream hat and gloves. On my way to the University I called, as previously arranged, for my colleague, Norman Guilding. As I rang his doorbell I heard the eager voice of his three-year old son, who could see me through the glass door, shout: 'Quick, daddy, quick. She's here!' On being asked 'Who is *she*?' Peter, by now beside himself with excitement, and oblivious to the reprimand, replied: 'The Queen Mother, of course!'

At the meal protocol demanded that as the royal guest finished each course, everyone else had to stop eating simultaneously. With over 200 people present it was inevitable that many were served long after the guest of honour. I was amongst these and, being a slow eater, had barely taken up my knife and fork to the salmon course (in 1960 a great luxury) before it was whipped away from me! In the afternoon, before showing visitors round, graduate members of the Library staff had to change into gowns and mortar boards which we found oppressive on that hot summer's day. Larkin carried a packet of glucose tablets in his pocket which he slipped to any of us he noticed suffering from heat or fatigue. As photographs of the day show, he looked elegant and dignified in white bow tie and academic dress, and in spite of the anxieties which beset him beforehand – security worries, the responsibility of a royal visitor, apprehension lest anything should go wrong, the nervous tension of the occasion – he carried out his duties as principal host with innate courtesy and charm. He later recalled: 'This day was one of the happiest in the University's history' ('*A Lifted Study-Storehouse*' 9).

Once we were in the new building, Larkin turned his attention to quite a different matter. Previously, there had never been any pressure on the female staff, most of whom were totally unqualified or only partly qualified, to complete the Registration examinations of the Library Association. Even though a graduate, who had by this time been promoted to the academic-related scale of Assistant Librarian, I was no exception. We were young, unmotivated, disheartened by earlier failures and in any case more interested in marriage than career prospects. Larkin decided to take us in hand. Remembering his own struggles with these same exams a decade or so before, he therefore announced that he would give to those who were interested regular tuition during the lunch break. Seven or eight of us took up the offer. The subject was cataloguing and classification which some of us had already tried and failed and which Larkin himself had found tedious – as he complained in letter after letter to Sutton in the 1940s. Needless to say we did not find the going any easier now, especially the regular homework, which he insisted we must complete each week.

As far as I remember, the tuition started in the early summer but by the autumn all my colleagues had dropped out for one reason or another – they got married, or moved away, or became pregnant – and only I stayed the course. As the exam drew near, my ultimate success had become as much a personal challenge for Philip as for me so that when I passed in December 1960, his gratification was as great as mine. I had now completed three out of the four parts of the Registration course, and started to work with enthusiasm on the final section in January. It was a much easier part than the one I had just taken and I only occasionally had recourse to Philip for help before passing the following summer. Thus what had begun as disinterested encouragement of my career prospects, laid the foundations of a close friendship which thrived as much on mutual professional concerns as on more esoteric interests.

Years later I found it a remarkable coincidence when Ruth Siverns (née Bowman), the only woman to whom he ever became formally engaged, told me that her friendship with Larkin had begun in a similar manner. In her case the 'tuition' was in English Literature, a subject he, as the newly-appointed, 21-year-old librarian at Wellington, was only too happy to discuss with her. He encouraged her, and her school friends to talk about the authors they studied and read for pleasure, recommended others they should read, and ensured that the library stocked the books they needed.

3

⊙╳⊙

Romance

My close friendship with Philip began in 1960. It was not only the coaching for my Library Association examination which brought us into more regular contact: increasingly through 1960 I found myself making up a foursome with him on social occasions. At the time Philip was on friendly terms with David and Elizabeth Rex, a young couple who lived in the ground floor flat at 32 Pearson Park. In the early summer they gave a Sunday lunch-time party at which Philip and I were both guests. Before long Philip returned their hospitality, inviting me along too; and then I, in turn, reciprocated. From then onwards we quite frequently went out as a foursome; on one occasion Philip bought tickets for the four of us for an Acker Bilk concert. It was an enjoyable, innocuous arrangement which neither Philip nor I at that time had any intention of changing. He was deeply committed to Monica Jones; I had a steady boy-friend, by coincidence also called Philip. This had seemed a good liaison as we were both Catholics and our outlook on life was therefore similar. But ironically, as I was soon to discover, Philip Larkin and I were on a much closer spiritual level than Philip C. and I had ever been. In 1960, however, my friendship with Philip Larkin was still entirely Platonic and it seemed unlikely that the existing associations would be disrupted.

In December 1960 Philip took me to The White House (*the* place in Hull then for dinner) in token acknowledgement of the assiduous preparation I had put in for the exam for which he had so conscientiously coached me. I promised to return the compliment if I passed, and in early February, following the news of my success, I duly issued the invitation. We chose the Beverley Arms at the nearby town of Beverley, some seven or eight miles from my home. It was a bright, frosty night and after dinner the pavements were so hazardous that Philip had to support my arm as we sought a taxi (why he didn't call one from the hotel, I cannot think). Once in the taxi Philip kept his arm around me, and from that evening our friendship entered a new and headier phase which was to have greater significance than either of us could have envisaged then. The following morning he went to London for a few days during which time I was sure that he would have dismissed the memory of our evening together from his mind.

On his return, however, he called me up to his office where, once I was seated, he uncharacteristically sat on the edge of his desk opposite, but not directly facing, me. He seemed agitated and flushed, and in one hand he held a small parcel with which he fidgeted nervously. His stammer was extremely pronounced as he tried to explain that the recollection of our recent evening had indeed remained with him, as the token he held, I gathered, was intended to convey. The words stumbled out in painful confusion as I helplessly watched his distress. He then handed me the parcel without concluding his explanation. In a Harrods bag was a box containing a bottle of Elizabeth Arden perfume which, he said, he had chosen on account of its name: *Mémoire Chérie*. At 31 I was not inexperienced in these matters but never before had I been given so romantic a gift in such touching circumstances – and my quest for romance had always been strong, though hitherto a vain one. In analysing what nurtured this yearning, it is clear that three important elements were responsible: the anecdotes of my father's early life, my education and my Catholic upbringing.

Between 1955 and 1960 I had twice been engaged to be married but each relationship had foundered: the first on grounds of religious incompatibility; the second due to a combination of apathy and my increasing affinity with Larkin. Neither *fiancé* matched my idealistic aspirations. Nor had I any expectation that Philip would do so until February 1961 when I discovered how deeply sensitive he was, and that his yearning for warmth, affection and idealism was as great as my own. In spite of the rapport which had developed between us in the previous year, I don't think Philip anticipated a closer friendship, any more than I did. He was ever conscious that such a move would jeopardise his long-time friendship with Monica Jones. I, for my part, still felt a commitment to my former *fiancé* and hesitated to exchange one unsatisfactory situation for another. However, the following month, an unexpected blow overturned caution and caused us to clarify our feelings for one another beyond all doubt.

On Saturday 4 March we went to a U. C. & R. meeting at Leeds. British Rail had just introduced a new trans-Pennine service, one of the novel attractions of which was the Griddle Car dining coach where we had lunch. All I remember about the meeting is that the talk was extremely dreary and Philip fell asleep. To my amazement, as soon as questions were invited, he shook himself and raised a pertinent point as if he had absorbed the talk during his sleep. This was a facility I was to witness frequently in the years ahead and it never ceased to command my admiration. On returning to Hull that evening we had a drink before parting at the White House Hotel, where Philip talked about the problems he would have to address at the Library Committee meeting on Monday. Even though his preparations for these meetings were meticulous, he always anticipated them with a certain nervous anxiety. For the first time we also talked about his poetry and I had to confess that I did not possess a copy of *The Less Deceived*. The day marked a significant development in our relationship, even though Philip described it that evening in a letter to Monica Jones as 'A wasted sort of day, in that it's spent going to Leeds ... to an annual general meeting ... & damned dull it is too. Information retrieval if you don't mind' (*SL* 324–5).

On Monday he gave me a copy of *The Less Deceived*, as promised, just before lunch, at the same time complaining that he did not feel well. He did seem unduly apprehensive but I put this down to pre-Committee tension. I then went off duty for the rest of the day and did not know until that evening, when a colleague 'phoned to tell me, that Philip had collapsed during the meeting and had been taken by ambulance, unconscious, to hospital. I was stunned: it seemed to me that the bottom had dropped out of my world.

On my way to work the following morning, I fell in with John Saville, a member of the Library Committee who described Philip's collapse to me and speculated on the reason for it. He knew nothing of our growing friendship, but to my utter dismay, suggested that it may have been brought on by some private emotional worry, a view also advanced by Andrew Motion in his biography (*Life* 312). At the Library I found my colleagues equally shocked by the previous day's events. We were still a small, closely-knit staff of twenty-five or so, who all knew each other well and felt genuinely concerned when any of our number fell ill. But the dramatic nature of Philip's breakdown was outside our experience and we were apprehensive as we waited for a diagnosis. We feared a brain tumour. The next day I was somewhat heartened to receive his surprisingly prosaic account of events, written from 'Ward 5, Kingston General Hotel'!

> I don't really know what's wrong with me except that I fainted & had a headache & have a temperature. I gather that they are keeping me a little longer to look at, though nothing obvious is wrong. As you'll imagine, I felt awful when I was talking to you & I suppose if I'd had any sense I'd have called the meeting off. I hardly remember anything after about then.

Certainly none of the Committee … Perhaps I picked up a germ in the Griddle Car Coach? (7.iii.61)

A few days later, the novelty of his situation had worn thin, leaving him bored, lonely and fearful:

> I don't want to write very much at present. I don't feel in good enough spirits: I should only moan. Not that I have anything much to moan about. I'm still much the same this morning as I was yesterday – but with all this time to spare, & without getting better, I have not been able to keep from worrying rather. (12.iii.61)

Meanwhile I visited him in the company of one of my colleagues in spite of whose presence Philip did not conceal the warmth of his feelings. He was discharged on 17 March, still without a satisfactory diagnosis, and went to stay at Needler Hall, one of the University's halls of residence where his friend, Peter Coveney, was Warden. From there, the hospital authorities arranged for him to go as an outpatient to Wakefield for an electroencephalogram. But again the results were inconclusive. Consequently he decided to seek another opinion and on 9 April was admitted to the private wing of the London Hospital as a patient of one of the top physicians of the day, Sir Russell Brain. Over the next fortnight, further extensive tests were carried out, including two more EEGs and an audiogram.

His letters to me were full of hospital chit-chat, with mood swings ranging from humour to anxiety, from compassion to anger, from tenderness to impatience. He was not without concern for his fellow patients:

> One good thing, morally anyway, about hospitals is that you can see so many people worse off than yourself: this makes you ashamed of any feelings of self pity or undue self regard. There is a girl of 14 just across the passage from me – don't know what's wrong with her, but she looks pale & thin. And then you meet awful cases being helped or trollied about the corridors. (*SL* 327)

By this time, he had become somewhat whimsical about the cause of his breakdown, making him wonder if '. . . this ailment I'm undergoing is God's way of putting a stop to something He thought might be getting out of hand' (10.iv.61) – in other words, our deepening intimacy.

Three days later he remembered several sick colleagues at home:

> A letter from Wendy this morning, saying she isn't in hospital any longer but is still in bed. We should form a Club of Library Invalids. Qualification: hospital residence. Tie or brooch: a book on crutches. Object: to stay well.

> Means: Regular Drinking Parties. I can't think at the moment who wd. qualify. Myself, WM, MC, JF & who else? (13.iv.61)

In the same letter he illustrated his increasing concern, as he awaited the results of yet another EEG, with an amusing drawing: 'I have four whole days to build up anxiety. Don't take all this too seriously but it is quite a strain not knowing what the great Brain will pronounce.' Later in the letter his mood swung violently to one of rage and self-pity as he blamed tests done by

> those hamfisted unhygienic swine in the Ear Dept. – I have infection & inflammation in *both* ears, *fearfully* painful, shots of penicillin in the backside, feeling absolutely rotten, confined to bed, *ill* ... So now I am *not* cheerful but in a great mood of fury & irritation & wishing I'd never set foot in this lazar house. (13.iv.61)

And considerably more in the same strain.

One benefit of being in hospital in London was that he had several literary visitors, amongst them Stephen Spender: 'I doubt if he'll find the hospital. Poets are so vague, you know!' (13.iv.61); Kingsley and Hilary Amis: 'I envied them as they walked away into the evening sunshine,' and John Betjeman: 'He was much gentler & quieter than I'd expected' (18.iv.61). Philip enjoyed these attentions which helped to offset his loneliness and anxiety; besides, at this stage, he was not, as he later became, cynical about the London literary scene. It did not occur to either of us that I should visit him. I did not consider our friendship justified such a public gesture and he did not expect it on account of the distance involved. Instead, we took great comfort from each other's letters which, in themselves, constituted a gentle wooing.

> It has meant a great deal to me to have your sympathetic letters. I don't connect them with flirtation or my taking advantage of you ... or any other cliché of human relations: they were just one person showing kindness to and concern for another. And this is a jolly rare thing in my experience. Thank you, dear, thank you with all my heart. (18.iv.61)

As at Hull, the tests and scans revealed nothing sinister and Philip was discharged on 24 April, returning to work, to my immense relief, a fortnight later, after an absence of nine weeks. He himself concluded that new spectacles, prescribed in February, were too strong, thus causing incorrect focus which affected his vision and balance. In fact, four days before his collapse, he had described this experience to Monica Jones. 'I meant to start a letter to you last night but my eyes went peculiar about

4pm & I couldn't see to write or type. In the end I went to bed! This was awfully disturbing but seems to have cleared up now' (*SL* 324). He surprisingly quickly put the episode behind him and we resumed our relationship where it had so abruptly been interrupted.

In the months that followed it went from strength to strength, but not without concern for the distress it caused to our existing relationships. I dissolved mine on 1 April 1962. Philip did not resolve his situation until 1978 when he finally broke with me in favour of Monica. In the intervening years we became enmeshed in a triangular association which caused all three of us much anguish. For me, at least, the experience was well worth the pain I endured both during his lifetime and since his death, as this alone of all my relationships fulfilled my expectations of romantic love. Knowing, as I do now, of Philip's darker side, it seems all the more remarkable that his view of love coincided so closely with mine. (The discovery of the 'Moment of Ecstasy' letter was still thirty years in the future.) But I knew nothing of his *alter ego* then, nor throughout his life, and the Larkin I knew sought and gave affection in equal measure.

This he manifested in romantic ways, like reading poetry aloud – Hardy, Yeats, Sassoon, Wilfred Owen, Betjeman – one Sunday afternoon we read the whole of *Summoned by Bells*. We listened to records, classical as well as jazz: Philip was readily moved to tears by music. I taught him to dance – passably well – in the privacy of his flat. Some occasions have special memories, such as the time I gave him a present of Evelyn Waugh's *Unconditional Surrender*, which I knew he wanted. Waugh was one of his favourite authors. It was intended as a token of appreciation to mark the completion of my library exams. It also coincided with the intensification of our relationship in the late autumn of 1961.

Well aware that Philip would not be slow to spot the *double-entendre* of the title, I forestalled him by saying: 'Now don't think for a moment that this gives you the green light to go ahead because that's the last thing I have in mind!' The green light image was one he had used, in a rather more serious context in a letter to me, a few months earlier (10.iv.61).[9] Predictably he answered my retort with mock disappointment, saying that he naturally assumed that if a girl gave him a book with such a suggestive title, it could only have one meaning. Forty years later it astonishes me that this side of our relationship was conducted on such amiable, even artless, lines for so long, evidence of the quixotic sway we exerted over each other. After his death, when Monica Jones offered me

[9] See Chapter 5.

some of his books, I chose the trilogy of novels which *Unconditional Surrender* (1961) completed, the earlier volumes being *Men at Arms* (1952) and *Officers and Gentlemen* (1955). All three are first editions.

Another memorable event, which gave us both immense pleasure, was the 'hanging' of Philip's first art purchase. He bought it at a London gallery, early in 1963 as far as I remember, and had it delivered in the first place to the Library. Anxious to hang it at the flat that evening, he wanted me to share his excitement. For my part, I was only too eager to see what he had paid £750 for, an enormous extravagance in 1963! When he told me about the purchase I thought he had taken leave of his senses: in my experience ordinary people then just did not splash out that amount on a little-known painting.

Nevertheless, I shared his enthusiasm as he unpacked it to reveal a nineteenth-century pastoral idyll in oils of a young girl and small child observing sheep. The artist, Thomas Falcon Marshall (1818–78), although not well-known, exhibited regularly at the Royal Academy throughout his life. Philip hung the painting over the mantelpiece in his sitting-room, a position it later commanded in the Newland Park house until it was stolen about two years after his death. As far as I know it has never been recovered but I am very glad to have a photograph of it which Ted Tarling, editor of *Wave*, took for me shortly before its theft (see letter of 24.ix.70, fn. 19).

We went for long walks; sometimes in town; at other times we took a bus into the surrounding countryside and planned a circular walk, or spent a day by the sea. One summer Sunday outing in 1963 is etched on my mind because it showed Philip's attitude to children in quite a contrary light to that he generally claimed to hold. He had not so much given me to understand that he disliked children as that he felt ill at ease with them. Therefore I was all the more surprised by the following little charade in which he played an uncharacteristic part quite spontaneously. We had gone to Hornsea, a small seaside resort fifteen miles from Hull, by bus – the railway line had already fallen victim to Dr Beeching's early 1960s transport strategy which axed small branch lines.[10] The last bus back to Hull left in the early evening and as we waited at the appointed place for it – there was no bus station – several children were also waiting with their parents. A group of under-fives was playing with a large ball in the

---

[10] Richard Beeching (1913–85). Chairman of the British Railways Board (1963–65) and author of the *Beeching Report*, which advocated the closure of many rural and branch lines.

queue directly in front of us. I groaned inwardly at the scene, being sure their presence, not to speak of their ball, would irritate Philip and spoil what had been a perfect day. To my astonishment, he soon started fielding the ball to the children, then he actually joined in their game. Shortly he became quite talkative with them, asking them their names and where they lived. He was quite natural with them, but did not talk down to them. He simply spoke courteously and good-humouredly. Mesmerised by the scene, I was the one who felt awkward and excluded.

Otherwise, my experience of Philip's encounters with children was limited to the rare occasions he happened to come across my niece or nephews at my parents' or their homes when he occasionally kept me company as I baby-sat for them. As babies in the mid-1960s and 1970s they were not often at my parents' home at the times he visited, and they were invariably in bed when he joined me at my baby-sitting duties. I remember the occasion he first met my niece, Claire. It was the day of her christening when she was a few weeks old. I had not invited him to the ceremony, fearing an invitation would embarrass him, or his non-acceptance would disconcert me, but he certainly came to my home later in the day, where the family had gathered for an informal celebration. I surprised him bending over the baby in her carry-cot in my sitting-room where she had been left to sleep. He was fascinated as she tugged at his fore-finger as if it were a completely natural experience for him.

That he could be natural with children, even babies, on his own terms, was reinforced by an anecdote related to me more than thirty years later by a young woman I met at a mutual friend's. Gillian Scott told me that her son, Jo, was born at the end of December 1983. From being but a few days old she took him along to the local supermarket, Grandways, at the corner of Beverley High Road and Clough Road for the weekly shopping expedition, early on Saturday mornings. There she used to bump into Philip, also bent on doing his shopping before too many people were about. As a student she recognised him as the University Librarian although he did not instantly place her. However, as Gill emphasised when telling me the story, Philip's interest was not in her but in the blonde-haired, blue-eyed baby in the pram. Of course, he would acknowledge Gill while bestowing a broad smile on the child and after a few weeks he asked her if she would object if he gave Jo, whose name he now knew, a bar of milk chocolate. She consented and from then until his illness the following year, the presentation of a bar of chocolate to Jo became a weekly ritual, eagerly anticipated by both donor and recipient.

Mrs Scott ended this anecdote by adding that she could not help noticing how extremely courteous Philip always was to the assistants at the check-out as he paid for his purchases. About the same time, my reflexologist, Angela Myers, told me that as a schoolgirl she had a Saturday and occasional evening job at a small general store near the University where Philip frequently shopped. She had often served him when, she said, 'he always came over as such a gentle man', deliberately dividing the last word. I could not help contrasting these views with that of the assistant in the University bookshop whom I met the day before he died who had found him so churlish and bad-tempered. I think the explanation for these contrasting attitudes was that the bookshop staff did not measure up to his high expectations of efficiency and service, while, on the other hand, he did not judge the food stores' assistants by such exacting standards.

Once Philip had a car, we went further afield on summer evenings and fine Sundays. We sampled new places for meals, often pubs, occasionally more sophisticated restaurants. However, whether we had a meal or simply a drink and a talk, our favourite place was always the Beverley Arms. Sometimes we went to the cinema. We saw all the James Bond films. Philip's enthusiasm for the macho escapades of 007 both amused and puzzled me. Most of all I loved the autumn rituals we observed. First in early October came Hull Fair, although we preferred the off-duty sights and sounds of the fair-ground on Sunday afternoons to the cacophony of noise and the harsh lights of the Fair in full swing. At the end of the month came Hallowe'en when Philip customarily made mulled wine, the warm, heady smell of which pervaded his flat and half intoxicated me before I even tasted it. We drank it by candlelight under the caustic grimaces of little models of witches on broomsticks he had suspended from the ceiling, and threw apple peel over our shoulders but it never formed our initials as superstition ruled. The only time I saw children carrying pumpkin lanterns was when I was with Philip. The romantic significance of the encounter added to the magic aura of the occasion. After Hallowe'en came Guy Fawkes Night, when we sometimes strolled across the Park to watch the public bonfire and fireworks display but more often the 'high windows' of his sitting room provided a cosier vantage point.

In between these dates fell the religious festivals of All Saints and All Souls which I observed and Philip therefore acknowledged, usually with some reminder of Frances Cornford's sestet commemorating All Souls' Night:

My love came back to me
Under the November tree
Shelterless and dim.
He put his hand upon my shoulder,
He did not think me strange or older,
Nor I, him.

The feast of All Souls, 2 November, following that of All Saints, is a day set aside by the Church when the faithful are asked to pray for the souls of the dead still in Purgatory. Out of this tradition grew the superstition that a dead lover would appear to a still faithful partner on All Souls' Night. Already a favourite poem of Philip's, it acquired a special significance for both of us when, in 1974, after a parting of sixteen months, we resumed our affair on this day. He included the poem in the *Oxford Book of Twentieth Century English Verse*.

In early December on several successive years in the mid-1960s, we went to Scarborough to do Philip's Christmas shopping. These were very happy occasions. On arrival we had lunch at the Pavilion, a Charles Laughton hotel, long since pulled down, then shopped – always successfully – before finishing with afternoon tea at Marshall and Snelgrove's elegant café, also now long gone. Best of all, I liked the quiet autumn and winter afternoons (usually Sundays) when we ate toasted crumpets, spread with Gentleman's Relish, in the firelight, and drank Earl Grey tea. On Saturdays after work we had lunch at the Hoi Sun Chinese restaurant in town, a relative novelty in the early 1960s, or went out to dinner in the evenings. In more gregarious moods, we went to parties. Often we stayed at home and cooked for one another. Our companionship was exhilarating and stimulating; we had fun; we enjoyed life and refused to let thoughts of the future mar our happiness.

While our leisure activities were mostly confined to Hull and the East Riding, occasionally we took the opportunity to meet at pre-arranged venues as we crossed the country on business or on holiday. In September 1963, for instance, on my way back from Grenoble, Philip met me in London where we spent the night and following day so that he could fulfil a long-standing promise to take me to Overton's fish restaurant for lunch. My flight was delayed and I did not arrive at Cromwell Road air terminal – at that time the arrivals and departures check-in point in central London for passengers flying into and out from Heathrow, and where Philip had promised to meet me – until after midnight, three hours later than scheduled. I did not expect him to be there but to my delight and relief he was, even though somewhat bleary-eyed in that comfortless, smoke-filled waiting room. I found the lunch at Overton's the following day a thrilling experience as I thought of all the writers who had frequented it in the past, not to speak of the one whose guest I now was. Philip was a wonderful host on these occasions and made one feel very special. Afterwards we went to Liberty's in Great Marlborough Street, a shop I had not previously (or subsequently) visited. I still have two small souvenirs Philip bought me there. One is a smart black and grey coaster portraying Liberty's escutcheon; the other is a foot-long presentation of book-matches, showing on the front the London sky-line, and on the back Liberty's Tudor frontage with a brief history of the store. We both had a liking for novelty book-matches and vied with each other to find unusual ones. One Christmas we surprised each other by exchanging the same stocking-filler, a perspex box containing perhaps two dozen smart book-matches; mine were arranged alternately with bright red and green covers with my forename on the front in gold: Philip's had black or cream covers and each bore his initials. After his death Michael Bowen, a close friend in the last decade of Philip's life, produced one from his pocket. I explained that they had been a gift from me and that I should love to have one. But unfortunately he said there were none left. I now only have one left of those that Philip gave me.

Another time we engineered a rendezvous as I returned from a holiday in South Wales when we met and spent a night at Woodstock in Oxfordshire. We stayed at a very ordinary country pub of my choosing, which was awful in my opinion but Philip did not seem to mind. Fortunately we had the more sophisticated distractions of a visit to Blenheim Palace and dinner at the Bear in Woodstock where again Philip played the rôle of impeccable escort. By this time, 1964, he was driving whereas I had not yet thought of learning, so part of the plan in meeting at this half-way point was to drive me the remainder of the journey home.

I passed my driving test in November 1967 and although I had often driven long distances, it was not until the summer of 1971 that I drove more than 150 miles alone. That summer I drove to South Wales, breaking my journey overnight at Oxford. I was very touched when Philip insisted on accompanying me on the first stage of my route, as I followed him to the service station on the M1 where our roads were to separate. I can see him now, leaning over a parapet, admonishing me to remember this and not to do that, clearly anxious, as he said he would remain, until I let him know I had arrived safely. On parting he continued southwards while I turned westward. It was an intrepid undertaking which I did not attempt again until 1997. In 1971, thanks, no doubt, to Philip, I had not minded the M1 motorway but found the M4 which was still in the process of construction, terrifying. Twenty-six years later I found the positions reversed with the M1 much busier and the drivers on it much more aggressive.

Occasionally when travelling by train across the country, if it was at all possible to contrive that our paths should cross, we met for a few hours at a convenient meeting place, like Manchester or Oxford. Apart from these rather more adventurous exploits which always generated an air of esoteric excitement, we occasionally attended professional conferences together. SCONUL's[11] spring conference, at which Philip was a consistent delegate throughout the 1960s, was followed at the same venue by the University, College and Research Section annual conference where I joined him on at least three occasions – at Bangor, Reading and Liverpool. As Philip's deafness increased, he ceased to stay on for the U. C. & R. conference, and as my own interests became more specialised, I transferred my allegiance to the UK Serials Group. This organisation was formed by Blackwell's in the mid-1970s for librarians responsible for periodicals, an area of publication which was fast absorbing the major part of university and special libraries' expenditure. I very much enjoyed these conferences and served on the committee of the UK Serials Group for at least ten years from the time of its formation. Philip was always rather suspicious of my interest in this professional body, particularly as I became quite friendly with some of Blackwells' staff whom he suspected of wanting to lure me away from Hull to work on the commercial side of the periodicals business. His fears were not entirely unfounded as Blackwells did in fact put out feelers one time when they had a suitable vacancy but both they and I decided I was not tough enough for the cut and thrust of the business world.

My relationship with Philip always had something of a fantasy element about it. At one level it was entirely frivolous, even childlike; at a more significant level it was unalloyed, romantic escapism. The first grew out of Philip's nickname for me, 'Miss Mouse', or simply 'Mouse'. The name had actually been given to me by my previous boyfriend (Philip C.), but since Larkin liked to identify his women friends with (cuddly) animals – Monica was Bunny, Ruth Cat, Patsy Honey Bear – so it suited him to take over the ready-made name of Mouse for me. Around each of us he created fanciful worlds inhabited by our animal namesakes, and over the years his letters to me were adorned with drawings of mice pursuing

[11] Standing Conference of National and University Libraries.

various activities – going on holiday, smuggling contraband goods through Customs, going to conferences, drinking champagne, looking gleeful, looking glum, as befitted the content of the letter. From time to time he gave me little felt models of mice. Two are in full choristers' dress of purple cassocks and white lace albs which he found on one of his shopping forays in London. He always regretted not buying enough of them to make up a full choir but was never able to track down any more. As far as I remember, these particular models took his fancy because of our shared affection for Betjeman's 'Diary of a Church Mouse'. Other replicas are of elegant lady mice in period dress.

Then Philip discovered Margery Sharp's *The Rescuers*, 'a fantasy for children' which chronicles the exploits of a very elegant, white, pet mouse who belonged to an ambassador's son. Her name was Miss Bianca, she lived in the Embassy schoolroom in a porcelain pagoda and 'wore a silver chain round her neck, and on Sundays a gold one'. Her initials and the gold chain were just two of the characteristics which identified her with me for I always wore a gold chain (with pearl pendant) which Philip had given me for Christmas 1961. An even greater affinity, however, was that we each held influential office in our respective organisations! Miss Bianca was Chairwoman (later President) of the Mouse Prisoners' Aid Society while I, at the time, was Secretary of the Senior Common Room, a fact which inexplicably impressed Philip. The other main character in the book was 'a rather commonplace-looking mouse named Bernard' who was, of course, Miss Bianca's devoted slave, though his status as a mere pantry mouse forbade him to declare his love. Between 1962 and 1972 five more of these fantasies were published, each carrying Philip and me further into this particular realm of fancy. My copy of *Miss Bianca in the Antarctic* is inscribed in a childish hand 'To MB with love from Bernard', while in the last story in the series, *Miss Bianca and the Bridesmaid*, he wrote 'For Maeve, this last tale of Madam President who also wore a pearl. With love from Philip.'

As time went on, however, the romantic dimension of our fantasy world provided a subconscious escape from the growing futility of our predicament. Philip's fundamental ambivalence towards marriage, in spite of occasional assertions to the contrary, prevented him from making a decisive choice between Monica Jones and me, and in effect, put a stop to any significant development in *our* relationship. As long as Monica was in Leicester and I in Hull the choice was not forced upon him. Furthermore, I too refused to confront my instinctive misgivings about marriage with Philip; still less did I want to contemplate the future without him.

Nevertheless we were content with this state of affairs and intuitively shelved the issues of a deeper commitment, preferring the happy unmarried relationship we enjoyed to the risk of an unhappy marriage – or the termination of our affair. By locking ourselves into a complex dream world, we shut out the pressures of the real world, and apart from a sixteen-month separation in 1973–74 our friendship continued on this heady course until 1978.

Philip had apparently identified its essential illusoriness as early as 1965, somewhat earlier than I had. As he explained in a letter to Monica, it simply followed the pattern of his relationships with her, and with Ruth before her. 'I think there's something unreal about my relation with her [Maeve], as indeed there is with ours and mine with Ruth – in that it isn't "serious" in the world sense of the word, i.e. leading to marriage and children' (*Life* 357). As time went by, he became increasingly conscious of this lack of direction and would say with mock seriousness: 'I fear your father pulling me aside and asking (here he adopted a stage Irish accent): "Now Philip, when are you going to do the right thing by my daughter?"' Of course, my father never did anything of the kind, but years later, he told me that he had always thought that we would marry.

Actually, Philip got on surprisingly well with both my parents and was always relaxed in their company. I once cut myself short while relating some rambling, domestic anecdote: 'I'm sorry, this can't possibly be of interest to you', I said, to which he replied 'Oh, don't stop: it fascinates me. I *love* hearing anything about your family life.' Undoubtedly, there were some similarities with his own family: professional, articulate, authoritarian father; mild-mannered mother; a home full of books and records. However, my family interacted with one another a great deal more cordially than Philip's did – although I was unaware then of the underlying antagonisms within his family. My mother, in particular, who emanated warmth and hospitality, had a remarkable facility for putting everyone she came in contact with at ease. With my father, Philip discussed literature; they also shared an interest in boxing and rugby. Even though we did not acquire television until 1967 or 1968, we had it several years before Philip, who therefore used to come and watch the big fights and the Five Nations Rugby Union Championship matches with my father.

Another attraction was the piano, which only my mother played. It drew Philip like a magnet. Whenever he was alone in the room, he would sit at it and improvise a medley of classical and jazz tunes or syncopate the drawing room ballads my mother played. Occasionally he would ask her to play these, songs like 'Where'er You Walk' and 'The Last Rose of Summer'. They reminded him of the pile of sheet music on his mother's piano which inspired the bitter-sweet nostalgia of 'Love Songs in Age'. When Philip bought a high-fidelity Pye Black Box record player, just before he started writing his monthly jazz feature for the *Daily Telegraph* in 1961, my father, who was also a keen record collector, expressed great interest in it. Today's music-centres make this generation of record players appear primitive, but the sound they reproduced was much more faithful to the original than anything hitherto. They incorporated a diamond or sapphire stylus which gave a sharper, cleaner tone than the fibre needles which preceded them. Moreover, a stylus, although it had to be replaced eventually, did not require sharpening after each playing as fibre needles did, a significant innovation which appealed to my father. Consequently, Philip invited my parents to Pearson Park in order to demonstrate his new toy. My father was duly impressed but did not buy a Pye Black Box – it was probably more than he was prepared to pay. He nevertheless updated his equipment with advice from Philip. In return, when Philip came to buy a car in 1964, he was influenced by my father who had also learnt to drive late in life.

The music which Philip preferred as solace and respite from outside pressures, was of course jazz. 'Few things have given me more pleasure in life than listening to jazz' he wrote in 1968 (*All What Jazz* 1). Until 1961, when he started reviewing new record releases for the *Daily Telegraph*, he had coasted along with the comfortable style of Humphrey Lyttleton, Acker Bilk and Chris Barber, all of whom gave concerts in Hull or other nearby towns to which Philip often invited friends. Moreover, deprived of his gramophone during the years he had lived in digs, he had not kept pace with the new developments that had taken place since his youth. Consequently, in 1961 he found the dichotomy between pre and post-war jazz an unpleasant cultural shock. Modern jazz, he complained, 'wasn't like listening to jazz at all ... Something fundamentally awful had taken place to ensure that there should be no more tunes' (*All What Jazz* 6–8). It seemed in sharp contrast to the jazz that had excited him in the 1930s, and at Oxford, which evoked 'memories of vomiting blindly from small Tudor windows to Mugsy Spanier's "Sister Kate" or winding up a gramophone in a punt to play Armstrong's "Body and Soul"' (*All What Jazz* 18).

But while traditional jazz remained his most abiding musical love, Philip's taste included a more eclectic repertory. In one of the earliest letters to Jim Sutton he talked of listening to Beethoven's *Coriolan Overture*, and commented:

> You simply can't think of Jazz after Beethoven. It's a physical impossibility...
> Not that I pretend to 'understand' it. It conveys nothing definite. But it's
> just 'big', that's all. Jazz isn't big ... (9.viii.[1939]).

Later he changed his views, conceding after listening to a late Beethoven quartet: 'I stick to jazz firmly, not as being supreme, but as being more honest' (10.xi.41), and later still observed 'I can see myself as liking Mozart *in time*. Not yet' (5.iv.43). He never grew to like Mozart, although I understand he bought records of his symphonies, conducted by Christopher Hogwood on original instruments. However, at the time I knew him he appreciated many classical works to which he listened in the privacy of his home.

It is not surprising, therefore, that of the eight records he chose as his 'Desert Island Discs' in 1976, only three were jazz items. The others were a Northumbrian folksong, the sixteenth-century 'Coventry Carol', and works by Tallis, Handel and Elgar. Of these Handel was Larkin's particular favourite, with a special preference for his oratorios. In the mid-1970s, he discovered a more frivolous Handel composition, arranged by Beecham who gave it the title *Love in Bath*. A skilful orchestration of arias, choruses and dances from Handel's operas, it narrates the elopement of Elizabeth Lindley and Richard Brinsley Sheridan from eighteenth-century Bath. This record, a copy of which he gave me, gave us both immense pleasure, and still evokes for me very happy memories of that period of our friendship.

We also shared a love of Elgar, whom Philip found nostalgic and intensely moving. One of my earliest insights into his esoteric side was seeing him in tears while listening to Elgar's *First Symphony*. Perhaps it was not without significance that the first item on the programme which inspired 'Broadcast' was this composer's *Introduction and Allegro for Strings*: 'A snivel on the violins' (*CP* 140). He liked 'church music ... in the same way as jazz', he explained when choosing the Tallis motet, *Spem in Alium*, as one of his 'Desert Island Discs'. This preference also extended to Gregorian chant which he enjoyed years before it gained its contemporary popularity. As a Catholic I was familiar with plainsong in church and school from an early age and was surprised that it should appeal so much to an agnostic. By request, I gave him several records of it for Christmas presents. Other favourites were Corelli and Vivaldi: a note to me accompanying a present of *The Four Seasons* read: 'I like this kind of thing very much indeed' (25.ix.63).

On a less serious plane, Philip fell under the sway of the Beatles in the 1960s, sufficiently to give them a memorable refrain in 'Annus Mirabilis': 'Between the end of the Chatterley ban / And the Beatles' first LP.' He was more circumspect in *All What Jazz* where he described them as the 'Original Sound of the Sixties' (161). Nevertheless, long after the group disbanded, their tunes held a special place in his affections, for they stood for a happy and successful period of his life ('Though just too late for me', *CP* 167).

The 1960s were very happy years, for Philip, as well as for me, highlighted by the enormous success of *The Whitsun Weddings*, the television documentary, *Down Cemetery Road* and the award of the Queen's Gold Medal for Poetry. By 1965 he was second only to Betjeman as England's most popular poet. Simultaneously, he was at the peak of his professional career, with Stage II of the Library well under way. Consequently his advice on new buildings – of which there were many being built during those boom years of university expansion and prodigal capital expenditure – was widely sought. These literary and professional successes projected him into the limelight, which in spite of his natural reticence, flattered him, while his unique blend of modesty and charm endeared him to both strangers and colleagues. By the end of the decade, however, a combination of factors, literary, professional and personal, triggered a restlessness and depression which he was unable to conceal.

The fact that he had been in Hull for fifteen years was the largest single contributory factor to his restiveness. At 48 a career move was still feasible but the memory of a fudged interview at Reading University in 1967 haunted him. On presenting himself at the appointed time he inexplicably took fright and fled. No-one was more surprised – or relieved – on his return, than I was by his confused explanation which he said had much to do with the emotional appeal Hull still held for him. In any case, by 1970 a career change appealed to him rather than a career move and he toyed with the idea of finding some literary sinecure in Oxford. In the event, he was given two terms' sabbatical leave at All Souls' College in the autumn and winter of 1970–71 which, although it provided a change of company and occupation, did not resolve his problems.

Secondly, his mother, now in her mid-eighties and still living alone, was finding it increasingly difficult to cope. Her gradual deterioration had worried Philip for some time but by 1971 it was clearly necessary to make alternative provision for her care. After a period of trial and error, in January 1972 she became a permanent patient in a nursing home near Leicester where Philip visited her every two weeks, at the same time maintaining her garden as he had done since 1955, and keeping an eye on her home. He worried about her continuously:

> Mother doesn't speak of any more falls, but she does say that someone tied her to her chair yesterday, wch. is rather disagreeable. Showed me the string. No doubt it was all done with the best intentions, just to remind her she wasn't supposed to walk unaided, but I didn't like it ... she is also muddled, as usual, though kind and patient enough in dreary circumstances. It leaves me feeling *very* wretched as you know. I can't imagine how it will go on. (26.iii.72)

In 1958 he had written 'Home is so Sad'. How much sadder was it now: 'I am not happy about my mother ...' he wrote to me, 'I am going "home" (as I still call it) this weekend as of course I must & want to, but it is saddening to face the sad situation again' (13.ix.72).

4

Poetic occasions

I have to confess that the publication of *The Less Deceived*, six months after Larkin's arrival in Hull, made little impact on me, or indeed on most of my colleagues in the Library. More than 40 years on such an admission must seem very *naïve*. We knew that he wrote poetry and had had two novels published, but in 1955 Larkin was very diffident about his creativity. He had virtually no literary standing. *The North Ship* had attracted only one review while *XX Poems* had failed to elicit any: the novels had long been forgotten. Consequently, in October 1955 he was not anxious to herald *The Less Deceived* before he knew if, or how, it would be received by reviewers. He had told his publishers, George and Jean Hartley, that he did not want it to be known in the University that he wrote poetry. Among Library colleagues, possibly only his secretary knew of its pending publication. Once again he must have been disappointed by the literary world's slow response, for it was not until Christmas, when *The Times* listed it as one of the year's best books, that favourable reviews began to appear. For my part, although I read *A Girl in Winter* (a book sale bargain) soon after his arrival, I tended to eschew contemporary poetry and did not own a copy of *The Less Deceived* until Philip gave me one some time later. Even then, I always found it less accessible than *The Whitsun Weddings* with which I was privileged to be so closely involved.

As my friendship with Philip grew in the early 1960s we discussed many of the poems in the latter collection either retrospectively or while they were being written. Consequently, I was often aware of the circumstances which gave rise to them. 'The Large Cool Store' was the first poem he ever showed me, for the simple reason that I had unsuspectingly inspired it. I had been shopping in town on my 'split day' and returned early to the Library for evening duty with my purchases. Anxious to gain the commendation of colleagues, I was showing them what I had bought when Philip came through from his office to give his verdict. He was very taken with a smart summer handbag I had bought at Marks and Spencer's. He found it hard to believe that I had found anything quite so stylish there: in 1961 their merchandise was generally less well designed than in later years. The following Saturday Philip went along to 'the large cool store' which he saw through the eyes of working-class women whose humdrum existence was far removed from the tantalising world represented by the store's 'Modes for Night'. Caressing the 'Bri-Nylon Baby-Dolls and Shorties', ethereal in colour, texture and design, the women imagine how possession of such a garment might transform their lives, showing: 'How separate and unearthly love is, / Or women are, or what they do' (CP 135). Although in some degree flattered, the treatment of love in the poem did not strike me as commensurate with *our* deepening feelings for one another.

Naturally, I felt very differently about the much more personal poem 'Broadcast' (CP 140) and never now attend a concert without recalling its opening and concluding lines, and the performance which inspired it at the City Hall in Hull. I had been present at a live concert on 5 November 1961 which was simultaneously broadcast on the radio. Philip, who knew I was in the audience, listened at home. The inscription in my copy of the *Listener* (25.i.62), where the poem first appeared, reads: 'To Maeve, who wd. sooner listen to music than listen to me', accompanied by a caricature of himself, enveloped in gloom beside his radio, while I sit nearby, lost in my own musical world, one of my gloves unnoticed on the floor. 'Those new, slightly outmoded shoes' were a private joke, whose formulation, if not the specific adjective, was mine. They were an unusual colour of pearlised bronze, very smart, with stiletto heels and long, pointed toes, popularly known as winkle-pickers. I had bought them (and the gloves) that autumn to go with a new coat. Philip raved about the shoes. He used to take them off my feet, hold them up, stroke them, put them down on the sofa and continue to admire them; not just once, but every time I wore them. He thought they were the last word in fashion, until one day, slightly exasperated, I teased: 'I don't know why you go on so about these shoes. They're almost out of fashion now. You know how I haven't the nerve to wear anything until it's been in vogue for six months.' He laughed and said: 'Well. I still adore them even if they are slightly outmoded!'

The description of my face, although an entirely poetic perception ('It's seeing you poetically' as he put it some years later in a letter to me: 25.vii.65), nevertheless for me expresses the transcendental quality that marked our relationship from the beginning. I was deeply moved that Philip commemorated it in this way. For some years afterwards, he would add one of the following notes to Christmas cards, depending on the nature of the illustration: 'Devout but not beautiful'; 'Beautiful but not devout' or, more rarely, 'Beautiful *and* devout'.

In March 1962 Philip went to the funeral, in Oxford, of Miss Agnes Cuming, Hull's former librarian, and when he returned I remember, with vivid clarity, how he recalled the incidents described in 'Dockery and Son' as we met by chance at the foot of the main staircase in the Library. '"Dockery was junior to you, / Wasn't he?" said the Dean. "His son's here now"' (*CP* 152). The recollection is so strong even now that it surprises me that the poem was a whole year in gestation before its completion although I must have known it at the time. Shortly after the visit to Oxford, he produced from his wallet the 'two snaps / Of bosomy rose with fur gloves on./ Unlucky charms, perhaps', before showing me the typescript of 'Wild Oats' (*CP* 143). Unlucky, because when Philip was younger at any rate, he was constantly torn between wanting to be conventional, to be married and to have children, and the even stronger desire of wanting to be alone. This tension produced the cynical little poem 'Love' (*CP* 150) when, on the verge of falling seriously in love again, he confronted these opposing desires.

I was well aware of the protracted struggle to finish 'The Dance', begun in May 1963 and which he would have liked to include in *The Whitsun Weddings*, but was unable to complete. On this occasion Philip went against his better judgement in following me to a Senior Common Room dance. I was in the habit of going to these mid-term hops with my 'own sad set' – why sad, I don't know for we were a jolly, lively group – and I made it quite clear I intended to go to this particular dance whether or not he accompanied me. He was not a dancer and felt ill at ease on a dance floor. Although very torn, he made no commitment to come and I really thought his reluctance would win the day. I was therefore surprised but elated when he appeared towards the middle of the evening. The events and emotions that followed were every bit as intense as he describes them in the poem which, for the next year, not only arrested his poetic output but also created a significant watershed in his emotional life. Several months later he wrote to me: 'I am beginning to think this is a great obstacle in my creative life: shan't write anything till it's out of the way' (27.xii.63). Philip had in fact reached an emotional *impasse* which prevented him from either securing or severing the bonds which ensnared him. 'I feel / The impact open, raw, / Of a tremendous answer banging back / As if I'd asked a question' (*CP* 155). Interpreting my body language as challenging, even threatening, his reaction at 41 was as gauche and inadequate as that of a youth of 20:

> ... It's pathetic how
> So much most people half my age have learned
> Consumes me only as I watch you now.

The dance was equally unforgettable for me. Having enticed him to it against his will, I judged his coming as a measure of his feelings for me and recognised, with some surprise that I exercised considerable emotional sway over him. I should not have been so surprised for throughout our friendship he frequently said as much: 'Emotionally, I'm very dependent on you', or 'You have enormous emotional power over me.' However, even though he showed me 'The Dance' at intervals in the ensuing months, it was not until he gave me a typed copy, 'long afterwards with undimmed memories' – in fact a decade later – that I realised just how turbulent his emotions had been on that memorable evening.

My transcript does not include the eight lines he added to the work-book version on 12 May 1964,[12] a year after he began the poem, nor are they included in the *Collected Poems*. In my case it is perhaps not surprising, since my copy was given to me on the spur of the moment on the eve of a more serious parting than we had hitherto contemplated. On asking if I had a copy, he was surprised to learn that I had not, and simply extracted a duplicate from a file on which he hastily scribbled its moving dedication. I was astonished that the dance still, ten years on, seemed to be such a significant milestone in his life. Nevertheless, the additional lines do not complete the poem. The last line breaks off, without a full stop – 'I see for the first time as something whole / What earlier seemed safely divisible' – almost as unsatisfactorily as the *Collected Poems* version.

Some years after his death I learnt that amongst his papers in the Archives Department of the Library, there is an audio-tape of Philip reading 'The Dance' at home, to the accompaniment of carefully-chosen, strict tempo dance-band music. He includes the additional lines. Hearing Philip reading the poem for the first time, in clear, strong tones, was an emotional shock, leaving me in my turn 'desperate' to know when and why he recorded it.

Apart from these poems with very personal connections, I distinctly recall Philip showing me 'An Arundel Tomb', 'Ambulances', 'Here', and 'Toads Revisited' which, because of their private associations, remain enduring favourites. I remember equally my indignation when he showed me 'Breadfruit', written, he said 'out of frustration when you refused to come round last night!' and my protest at the strong language – which

---

[12] See A. T. Tolley, *Larkin at Work* (Hull: University of Hull Press, 1997).

he had not used before – in 'Sunny Prestatyn'. His response was: 'That's exactly the reaction I want to provoke, shock, outrage at the defacement of the poster and what the girl stood for.' I was not convinced and dismissed the poem's subject matter, along with 'Essential Beauty', as unfitting for poetry.

The publication of *The Whitsun Weddings* in February 1964 ushered in a personal *annus mirabilis* for Philip. The first triumph was somewhat esoteric. At the beginning of February he passed his driving test and on publication day he bought his first car. The success of the collection, on the other hand, was instant and very public. Overnight, he became a popular poet, 'the John Clare of the building estates ... He has certainly closed the gap between poetry and the public which the experiments and obscurity of the last fifty years have done so much to widen' (John Betjeman in the *Listener*, 19.iii.64). Christopher Ricks, writing in the *New York Review of Books* claimed Larkin was 'the best poet England now has ... [His] poetry is a refinement of self-consciousness, usually flawless in execution ... [his poems] deal with the world of all of us – the place where, in the end, we find our happiness, or not at all' (14.i.65). In April 1964 Larkin was elected a Fellow of the Royal Society of Literature and the following month, Patrick Garland, a young film producer working with the BBC, negotiated to film him both at work and at leisure in Hull.

Garland and his support team arrived for a week in June, their trailing cables and ubiquitous cameras confronting the Library staff at every turn. Most of us were caught on camera going about our daily tasks but only a few of us appeared in the film. The Library's photographer, however, had a field day, photographing the television crew filming Philip – and whoever happened to be with him – so that the Library has its own record of the event.

One evening I accompanied Philip and the team to an outdoor location, a watery, run-down hinterland between Beverley Road and the west bank of the River Hull. It is a heavily industrialised area, bisected by man-made drains which run parallel to the river. At its southern extremity the Hull flows into the Humber which at this point Philip describes in the poem 'Here' as 'barge-crowded water' (*CP* 136–7), but where we were that evening, a couple of miles upstream, it was more reminiscent of 'Canals with floatings of industrial froth' (*CP* 114).

I remember very little about our precise location or, other than where we turned off Beverley Road, how we reached it, or what I did. I seem to remember just standing around or following the film crew on a cool, sunless June evening. I have always been convinced that the film sequence, with Philip's recorded voice reading 'Wants', took place on the west bank of the River Hull, against an ugly backdrop of gasometers and cooling towers. But others, more familiar with the area than I am, believe that Barmston Drain is the waterway featured. Possibly both locations were used – they are certainly within easy walking distance of one another. It matters little since the view from either point is similar: murky waters and slimy banks, offensive to both sight and smell. A polluted backwater, aesthetically, it was a world apart from Pearson Park although in actual fact the distance is little more than a mile.

The 'Church Going' sequences were not filmed the same evening, nor was I present when they were. Nonetheless, I'm fairly sure that the derelict church featured in the programme, 'this special shell' where 'so many dead lie round' was also in this area, in or near Sculcoates Cemetery. By contrast, the early morning fish dock scenes bustled with feverish activity while the rest of the city still slept, an experience Philip enjoyed in spite of his protestations at having to rise so early.

As the date for the programme's transmission approached (15.xii.64) he became increasingly uneasy. Neither he nor I had television at the time, therefore his friends, John and Angela Kenyon, thoughtfully invited us both to dinner, before watching the film. In a winter of bad fogs, the one that night was particularly dense, and as Philip had only had a car since February, it was his first experience of night-driving in fog. Describing the ordeal to Garland afterwards, he complained:

> *Monitor* was nearly the price of me on Tuesday, as I had to drive six miles into the country to see it, get three-quarters drunk in order to withstand its impact and drive back in even thicker fog than had reigned earlier. All in all it's a wonder I'm still alive. (Patrick Garland: 'Filming with Philip Larkin', the *Listener*, 12.xii.85)

More than thirty years later I still remember that nightmare drive vividly. At times I had to walk in front of the car with a torch! When we arrived at the Kenyons', distressed and apologetically late, we discovered that our hostess had been involved in an even more frightening experience. Earlier in the evening, driving home with their two-year old daughter, poor visibility had caused her to run into the back of a lorry. Thankfully neither mother nor child was hurt although both parents were still shaken by their narrow escape from possible tragedy. How Angela produced a meal in the circumstances, I cannot now imagine, but the food and drink relaxed us all so that even Philip enjoyed the programme, not inappropriately named, as events turned out, *Down Cemetery Road*.

It was an immediate success and as it was virtually the only television appearance to which he willingly (but diffidently) consented, its future popularity was assured. It is perforce shown whenever his work, life and death are discussed. Wistful, speculative, sensitive, the film portrays Philip as he then was, a thoughtful observer of society and his surroundings. Garland captured the essence of the man Larkin wanted his readers to know and remember: gentle and compassionate, albeit melancholy; not the acerbic misanthrope of more recent appraisals.

Other honours followed. His pleasure on being awarded the Queen's Gold Medal for Poetry in June 1965 was equalled by his disappointment at its unceremonious delivery by post! He had expected to receive it personally from Her Majesty. Nevertheless, I recall the shy pride with which he exhibited it to chosen friends at lunch in the Refectory, and the unaffected description of his mother's joy when he showed it to her. 'Mother looked at the medal & says what she always says, that she wishes Father could know (it always touches me): I think I shall leave it here [at his mother's home] for a while' he wrote to me some days later (20.vi.65). He was increasingly sought after for newspaper interviews (John Horder, 'Poet on the 8.15', *Guardian*, 20.v.65; Philip Oakes, 'The unsung Gold Medallist', *Sunday Times* magazine, 27.iii.66); and for contributions to literary periodicals. He became a regular book and jazz record reviewer, and from 1961–71 wrote a monthly column on new jazz releases for the *Daily Telegraph*.

In January 1966 he was asked to edit the *Oxford Book of Twentieth Century English Verse*, an invitation he regarded as particularly prestigious as its forerunner, the *Oxford Book of Modern Verse*, had been edited thirty years earlier by his youthful model, W. B. Yeats. It was a larger task than Larkin had anticipated and took five years to compile, necessitating a period of sabbatical leave in Oxford, with the facilities of a copyright library. Publication day, 29 March 1973, coincided quite by chance with an invitation to lunch with the Queen at Buckingham Palace. In order to fulfil this honour, he had to absent himself for a day from a SCONUL conference at Southampton. On returning there that evening, he wrote to me of 'this really quite extraordinary day'. At the Palace, he admitted: '[I] felt a bit out of my element', having been placed opposite Princess Alexandra whom he described as quite 'fierce'.

About the publication of the *Oxford Book*, he confessed that he was relieved by the 'good reviews in *The Times, The Daily Tele[graph], The Guardian & The Financial Times*', but equally disturbed by 'bad ones in *The Listener, The Spec[tator] & The N[ew] S[tatesman]* ... But all leaders

& so indications of importance' (29.iii.73). The reviews were indeed mixed. Among the many critics Donald Davie, writing in the *Listener*, was particularly critical of Larkin's choices and *ipso facto* his omissions, and attacked his stance on the modernists. On the other hand, as Larkin intended, the anthology was a success with the 'gentle reader', in which light he regarded me, as the inscription in my copy shows.

No matter how controversial the reviews of the *Oxford Book of Twentieth Century English Verse* were, his popularity was at a peak when his final collection, *High Windows*, appeared in June 1974 to almost universal acclaim. In spite of the fact that we remained very close during the writing of this collection, Philip did not talk about, or show me, the poems while he was working on them to the same extent as he had done those in *The Whitsun Weddings*. One of the exceptions was 'Friday Night in the Royal Station Hotel' where we often sat over a drink in its formal, lofty lounge. It was a more forbidding place then than it is now. Another was 'The Trees' which he showed me one lovely summer evening when he pulled up at a beauty spot on the Wolds. In 1967 he had certainly not lost his sense of the romantic. On the other hand, until he gave me a copy of *High Windows* in May 1974, I knew nothing about 'Forget What Did', an enigmatic poem which hints at an emotional wound, of such significance, sustained by the poet, that he stopped writing up the daily entries in his diary. He merely said as he handed me the book: 'There is one poem in this collection which directly concerns you: it is called 'Forget What Did'. As the presentation took place during a lengthy break in our friendship (July 1973 to November 1974) I did not ask, then or subsequently, what I had done to upset him to this extent. I have always assumed that jealousy, real or imagined, inspired the poem.

A possible reason for not discussing the poems in *High Windows* with me may have been a certain sensitivity about showing me the harder-hitting poems like 'Annus Mirabilis' – a somewhat thinly disguised account of our relationship – or 'This Be the Verse'. I should have shrunk from the personal implications in the first and the cynicism of the second, and he in turn would have recoiled from my reproach. I did not therefore share the general approval of *High Windows* which seemed to me to lack the warmth and compassion of *The Whitsun Weddings*. Nor could I regard it with the same affection as its predecessor, which Philip used to refer to in private as 'your book', and said he would have liked to dedicate to me. By contrast, the voice with which Larkin spoke in the new collection was angry, iconoclastic, loveless: 'in *High Windows* there is a deafening silence about love' (Swarbrick 143), while Booth points to the difference between the younger and the more mature Larkin:

> The earlier poems philosophise ironically over the sense of lost opportunities ... Then in the later 1960s ... his philosophical composure cracks and he begins to express a raw jealousy of the young. Finally in the early 1970s he turns his attention ... to the prospect of physical and mental senility. (149)

Always obsessed with the thought of death, Larkin began to write his last major poem, 'Aubade', just as *High Windows* was about to be published. But it was not completed until November 1977, ten days after his mother's death. It appeared in the *Times Literary Supplement* the following month, but was largely overlooked until his own death eight years later. We had often exchanged views on our respective ideas about death and our discussions invariably concluded with Philip pointing out the advantage my religion gave me over his outlook, namely the Christian expectation of an afterlife. But in the days following his mother's death, I was not prepared for a threnody on the subject. I too was in subdued mood as my mother had died only six months previously. At first I did not realise that his repetition, over two or three days, of the views I had so often heard him express before, was in fact a recital of 'Aubade'. When I did recognise it for what it was, I was stunned by its bleakness, its total lack of consolation. I suggested it was the agnostic's response to Newman's *Dream of Gerontius* which we had read together some years earlier when we borrowed (at Philip's request) my father's recording of Elgar's oratorio. He did not dispute this view but turned away, overcome by his recent bereavement and thoughts of his own end.

> Unresting death, a whole day nearer now,
> Making all thought impossible but how
> And where and when I shall myself die. (*CP* 208)

Larkin's poetic output, never prolific, was decidedly meagre after the appearance of *High Windows*. In his remaining eleven years, he completed only seventeen poems and of these only seven were published in his lifetime. One of the reasons he gave for his diminishing output was that he did not find the new house he had exchanged in 1974 for the flat in Pearson Park conducive to writing.

Of the handful of published poems, the seldom noticed 'The Mower' (*CP* 214) describes the accidental killing of a hedgehog by the poet in his Newland Park garden. He told me about the incident and the poem, knowing that I had not forgotten the occasion when, a few years earlier, he ran over a hedgehog while driving me home late one night. We had been to a party and as Philip turned into a side road close by my home, he slowed down then suddenly accelerated just as a hedgehog was crossing in front of the car. I was shocked for the action seemed almost deliberate. Philip braked and we both got out of the car but could find no trace of the poor creature. The following morning I went out to see if I could discover its fate and found its lifeless body in the gutter. When I saw Philip later I said accusingly: 'You killed that hedgehog,' knowing that alcohol had almost certainly impaired his judgement. 'Yes, I know,' he replied very humbly; 'I went at 7.30 this morning and moved it to the side of the road. I couldn't sleep for thinking of what I had done.' However, there was no elegy to mark that particular hedgehog's death.

A more important poem published in those lean years was the commissioned work, 'Bridge for the Living', the writing of which caused him particular anxiety. The work was a joint venture, Larkin supplying the words for a cantata composed by Anthony Hedges, of the University's Music Department, to mark the opening of the Humber Bridge in 1981. From the beginning, Larkin was a reluctant participant. Emotionally, he was not in favour of a bridge linking the north and south banks of the river: he resented its 'stride into our solitude' (*CP* 204). In the preliminary negotiations, Hedges explained that he envisaged a musical composition lasting 40 minutes, which indicated a poem of some 250 lines, a proposition Philip 'went away to ponder on for several months'. In the meantime *High Windows* was published, a copy of which he sent to Hedges, inscribed 'Friends before …!'

When the long-awaited text was eventually submitted, it was only 40 lines long which, not unnaturally, Hedges assumed was the first instalment. 'It's absolutely marvellous, Philip' he enthused. 'When shall I get the rest? "That's it", he said, "I can't add a word more".' Stalemate. Since 40 lines of verse could not by any stretch of the imagination be made to fill 40 minutes of playing time, the composer had no alternative but to reduce his setting to 20 minutes. But, as he explained in his contribution to the Thanksgiving programme for Philip after his death,[13] even to fill this performance time, he had to write 'a long, slow atmospheric, orchestral introduction' and have the chorus repeat the opening words '"Isolate city" so slowly and so often'. Philip told me that he was dissatisfied with the title, which had been insisted on by the commissioners. In fact it

[13] A tribute produced by Donald Roy, Head of the University Drama Department, in June 1986 (see Chapter 7).

pleased neither artist. Hedges recalled that Philip 'in his most Eeyore manner' had said '"Bridge for the Living" sounds like some card instruction manual for adults.' As the opening of the bridge was delayed, the cantata was not performed until 1981, several years after its completion.

Larkin also remained dissatisfied with the poem's ending. Normally he prided himself on the compact force of his closing lines. In the case of 'Bridge for the Living' he admitted to me that its conclusion was metrically weak and its sentiment trite – 'Always it is by bridges that we live' – even though he had spent several weeks trying to improve it. It confirmed his aversion to writing to order and strengthened his growing conviction that he would be unable to fulfil the duties of Poet Laureate should he be offered the post which, ironically, he had privately coveted since the early 1970s. As he grew older, an added disincentive was the glare of publicity which the office had increasingly attracted. However, he did not decline the honour in 1984 without acknowledging that he had been offered the highest accolade the nation could bestow, a tribute which completely negated his youthful prediction 'that I should never even at my best be much more than a minor artist – and indeed if I start thinking about it I see that I shall never be anything at all – but I want to be that and write anyway' (PAL to JBS, 20.vii.41). Few aspirations can have been so richly consummated.

Finally, when, after Philip's death, Anthony Thwaite discovered three unpublished love poems written between 1975 and 1979, he wrote asking me if Philip had ever shown me or talked about these poems which he had found folded together and tucked into the back of the final workbook. He wrote 'indeed I feel sure all three have to do with you. All were typed out by Philip ... as well as clearly being there in pencil-written drafts in the notebook' (11.xi.87). My simple answer was 'no' but since Anthony had given me an outline of each of the poems, 'When first we faced and touching showed', 'Morning at last: there in the snow', and 'Love Again', I replied that each poem seemed to mirror a significant stage in our relationship. When Anthony sent me copies, this impression was reinforced. The final stanza of 'When first we faced' sharply resembled Philip's actual words to me on that February evening in 1961 when we embraced for the first time.

> But when did love not try to change
> The world back to itself – no cost,
> No past, no people else at all –
> Only what meeting made us feel,
> So new, and gentle-sharp, and strange? (*CP* 205)

Although not written until fifteen years later (December 1975), I supposed the very intense renewal of our friendship between 1974 and 1976 may have prompted this recollection of its beginning. However, it may be that it could equally have been written to celebrate his mature affair with Betty Mackereth (*Life* 454).

On the other hand, 'Morning at last', written a few weeks later, was prompted by my winter boots one snowy night in January 1976. As I was pulling them on in front of the fire at 105 Newland Park prior to going home, Philip observed how the boots distorted my feet. 'How short and stubby they look' he said (not unkindly) when in fact my feet are long and narrow. The following day he told me how, first thing, he had looked out of an upstairs window and been mesmerised by 'your small blunt footprints' imperceptibly dissolving in the melting snow. He said nothing about the deeper thoughts this scene gave rise to, how my vanishing footsteps would leave 'only this sign / Of your life walking into mine' (*CP* 206). As always, when he reflected realistically on our association, there was no conventionally happy solution – as indeed there wasn't with any of his sexual relationships. Knowing this makes me content with what I had.

The genesis of 'Love Again' proved more difficult. The copy which Thwaite sent me only gave its completion date, 20 September 1979, which suggested to me that the poem was stimulated by a new relationship, the first since the break with Philip eighteen months previously, which I had started in mid-August 1979. I did not appreciate until much later that the poem had been started in August 1975 when, after a separation of many months, my renewed intimacy with Philip had reached a new peak. However, before I was aware of this, new biographical evidence came to light which, Anthony Thwaite concluded, indicated that 'Love Again' almost certainly did not concern me (AT to MMB 3.vi.88).[14] After studying the penultimate draft of the biography in 1992, I let Andrew Motion read Philip's letters to me in order that it might give him a better insight into our relationship. Amongst them he discovered a letter written on 7 August 1975 in which he detected the inspiration for 'Love Again'. I had only that day left for a family holiday in Ireland with my sister and three-year old nephew and that evening Philip wrote:

I wish you hadn't gone away just when you did: I miss you. A fearful boiling

---

[14] It was in fact this intimation that led me to the discovery, a few days later, of the relationship with Betty Mackereth, and not, as has often been stated, the revelation in the draft biography five years later.

night was diversified by two dreams about you, both 'losing dreams' – you going off with someone else – wch was all very silly, for how can one lose what one does not possess?

Motion concludes: 'Hours after posting it, he began one of his most powerful last poems, "Love Again", discovering that beneath the calm surface of his affair lurked feelings as turbulent as those he had known as a young man' (*Life* 454).

If this letter does link the beginning of the poem with me, I think it is all the more likely that the immediate motivation for finishing it was not the influence of his 'muse-mother' (she had been dead almost two years) as Motion believes (*Life* 476–7) but rather the new relationship I had formed in August 1979. Knowing Philip as I did, pure jealousy, it seems to me provoked the speculation 'why it [love] never worked for me'. After all, in the poem he traces the root of his anguish to *both* his parents, and the effect of their hapless marriage on him from his earliest years. In particular, it seems that the memory of 'the terrible neutralising effect of a quarrel' between his parents when he was twenty haunted him for the rest of his life. This is how he described the incident to Jim Sutton: the same sentiments are discernible in the poem.

> I realised that I contain both of them, and that this is the cause of my inertia, for in me they are incessantly opposed ... It intrigues me to know that a thirty-years struggle is being continued in me, and in my sister too. In her it has reached a sort of conclusion – my father winning. Pray the Lord my mother is superior in me. That is as it should be. (12.iv.43)

5

Religion

Since someone will forever be surprising
A hunger in himself to be more serious,
And gravitating with it to this ground. (*CP* 97)

When I came to read the Sutton letters, one thing I found fascinating
was Larkin's frequent expressions of ambivalence towards religion, rang-
ing from the cynical and profane to the mystical and spiritual. Generally,
his attitude is thought to have been harshly dismissive – as indeed for
the most part it was – but privately Larkin gave religion more serious
thought than he publicly admitted. Ever-mindful of his father's exhor-
tation never to believe in God, there were, nevertheless, occasions when
he questioned the wisdom of this advice.

He described himself as 'an agnostic – but an Anglican agnostic of
course' (*Life* 485). Anglicanism was in fact the key to Larkin's singular
outlook. He had been baptised in Coventry Cathedral, a fact of which he
was privately proud. He related readily to the Anglican tradition and
admired the simplicity of its ritual. He was knowledgeable about the
Church's year, the significance of its seasons and feast-days, the occurrence
of ember days and ferial days. Ray Brett, a close friend, has observed:
'He never had any religious faith, but like Hardy, whom he resembled in
so many respects, he felt a reverence for the familiar forms of Anglican
worship and would have liked to believe they rested on truth' (Brett 111–12).
Among favourite poems he numbered John Meade Falkner's 'After
Trinity'. To mark Trinity Sunday 1966 he gave me John Betjeman's
miscellany, *Altar and Pew*, which contains this poem.[15] Another preferred
poem was Frances Cornford's short love lyric, 'All Souls' Night', the
religious significance of which is central to its meaning. In short,
the Church of England was part of his middle-class heritage.

His formative years, however, were spent in the climate he described

---

[15] London: Vista Books, 1959.

in *High Windows*, with '*No God any more, or sweating in the dark / About hell and that, or having to hide / What you think of the priest.*' (*CP* 165). Typical of his generation, Larkin exulted in this new-found freedom which he expressed in blasphemous expletives such as 'Christ fucking Jesus' (26.vi.46), or, when fulminating about the delay of *Jill*, 'God bugger me blue, where *is* the sod?' (*SL* 122). More positively he declared: 'All this Christian bunk is denying half of oneself as L[awrence] will tell you' ([summer 1941]). Jazz, he suggested to Sutton, was their generation's substitute for religion: 'One can't be a Christian in these days either; that may connect up with it [jazz]' (10.xi.[41]). Art indeed replaced religion for Larkin: 'art is as near religion as one can get' (5.vii.44), and 'the only worthwhile theories, or statements of belief, are works of art' (*SL* 125).

One of the aspects of the Sutton letters which seemed quite familiar to me was the sensitivity and grace of the lyrical passages with which they are liberally interspersed. These stand out in sharp contrast to the distinctly more rumbustious outpourings of earthier interests. Outdoor scenes particularly generated a mystical state, like this evening vignette of Oxford:

> It is now nearly 9 pm and raining ... A single reading lamp lights the whole room. Beyond the window, the classic and associated spires, turrets and cornices stand motionless, but grey; the enormous impact of war has given Oxford a fundamental shock, so that its axis has been shaken from the Radcliffe Camera to Carfax. Army lorries thunder down Cornmarket Street in an endless procession ... Away in the depths of university quadrangles, I gain the impression of being at the end of an epoch. Will the axis ever return to its normal position? (21.v.41)

Motion says of Larkin's genius: 'the flower of art grows on a long stem out of some very mucky stuff.'[16] It could equally be said that Larkin's talent was nurtured in some very rich soil.

Sometimes the beauty of the world and its inhabitants seem 'meaningless' to him, though still capable of filling him with a sense of well-being and awe:

> It is half past nine at night, and I am sitting in a pool of light hollowed from the darkness ... Birds and blossom are out, lambs, daffodils, almond trees, all very beautiful. I am in a state when I can wander through the streets, letting my gaze slip from one face to another ... delighting passively in the

---

[16] Mark Lawson, Interview with Andrew Motion (*Independent on Sunday*, 7.iii.1993).

meaningless beauty of each one. I found myself in a little pocket of silence crossing Cornmarket Street this evening and felt afraid and exhilarated. (25.iii.43)

Hearing the dawn chorus also fills him with wonder:

> But what I really like is hearing the birds singing at dawn: I very rarely do, but if I wake up before 5 & 6 [*sic*] in the half light I can hear them chattering away outside: led by a blackbird. The very fact that they are unintelligible seems to make them doubly beautiful to me. Planed-off shavings of sound! (17.iii.50)

His dismay, when deafness robbed him of this pleasure in his late thirties, is not surprising. On another occasion, after a day's walking on the hills around Wellington, everything seems bathed in mystical light as he contemplates

> the graveyards and the different houses all quiet on Sunday afternoon. You can remember, I expect, days like this, when everything far or near at hand seems specially graced by the light. Sheep, railway engines, yards, lanes, distant hills, iron gates, drinking pumps.
>   I was not in the mood when I wanted to make anything out of it: I was quite happy to let it alone. (*SL* 114)

At other times he resorts to the language of religion, if not the substance, as in this description of an early January morning cycle ride in the Warwickshire lanes near his home:

> Do you know the kind of morning – cold, with a pale, diffused light over everything, with frost in the grass and hedges, and ice in the puddles and cartruts? ... The sky was half ice-blue, and half misty and dovecoloured. Occasionally an aeroplane swam across. And the land was so richly brown and green, with occasional flocks of grey and golden sheep and red brick farms rising up ... Everything seemed filled with the 'Glory of God' ... (*SL* 54)

On some occasions Larkin is conscious of spiritual experiences he is unable to fathom. A walk one evening, for instance, fills him with

> an emotion of an intensity never surpassed by anything else, and unlike anything else. I know no explanation of it: Wordsworth, I imagine, had it even stronger. (9.vii.43)

At times like these he admits that he is at a loss to explain the mysterious force which suffuses him:

> Everything that my personality colours is a balls-up – my own affairs and

so on. But when I am being 'no more, no less, than two weak eyes' everything is filled with a blessed light, bells, bugles, brightness and the Lord knows what. (24.v.44)

Interestingly, he defined Lawrence's creativity in specifically theosophical terms: 'the key of the matter is that he had more genius – more of God, if you like, – than any man could be expected to handle' (*SL* 101). In short, certain experiences made Larkin aware of forces outside his control which defied explanation. However, he did not pursue these fleeting insights to formulate any particular creed and continued to uphold agnosticism.

Then, shortly before his father's death, he made a surprising disclosure to Sutton:

I am being instructed in the technique of religion by an old chap called Leon. A very nice chap but a bit apt to take things cut & dried for granted, you know – things like good & evil & faith etc. (*SL* 146)

Two weeks earlier, having been exhorted to do so by Sutton, Larkin had visited a major Van Gogh exhibition in London which made a deep impression on him. 'Certain of the landscapes, *View of Arles* for instance, seemed to tremble with packed life: the structure of them seemed entirely organised by the intensity of his vision rather than any mental plan' he told Sutton (24.ii.48). A fortnight later, as his father's final illness progressed, he recalled the impact another of the paintings had made on him:

On the Threshold of Eternity – you remember the old man with his head in his hands. That has a quality I admire. I wish I could write a book like it. A quality of rough, shrunken suffering. Truly old age seems a terrible time, but I suppose one reaches it by easy stages. (*SL* 146)

The letters to Sutton contain no further reference to formal religious instruction but in the months following his father's death he told Sutton he was studying the Bible. Passages he found interesting or moving he quoted at some length, such as this one from *The Apocalypse*:

How lovely those verses are – 'And God shall wipe away all tears from their eyes: and there shall be no more death, neither sorrow nor crying, neither shall there be any more pain … And he said unto me, Write, for these words are true and faithful.' (*SL* 149)

Larkin again read the Bible in its entirety two years before his death, but this time his verdict was more trenchant. 'Really, it's absolute balls. Beautiful, of course. But balls' (*Life* 486).

During the twenty-five years or so I knew Philip Larkin well, he probably talked about religion as much to me as to anyone. As a practising Catholic it was natural that I should talk about my beliefs. I was never circumspect about this because at no time did he display any hostility towards them although he may at times have found my strict adherence to the Church's teaching on sexual ethics disconcerting. However, he understood and respected my principles with a facility which struck me as remarkable until I discovered the 'Moment of Ecstasy' letter, written to Jim Sutton on 17 August 1943. In this letter, in which Larkin argues against instant sexual gratification with a surprising urgency, it became clear to me that although he was unable to endorse my beliefs theologically – when contemplating marriage he admitted to a mutual friend that my religion was a serious obstacle – at least he had grasped morally, long before he met me, the principles on which they were based.

At the age of twenty-one love was still a remote ideal, about the conduct of which Larkin had very romantic ideas. These he set down in an essay in which the key phrase is 'The Moment of Ecstasy' and which he transposed the following morning into a seven-page letter to Sutton. Its ethos is in great contrast to the uncouth stance he took on love at other times, and the entrenched cynicism he upheld in public in later life. Its unworldliness and virginal arguments have nothing in common with 'Annus Mirabilis' or 'High Windows' but portend the lyrical strain of 'First Sight' or 'The Trees'.

The principal argument of 'The Moment of Ecstasy' is that at every sentient level of human experience, and particularly in sexual relation-ships, the modern trend is to cut out the preliminaries in order to reach the moment of ecstasy as soon as possible. Inevitably the result is rapid disillusionment and disappointment. In the context of love, for instance, the ritual of wooing and courtship, he explains, has been abandoned:

> Once man, like the elephant, was 'slow to mate'. There were addresses to be paid, gloves to be picked up, dances to be requested ... Now there is nothing but a desire to get on to the moment of ecstasy, whether it is the 'security' of marriage, or the sexual consummation ... the ritual has been cut out ... And birth-control, sex doesn't mean children, families, living, growing, lives twisting more and more richly together ... Sex means nothing – just the moment of ecstasy, that flares and dies in a few minutes. (17.viii.43).

From there he moves swiftly to another increasing phenomenon of the present day: 'The result of speeding up the approach is speeding up the departure – quick divorces. Do you realise how *modern* a thing divorce is?' The moral, Larkin concluded, 'lies in abnegating the technical power that enables us to cut the cackle and get to the moment of ecstasy without paying for it'.

Another striking feature of this letter is its imagery. Larkin begins by comparing man's life to a flower which, in its seminal stages, spends months in the ground, unseen and forgotten, until it blooms and has its moment of ecstasy. Unlike man, the flower does not seek to hasten its moment of glory – or didn't before man introduced methods of intensive horticulture. Other analogies are drawn: from religion, where the gradual erosion of ritual has given way to more ascetic – and shorter – forms of worship; from modern literature, where the tendency is to cut out long descriptive detail so that the impact 'is sharp and immediate: it goes straight to the raw senses ...'; from travel, where the aim is to reach one's destination without delay, eschewing the pleasure of the journey. All these examples illustrate the moral that by hastening fulfilment we court disappointment, and our experience is consequently impoverished. A fine sermon in true Christian tradition, delivered by an agnostic, celibate idealist of 21!

Over the next few months, occasional references were made to the essay in the correspondence between the two men. The last time it was mentioned, in an undated note, Larkin rejoices that a letter received from Sutton that morning is 'full of the "moment of ecstasy" and little lyrical passages like the spontaneous dance-steps of a negro child strolling down the sidewalk with its hands in its pockets. It was quite like old times to have you writing like that ...'. A little further on he wrote: 'I have not been thinking about the moment of ecstasy recently, but I have no doubt if I read the letter I sent you I should agree with it still. That and the jazz business, I stand by sincerely', adding somewhat randomly: 'NB Katherine Mansfield's letters and diaries = the fallow period: her stories = the moment of ecstasy' ([Jan. 1944]).

In spite of Larkin's subsequent – and for the most part publicly proclaimed – disillusionment with love, it struck me, reading this letter almost 50 years after it was written, that he never entirely lost sight of the ideals he extolled in it. They certainly propelled and sustained his deeper sexual relationships and – more permanently – found expression in the lyrical poems. Perhaps love failed him because his ideals were so high: it never matched his expectations.

In 1961, just as our friendship was developing, Philip suffered a mysterious illness which necessitated a spell in hospital both in Hull and in London. This was how he interpreted the abrupt interruption of our association:

Do you think this ailment I am undergoing is God's way of putting a stop
to something He thought might be getting out of hand? If so, I wonder why
He shd. pick on me when so many others get the green light all the way.
But perhaps He is very fond of you. If so, I can understand it more readily.–
Looking over that I see an ambiguity: I don't mean a green light with you,
just other pairs of people in general. (10.iv.61)

This is an unexpected speculation for an agnostic, but one I confess I
had myself examined. It supports Booth's view that Larkin's attitude
towards religion 'is emotional rather than spiritual.' As I have already
demonstrated, illness, death and external beauty produced similar re-
sponses. But Booth's extension of this theory, that Larkin only saw religion
'as another of the pathetic ideals by which we live' (Booth 137), is to
overlook his sensitivity, idealism and susceptibility to mystical experiences
– 'Everything seemed filled with the "Glory of God".' These characteristics
enabled him not only to recognise another person's spirituality but also
to share it.

In the early days of our friendship he used to encourage me to take
my missal along when we met on Sundays. We would then compare the
readings for the day in the *Small Roman Missal* with those in the *Book
of Common Prayer*. This was before the deliberations of the Second
Vatican Council (1962–65) were implemented, when the only readings
included in the liturgy of the Mass were the Epistle – usually a passage
from the letters of St. Paul – and the Gospel – an extract from one of
the Evangelists. Very seldom was a reading from the Old Testament
included, a fact which frequently drew comment from Philip, who con-
sidered my Catholic ignorance of the Bible abysmal, as indeed it was,
compared with his knowledge.

Partly to remedy this deficiency he gave me the recently published joint
Oxford University/Cambridge University Press's complete *New English
Bible with the Apocrypha* for my birthday in 1970. Its publication had
been a long awaited literary event as it was the first authorised translation
for a hundred years and took twenty years to complete. The intention
was to produce a translation in good modern idiom to replace the 1611
King James's version, still the most commonly used version in the Church
of England, but considered archaic and difficult to interpret. The new
version did not fulfil its ambition and was met with much hostile criticism
on account of the looseness of the translation and its commonplace and
unimaginative idiom. Philip, who had keenly awaited its publication, must
have voiced his disappointment in the appropriate quarter, no doubt at
Oxford during his sabbatical leave there in 1970/1, for he was subsequently

invited by the Joint Committee of the New Translation to join a panel to turn it into more dignified English. This project never got off the ground. Personally, I think some of the modern idiom is successful and much prefer the form: 'Love is patient; love is kind and envies no-one', with which my copy is inscribed, to the more pompous 'Charity suffereth long and is kind; charity envieth not ...' (Corinthians 13.4)

However, as a result of Vatican II's deliberations in the early 1960s, many changes were gradually introduced into the liturgy of the Mass, and amongst the earliest were an Old Testament reading and a Psalm which preceded the Epistle and Gospel readings. But the biggest change was from the Latin Mass, with very few responses (also in Latin) by the congregation, to the Mass in the vernacular with much greater participation by the laity. It surprised me that Philip showed any interest in these innovations, and while I would not maintain that his curiosity was sustained throughout the period of change, in the early stages he was probably better informed about the liturgical alterations ushered in by Vatican II than most church-goers of other denominations.

About this time, shocked by the sudden death of Evelyn Waugh on Easter Sunday 1966, Larkin confided that he felt moved to go into a church to pray for him. I found his reflections very touching:

> It's very hard for me to imagine a world without Evelyn Waugh – he was one of the few really good living writers & is a great loss. I went in the church again today [17] & thought I shd. have liked to pray for him if I'd known what to say & if he hadn't been a RC! Perhaps some strangled supplication escaped me & voyaged to the right destination. (Easter Monday 1966)

Before his next letter to me he had '. . . bought at last *The Father Brown Stories* [by G. K. Chesterton] in memory of Evelyn Waugh. I've often meant to buy them & this seemed a good excuse. Good Catholic literature.'! (13.iv.66).

These confidences in no way encouraged me to believe that Philip was about to embrace Christianity, let alone Catholicism, but ironically, far from my religion dividing us, it added a spiritual dimension to the relationship which greatly enriched it. Sometimes his response to my faith led him to anticipate my religious needs before I had even considered them. When he was on sabbatical leave at All Souls in 1970/71, I spent a weekend in Oxford with him. I had scarcely stepped off the train before

---

[17] Philip had already accompanied his mother to church the previous day, Easter Sunday.

he volunteered that he had located the Catholic church nearest to my hotel and had noted the times of Sunday Masses.

The following morning (Saturday) he insisted that we went to the church, Greyfriars, so that I would know its exact whereabouts in relation to my hotel on the Iffley Road. Then he took me to two more churches. The first was Blackfriars in St. Giles which he erroneously introduced as the University Catholic Chaplaincy, a common misapprehension. The second was St. Aloysius's church on the Woodstock Road. I do not now remember why Larkin wanted me to see this church. It is possible that he had discovered during recent research for the *Oxford Book of Twentieth Century English Verse* that Gerard Manley Hopkins had spent a year there in 1878–79, and was therefore curious to see the church himself. A holy water stoup commemorates the poet-priest's stay. I had not asked to be taken to any of these churches. I had not even mentioned the need to enquire about Mass times on Sunday. But I was greatly touched by Philip's forethought and sensitivity in thus introducing me to Catholic Oxford.

Visits to three Catholic churches on a wet Saturday in Oxford is an uncommon diversion for most lay people; for Philip it was unprecedented. Apart from this occasion, however, our shared church-going was limited. I recall that he accompanied me to Mass in Hull once or twice, and more distinctly I remember a Good Friday Service we attended at Ampleforth Abbey in North Yorkshire. The austerity of the ceremony and the simplicity of the church appealed to Larkin, but I realised that his motivation in escorting me was not so much an interest in the Catholic faith as a willingness to remain with me rather than wait elsewhere while I went to the service.

Otherwise, until he met A. N. Wilson in the early 1980s, Philip's church-going in middle life was mainly restricted to fulfilling social obligations and occasionally escorting his mother when they were on holiday. Wilson had a friend who was the priest-in-charge of St. Stephen's, an Anglo-Catholic church in Hull. He persuaded Philip to go along there to Evensong one October Sunday in 1983. Describing the service afterwards, Philip told me he found the liturgy impressive but the atmosphere was too High Church and he did not go again. It was at this time, also under Wilson's influence, that he re-read the Bible from beginning to end, dismissing it as 'absolute balls.' As a result, he thought he had finally rejected Christianity.

In June 1985, however, faced with death at the time of the operation on his oesophagus, Philip again felt drawn to the Church, just as he had during his father's last illness. After several weeks of convalescence he confided that he was anxious to attend Evensong in thanksgiving for his recovery, incomplete though it was. Diffident about going alone, he twice told me that he had been unable to persuade Monica Jones, his now constant companion, to go with him. However, it did not occur to me until it was too late that he was probably hoping that I would volunteer to accompany him. Nevertheless, shortly afterwards he went, not to St. Stephen's but to St. Mary's in Cottingham, the church in which his funeral service was held barely two months later. I do not know if he went again, but suspect he probably attended once or twice more before his illness finally overwhelmed him. Much though I should like to think he did, it is doubtful if Larkin derived any comfort from the Church in the weeks before his death. By his last words: 'I am going to the inevitable' (*Life* 521) he almost certainly meant 'the total emptiness for ever, / The sure extinction that we travel to / And shall be lost in always' (*CP* 208). At the same time, his intense fear of death almost certainly recalled to mind the agnostic's prayer he articulated to Sutton a month before his father died: 'God, if there is a God, have mercy on my soul, if I have a soul' (*SL* 145).

Larkin's skirmishes with religion over the years were but the quest of an enquiring mind for the fundamental truths about life, death and eternity. Just as the most convinced Christian at times doubts the existence of God and an afterlife, so Larkin occasionally wavered in his agnostic views. This point was made by one of the two priests – both incidentally Anglo-Catholics – who officiated at his funeral service. Acknowledging the conflict between Larkin's life-long views as a non-believer and his spasmodic search for religious truth, he concluded that Christian burial was entirely appropriate for Larkin who would have 'wanted to be on the side of the angels.'

Many who were familiar with his well-aired agnostic views were surprised that he was not cremated. Jim Sutton, in fact, was told that he had been. On enquiring the whereabouts of his grave at St. Mary's church, six months after Philip's death, Sutton was told 'by a lady I asked that his ashes would be at the crematorium' (JBS to MMB 25.viii.87). Later, when he discovered the truth, Jim's response was 'I thought it very strange that Philip should be cremated!' (JBS to MMB 17.ix.87). Like me, his old friend recognised instinctively that Philip would not have chosen cremation.[18] We never discussed it, but had we done so, I feel sure Philip's

[18] According to Graham Stroud, Larkin had bought a plot in Cottingham Cemetery some years before he died. *About Larkin* 9 April 2000, 13.

reaction, albeit irrational, would have been that cremation would merely accelerate the process of 'sure extinction'. As it was, I felt that his obsequies would have been entirely in accordance with his wishes, even though he died, as he had lived for the most part, a convinced agnostic, 'but an Anglican agnostic, of course' (*Life* 485).

My reading of the Sutton letters had a remarkable postscript. In the spring of 1991 I spent a few days at Ampleforth Abbey. As I was walking through the grounds to the nearby village of Gilling East, on one of those translucent April mornings of brilliant sunshine on hoar frost – all thought of Philip completely absent from my mind – suddenly and quite unbidden the 'Moment of Ecstasy' letter (17.viii.43) flooded my consciousness with blinding force. From that moment – having vacillated about it since his death – it came to me where and how I had fitted into Philip Larkin's life.

When I first read the letter I had been astonished to see set down in logical progression his views on society, sex, love and marriage, in precisely the same language as he had imparted them to me twenty years later. At the time I was surprised by their catholicity and orthodoxy, as well as their idealism, not knowing that Larkin had formulated, if not always observed, these opinions long before I met him. In that moment of revelation at Ampleforth it struck me that the sense of the numinous in me must have appealed to a like quality in him, recalling this youthful philosophy which, in turn, no doubt subconsciously, prompted him to test its endurance in our relationship. This incident, more than any other, restored my faith in Philip and in the love we had shared, confirming that the part I had played in his life had been not merely romantic and exhilarating, but as he himself described it: 'something that ... did at one time seem a different kind of experience from anything hitherto' (*Life*, 366).

Appendix:
the 'Moment of Ecstasy' letter

73 Coten End,
Warwick.

Aug 17th. 1943.

Dear Jim –

I received your airgraph this morning of July 24th, acknowledging some doctrine or other I had been spouting previously. You are unlucky, for I have just turned in despair from trying to pick up a thread of thought I had last night by writing an essay about it – the kind of thing Lawrence would do so well – and shall probably pour it onto you. Briefly, it is this: the title was to be 'The Moment of Ecstasy'. (don't go away). Man's life is a flower. But man's life is composed of innumerable experiences, and they are flowers, too. And the point about flowers is that they spend months underground, and dumb and flowerless above ground, and then for three days or so – they bloom, they blow, they have their moment of ecstasy. This moment is dependent upon months of preparation, as a musician's single miraculous rendering of a piece of music depends upon years of study, practice, and the rest. It is the same with man's own experience – years of unconscious preparation may be needed to prepare each little moment of ecstasy. (I am assuming, of course, we know what a m. of e. is – we as artists should be bung full of them.) The trouble is, that they are so pleasurable that we try to get more of them, by cutting the cackle and getting to the horses, or in other words by cutting out ritual and getting down to the moment of ecstasy. Take religion. The decay of ritual there is obvious enough – the Catholic dogma & high mass, replaced by Protestantism (speaking of England, of course) and then by Methodism – each time getting further from the cumbersome ritual, vestments, fol-de-rol, lah-de-dah, and so forth – towards the single expression of God to man – the naked contact.

> he who receives
> Light from above, from the fountain of light,
> No other doctrine needs

– Milton being a Puritan, of course. Take love. The chief difference between modern and less-modern love is the speeding up of the whole process. Once man, like the elephant, was 'slow to mate'. There were addresses to be paid, gloves to be picked up, dances to be requested.

80

Further back, there were lions to be slain, or deeds of derring-do to be performed by the lady's knight. You see what I mean? Now there is nothing but a desire to get on to the moment of ecstasy, whether it is the 'security' of marriage, or the sexual consummation. And so the ritual has been cut out, the horses got to, and the moment of ecstasy reached sooner. Take literature. We all know that the main thing about the old bastards is that they are unreadable. Chaucer, for instance: you may have read somewhere that 'Troilus & Criseyde' is a masterpiece. Very well: you try to read it. You are bogged in the first dozen pages – it's long, it's cumbersome, he natters on, it's boring. You chuck it aside and pick up 'Mr Norris' (or at least I do). Virginia Woolf has said: 'Undoubtedly there is a dullness in great books ... Opportunities occur and they neglect them. Shades and subtleties accumulate and they ignore them. They seem deliberately to refuse to gratify those senses which are stimulated so briskly by the moderns ...' That puts everything clearly – you will have found it in reading Jane Austen or even Dickens. Modern literature is sharp and immediate: it goes straight to the raw senses, with such a profusion and conflict of sensations that one is easily exhausted. One has only to think of Dylan Thomas – and as for his followers! – Again the *modern* art is the cinema – again, direct contact.

But there's no need to search religion, love, and art for examples that are shown clearly in everyday life. The difference between cleaning and lighting a lamp, or laying sticks, paper, and coals, and watching the flame rise, with turning a switch, is too obvious. So is the speeding up of travel – get there, cut the cackle. And birth-control, sex doesn't mean children, families, living, growing, lives twisting more and more richly together till a family is like a subtle tweed, with an indefinable *bouquet*, like a wine: – sex means nothing – just the moment of ecstasy, that flares and dies in a few minutes. Do you begin to see what I mean? (You: 'God fuck.')

Bert [sic] – *in cutting out the steps whereby conclusions are reached, we have falsified the conclusions.* Yes, sir. Consider: religion – well, nobody gives a darn for that any longer, not in England, anyway. Methodism caught on fine in the 18th century, but it's worn thin now. Love? The result of speeding up the approach is speeding up the departure – quick divorces. Do you realise how *modern* a thing divorce is? Art? Well, I'm not really competent to judge. Time will show if 'modern' art will survive. But Virginia Woolf says: 'the flash is soon over, and there remains with us a profound dissatisfaction. The irritation is as acute as the pleasure was intense.' And as for sex – well, out of all the pother and gabble and jabber and natter and Sunday paper articles and sermons and government leaflets and school hygiene classes and 'enlightenment' and so on, there remains a rock bottom conviction that the main thing about sex in the modern world is that there is something wrong with it. And all this is only to be expected. Take a bulb, a root. Put it on the table and fix it with your eye, and say 'Flower, you little sod, flower! Go on! Put forth!' It's 10 to 1 the root will reply 'You great oaf, I must lie in the ground, secretly, and be utterly forgotten. Snow must lie above me and the dragons of winter rage in the wind. The earth must be veined with frost. Then March must come, and rain, and sun, and wind. Then I shall put forth: a green sheath, a green hand clasping a folded Treasure, growing stronger and stronger as summer comes on. Then, for a few days, I shall unclasp my hand: the flower will unfold, more delicate, more beautiful and rare than anything you can conceive. Perhaps you won't even see it. Then that will vanish, and I shall be dumb again. But I shall have expressed myself.' (That is, if the bulb has been reading Lawrence.) And it's the same with experience: man's life is a flower, and man's every experience is a flower, and the flower will not put forth *unless* the months of waiting are patiently undergone. Dull weeks, silly weeks, stupid weeks – dull as 'Troilus & Criseyde', silly as roman catholic ritual, stupid as sexual convention. But *NECESSARY*. Jer see wot I mean? (You: 'Christ bugger') And the way of salvation lies in abnegating the technical power that enables us to cut the cackle and get to the moment of ecstasy without paying for it. Or something like that. I don't know what the remedy is. But that's what's wrong, unless I am talking unmitigated anus.

Thank you for your kind attention. I wrote to you yesterday, as a matter of fact, and so there is little more to say. I will include my third in the series 'Men Playing Jazz'.

My greetings to you, man!

Philip.

6

⟨×⟩

Towards the inevitable

In 1962, three years after we moved into the new Library building, the planning of Stage II had begun. This was to be a huge elevation, comprising a basement and eight floors above ground, to the rear of Stage I, linked to it at ground and first floor levels. Its planning, construction and furbishing, together with an interim addition in 1967, occupied most of the 1960s, as well as taking up much of Larkin's time and energy both within and outside working hours. The two buildings were finally integrated in 1970. This time, unlike in 1955 when there was no time for consultation about the plans for Stage I, Philip consulted library staff as extensively as possible. Section Heads, of whom I was one, made up a small working party which regularly studied the plans under his guidance – he, in turn, had frequent meetings with the architects. Comments, criticisms and proposals were not only encouraged but expected. The working party, in their turn, took the plans relating to their particular areas to colleagues who were also encouraged to voice their opinions.

At intervals Philip called together the whole staff to ensure that everyone was kept informed of developments throughout the planning and building stages. Every member of staff was made to feel free to put forward suggestions or raise objections. Every point, whether it came from an assistant librarian, a library assistant or a porter, was considered and adopted in the light of majority agreement. In the matter of staff consultation, Philip was ahead of his time. Although the structure was hierarchical, with the librarian firmly in control, communication on all matters affecting the Library was transmitted through regular committee meetings to all staff – long before the University made them mandatory, following the 1968 student riots – so that everyone was kept abreast of new developments. As for the new building, because we had been given so generous a representation in its planning and equipment, we certainly got the library we had asked for, in a way that probably few other library staffs can claim.

For my own part, it never crossed my mind, when I was studying for that part of the Library Association's Registration examination which covered the planning and equipment of new buildings, that I should ever be remotely involved with such matters in practice. The information I had then gleaned related for the most part to pre-war libraries so was of little practical use in the 1960s. But the subject became an on-going pre-occupation for me over the next eight years. The work was exacting, sometimes tedious, and short deadlines had frequently to be met. Once, when I was away, a large parcel containing detailed plans of the layout and shelving of the periodicals floor (my particular responsibility) was delivered to my holiday address! In a covering note, Philip asked me to check the floor areas and shelving capacity for 10,000 journals and to return the plans with comments as soon as possible – which meant the next day. None of us ever complained about these intrusions into our leisure time. We recognised their urgency and in any case we knew Philip never asked us to do anything that he himself did not regularly do.

Meanwhile, Stage I was rapidly filling up as the Library's stock more than doubled in size. Up to 1959–60 the Library's holdings totalled 153,750 volumes; in the next decade they increased to 333,185. In this period, Larkin thrived on the activity, the intellectual challenge, the steady expansion of staff, of student numbers, materials and services, simultaneously matched by seemingly unlimited funding. 'We built one new library in 1960 and another in 1970, so that my first fifteen years were busy' (*RW* 57), as he put it with characteristic understatement.[19] By 1970, however, the pressure of work had taken its toll and the completion of Stage II did not give Larkin the same exhilaration that Stage I had done. In spite of the accolade of a Civic Trust Award and a Royal Institute of British Architects Architectural Award, the official opening of the completed building in December 1970 was, by comparison with the corresponding event in 1960, a very low-key affair.

A period of disenchantment had already set in for Larkin which was not entirely dispersed by two terms of sabbatical leave at All Souls' College, Oxford in the autumn and winter of 1970–71 to complete the compilation of the *Oxford Book of Twentieth Century English Verse*. This was the only break from his salaried responsibilities Larkin was ever given to pursue his literary interests. Normally he practised them in his limited leisure time.

On the other hand, as a poet, he was able to use his influence to the benefit of the profession in at least one matter of national concern. In

[19] *Required Writing* (London: Faber, 1983). Subsequent references (*RW*) are bracketed in the text.

1 The Brennan family *c.* 1935. (I am on the left.)   2 At age 13 or 14, 1942/43.

3 Endsleigh Demonstration School Percussion Band. (Front row, left. I was the conductor!)

4 The first Library staff photograph taken by Larkin (with a delayed-action camera), 1957.

5 The Library move, September 1959. 'A certain hilarious excitement prevailed.' (The rope-handled wooden boxes (known as 'coffins') were designed to take a shelf and a half of books which were placed in the box in classified order and removed in the same order on to their new shelves.)

6 With H.M. the Queen Mother, at the official opening of the new Library, June 1960. Larkin described this occasion as 'one of the happiest in the University's history'.

7 At the high windows
of 32 Pearson Park,
June 1961
(taken by Philip).

8 Library staff photograph, *c.* 1960.

9 A portrait taken by Alan Marshall at Philip Larkin's request, February 1961.

10 A memorable day in October 1961 (taken by Philip with a delayed-action camera).

11 Afternoon tea at the Floral Hall, Hornsea, Summer 1963 (taken by Philip).

12 Studying the plans for Stage II of the Library, June 1964. Clockwise: Peter Sheldon, Arthur Wood, Philip Larkin, Betty Mackereth, Maeve Brennan.

13 Library staff photograph, July 1964.

14 Wearing an evening dress which Philip called 'your "My Fair Lady" dress', 1964 (taken by Philip).

15/16   Two dramatic poses on Ferriby Foreshore, October 1965.

17   Stylised staff photograph, taken from Larkin's first-floor office, 1967.

18 At 578 Beverley High Road, 1967 (taken by Philip).

19 'Here is unfenced existence': on the cliffs at Aldborough, E. Yorks., October 1969 (taken by the author).

20 Shades of D. H. Lawrence, Summer 1970 (taken by Philip).

21 Luncheon party to celebrate Larkin's 25 years at Hull, Spring 1980, to which the longest-serving members of staff were invited. Clockwise from left to right: Maeve Brennan, Philip Larkin, Wendy Mann, Peter Sheldon, Betty Mackereth, Alan Marshall.

22 Sally Boston's retirement party, October 1985; the last at which Larkin presided.

23 The launch of the *Collected Poems* (ed. Anthony Thwaite) and *Philip Larkin: The Man and his Work* (ed. Dale Salwak), October 1988. Left to right: Eddie Dawes, Anthony Thwaite, Maeve Brennan, John White.

24 The launch of the Philip Larkin Society, November 1995. Left to right: Maeve Brennan, Jean Hartley, Win Dawson, James Booth.

25 Two of the Miss Bianca books with some of the mouse figures which Philip gave to me.

the late 1950s more than one American library had solicited his manu-
scripts. Thus alerted, he became increasingly perturbed about the
migration of contemporary British literary manuscripts across the Atlantic
and the seeming lack of concern on the part of British librarians. Con-
sequently in 1961 he drew the attention of the Standing Conference of
National and University Libraries (SCONUL) to the problem and this in
turn attracted the notice of the Assistant Secretary of the Arts Council
of Great Britain, Eric Walter White, who had also begun to have similar
anxieties. As a result of further discussion with Larkin, the Arts Council
set up a committee in 1963 to purchase the manuscripts of living British
poets for the National Manuscript Collection of Contemporary Writers
(initially Poets) which was established in the British Library. Larkin served
on its Advisory Panel from 1963 and became its chairman in 1967, an
office he held until 1979. One of his first acts was to donate his first
Workbook, covering the years 1944 to 1950, to the Collection. I had a
postcard, post-marked London, [June?] 1964, stating he was about to
hand over the 'MS book I am presenting to the Arts Council.' [20] By
acquiring for Hull the literary papers of Anthony Thwaite, Andrew
Motion, Roger McGough, Stevie Smith, Douglas Dunn and others, Larkin
hoped to give SCONUL colleagues a lead. But they were slow to accept
their obligation, as he noted in a paper, 'A Neglected Responsibility',
delivered at a SCONUL Seminar on Modern Literary Manuscripts in 1979
(*RW* 98–108).

Another benefit to the University which came about as a result of
Larkin's influence with the Arts Council was the funding of a 'poet-in-
residence' post at Hull, commencing in January 1968. His choice was
Cecil Day-Lewis who, in the interval between accepting and taking up
the post, was appointed Poet Laureate, much to Larkin's delight. 'Hull is
the only University *in the world* where students will have a regular
opportunity of talking to the Poet Laureate' he boasted in a letter to
Day-Lewis (*Life* 379). However, it was a chance the students of that time
failed to appreciate, and to Larkin's acute embarrassment, disappointingly
few came to meet Day-Lewis at the fortnightly seminars he held in the
Poetry Room in the Library.

Fortunately, the academic staff were not so shy of welcoming him. To
enable as wide a cross-section of staff as possible to meet him, it had

[20] I donated this postcard to the British Library after seeing the splendid exhibition,
Chapter and Verse: 1000 Years of English Literature (March–October 2000), in which the
workbook was displayed.

been agreed that each Faculty would take it in turn to entertain the poet-in-residence, following the public lectures he gave each term. The Dean of Science, Professor George Cole, chose the relaxing surroundings of his home as a more suitable venue for colleagues to meet the Poet Laureate than the more formal atmosphere of the campus, and accordingly invited about 70 people on 14 February 1968 to a splendid buffet supper prepared by his wife, Tina. Day-Lewis was a very charming guest and surprisingly easy to talk to. My name alerted him to my Irishness and we talked at some length about Ireland. He had a very earnest conversation with Philip about marriage, the joys of which he extolled, following his own very happy second marriage to the actress Jill Balcon. I do not recall Philip's response – evasive no doubt – but he was not completely anti-marriage in those days. In May, Philip took his turn to entertain Day-Lewis at a dinner party for 10 or 12 at a local hotel to which the Coles were invited, also George and Jean Hartley. I wish I had realised then how privileged I was to be present on this as so many other equally illustrious occasions and consequently taken more notice of, for instance, who the other guests were and what the table talk was, but my friendship with Philip was quite unconcerned with his status as a celebrated poet – or distinguished librarian. On the contrary, it was for his warm, human qualities that I loved him.

Four poets-in-residence succeeded Day-Lewis: Richard Murphy, Peter Porter, Ian Hamilton and Douglas Dunn after whom the post was discontinued. I have no recollection of meeting either Murphy or Hamilton, but Porter was very gregarious, and often chatted to staff over tea in the Library common room. Douglas had the advantage of being known to most of us from his time as a colleague from 1969 to 1971.

Back in the library the growth of staff, stock and students continued steadily to 1975 when the first indications of retrenchment in Government provision for universities became manifest. In spite of intervals of temporary improvement, Hull was particularly hard-hit, a factor which Larkin felt very keenly. Staff numbers were reduced, the Library grant was drastically cut at the same time as inflation was running out of control. Even the Library's accommodation came under threat, a threat which, though ultimately realised, did not materialise during Larkin's lifetime. The golden age of university expansion was over, and before he died in December 1985 it seemed to him that all he had achieved in the last thirty years had gone into reverse. This greatly added to his wretchedness in the closing years of his life.

Following the death of the Poet Laureate, C. Day-Lewis, in 1972, Philip's name was mentioned in literary circles as a possible successor. At this time he very much coveted the honour – unlike twelve years later when it *was* offered to him – and he was deeply disappointed when Betjeman was nominated, thus increasing his melancholy. By July the following year, our relationship had reached an *impasse* which only a complete break could resolve, and in September the University announced its decision to dispose of the house in Pearson Park. This meant exchanging the comfortable tenancy of the flat Philip had enjoyed since 1956 for the responsibilities of house and garden ownership. He settled for a rather gaunt, unattractive post-war house with a third of an acre of land, close to the University. He moved into it in July 1974, and although he gave much thought to its furnishing and comfort (but not, it seemed to me, with anything like the same pleasure with which he had appointed the flat two decades earlier), he complained that it was not conducive to the writing of poetry.

The move coincided with the publication of *High Windows* which, after the mixed reception of the *Oxford Book of Twentieth Century English Verse*, re-affirmed his poetic reputation and bolstered his self-esteem. That autumn, even though nothing had been resolved, our friendship was restored to its heady state of a decade earlier, on which level it continued until tensions re-appeared three years later. In May 1977 my mother died unexpectedly, an event which devastated the family. Now only my father and I were living in the old home, which suddenly seemed very large and inhospitable. Or, as my father put it, 'since mother's death the house has lost its soul'. He did not wish to remain there and I readily concurred as its maintenance would have been a burden in addition to my job and new role of companion-housekeeper. Now 77, my father belonged to that generation of men who had never been trained in domestic skills and, although willing to learn, he was not very receptive to my teaching.

Within two or three weeks of my mother's death, a chronic health problem became acute and at the beginning of August I had to have major surgery. In the meantime we had found a house which, at the time appealed immensely to my father, although not to me. But by now I did not have the energy to continue the wearisome business of house-hunting. My convalescence, far from being a time to recuperate, was spent showing prospective buyers over the old house, not to speak of sifting and discarding or packing our household accumulation of 43 years. Meanwhile my father bargained with dealers over the sale of books, furniture – the new house would take less than one tenth of our possessions – and outdated dental equipment. Although he had retired in 1970, he had, ill-advisedly, neither sold the practice nor his equipment. At the same time, the eventual buyers of the house were constantly on the doorstep or the telephone, assessing, measuring up, haggling. In the week before we moved, Philip came each morning before work and changed all the round-pin plugs on our electrical appliances to square-pin plugs. In the evenings he helped us to pack books.

On the day of the move, 17 November 1977, he had again arranged to come early in the morning to drive my father to the new house while I supervised the removal men at the old. The previous afternoon, however, Betty Mackereth 'phoned to say that Philip had received news from the nursing home where his mother had lived for the last five years that she was dying. Consequently he had left immediately to go to her bedside. My assistant, Freda Carroll, brought me the news at lunch time the following day, in the midst of the move, that Mrs Larkin had died earlier that morning. It was with a deep sense of foreboding, which I could not help communicating, that I wrote my letter of condolence the next day. For each of us a long era had ended. I left the home in which I had spent 43 of my 48 years. The person to whom Philip had been most closely bound, both genetically and emotionally, for 55 years was no longer there. Even as a young man he had surmised that a 'mother complex' no doubt partly explained his 'permanent non-attachment' and ambivalence towards sex and marriage (PAL to JBS, 2.i.51). Now her house too, which he still looked on as 'home', would soon be sold. On that day, we both closed the door on significant parts of our shared and separate lives, a fact which Philip too acknowledged to me in a letter: 'Yes, it is odd our mothers should die in the same year, & that mine shd. die on the day you left your old home' (SL 572). For both of us, an enormous re-adjustment would be needed, a process which I had an uneasy feeling was going to estrange rather than unite us. Philip, also, as I discovered many years later, had felt similar misgivings when in February 1976 he had described my vanishing footprints in the snow as leaving 'only this sign / Of your life walking into mine' (CP 206).[21]

My presentiment proved to be correct. Four months later, Philip invited me to accompany him to *Larkinland*, the South Bank presentation of readings of his poems and favourite jazz pieces, which, as a tribute to him, was performed at the University on 16 March 1978. With Philip as

[21] I did not know of the existence of 'Morning at last: there in the snow' until November 1987, eleven years after the poem was written and two years after Philip's death.

the guest of honour, and me as his escort, it should have been an enjoyable evening for both of us. Alas, it turned out to be disastrous and resulted in the abrupt termination of our long intimacy. I still find it distressing to recall the details, let alone write about them. Suffice it to say that on the following day, anger about the previous evening's ill-fated outcome, together with the acute depression I had been suffering for some months, caused me to lose my temper and we quarrelled bitterly – something which had happened on only one previous occasion.[22] When we met a few days later, Philip had finally determined to end the vacillation of eighteen years and henceforth pledge himself to Monica Jones. I reluctantly accepted his decision: what else could I do? The situation had tormented all three of us for so long. We had had partings before, and all except the 1973–74 break had been of short duration. Throughout our association, I had always insisted that unless we were to make a decisive commitment, we should not feel tied to one another. Moreover, I was particularly anxious that Philip should not feel the sort of obligation to me that I knew he felt towards Monica. Consequently, I repeatedly dispatched him to sort himself out. But before long he would return, without a resolution, and we resumed where we had left off. Up to now, however, I had usually been in command of the situation. This time I was not.

Besides, I did not know then, nor indeed until some time after his death, that in spite of the ardour with which our friendship had been renewed in 1974, the threesome had become a foursome, and now with my elimination, Philip found himself once more at the apex of an albeit new triangle. Nevertheless, without this knowledge a still greater re-adjustment was now required than even our mothers' deaths had demanded. We still had to work together, and as a senior colleague, I had very regular contact with him. After a short time, he resumed the habit of dropping into my office at the end of the day to discuss library matters and exchange news or gossip, thereby giving the impression to our colleagues that all was normal. In due course I discovered there was life after Philip, but the intuitive sensitivity, the wit and sense of fun, above all, that unique transcendental quality, which had been such a vital part of our association, were lacking in new relationships, just as they had been prior to my knowing Philip.

Nearly five years later I wrote to a friend: 'I think now, looking back

---

[22] I fear that this account will not satisfy the prurient, or the merely curious. But I claim the right to privacy.

on the male influences in my life, that after a lifetime of exposure to my Father's mind and wit, and half a lifetime of close proximity to Philip Larkin's rare brand of intelligence and rapier wit (the two men are alike in many ways) it is little wonder that I am hard to please, although it ought not to be beyond the bounds of possibility for me to meet people with fine minds. Perhaps they lack the sensitivity and finesse of these two' (MMB to Molly Le Pape 7.xii.82).

For Philip provided a warmth and stimulation I had not found before or since and I was often astonished how effortlessly our thoughts and feelings were in tune. Frequently I had only to will him to answer an unspoken question, or supply unasked-for information, for him to volunteer it. That he felt a similar affinity is shown in the following passage in one of his letters to me:

> Considering the strains of our relationship, it's wonderfully harmonious! ... As I've said before, in some ways I think our natures [are] very similar in sort of basic ways, the ways we pick things up or instinctively do or don't say certain things. I don't mean our opinions are the same, or what we like necessarily. Anyway, I am very dependent on you ... I hope you feel, as I do, that despite all our differences there's a big area where we are alike. By differences I only mean where we aren't alike. (21.vii.71)

When it came to parting, these were intricate ties to sever and were, in fact, never completely dissolved, a truth borne out by the witness of a friend in whom Philip confided some years after we parted. Indeed, although no longer intimate, we remained close and occasionally had lunch together or a drink after work.

As time passed, it became very noticeable that he was increasingly depressed and dependent on alcohol. I remember how shocked I was when he confessed to regularly drinking half a bottle or more of sherry before going to work, just to enable him to face the day. Not surprisingly, I too was suffering from acute depression, and although we were aware of each other's melancholy, neither of us probed the depth or cause of the other's misery. Sadly, unlike the past when we each had a remarkable ability to dispel the other's despondency, now we were afraid to expose our feelings.

Gradually, the combination of excess alcohol and unrelieved low spirits undermined Larkin's health, so that by Christmas 1984 he had become deeply uneasy about more alarming symptoms which now appeared. In the new year he began a lengthy round of consultations and tests, proceeding from one specialist to another in a process of elimination. By early June, the source of the trouble had been identified and he underwent an operation for cancer of the oesophagus. To my surprise, before going into hospital he asked me if I would be willing to join the small rota of close friends he was organising to drive Monica to visit him. In return, he had asked her to notify me, as soon as she herself received news, when the operation was over. He also stressed that after Monica, he wanted me to be amongst his first visitors. This struck me as a very public acknowledgement of his regard when we had supposedly ceased to have any emotional claim on each other.

However, a serious set-back in the early post-operative period meant that I did not see him until the end of June when he was still in the Intensive Care Unit at the Hull Royal Infirmary. This visit was unexpectedly happy in spite of all he had been through. For more than a week he had been in a deep coma when it had been very much touch-and-go whether or not he would pull through. Once admitted to the ward, I had to wait as a nurse was ministering to him and the screen was drawn around the bed. Knowing I was there, however, he poked his head round the screen and pulled such a comical face, accompanied by a cheery wave of the hand. He was obviously delighted to see me and appeared in positively buoyant mood. I had expected him to be morbidly depressed about his condition instead of which he was almost dismissive of it. But what surprised me most of all was the intensity of his emotional response as he exclaimed: 'You look absolutely lovely.' It reminded me sharply of the occasion I had visited him in hospital in 1961 when our friendship ignited into love. I wondered if the same thought crossed his mind but did not ask him. Nonetheless, I was puzzled by this sudden relaxation of the unspoken rules we had imposed on each other in the last seven years but reasoned that it was no more than a bid for sympathy while he felt so vulnerable.

Subsequent visits, although emotionally charged, were not so propitious, especially on the only occasion I drove Monica to see him. For the brief period we were both at his bedside – by now he was at the Nuffield Hospital – the atmosphere bristled with emotional tension which could not have contributed to Philip's well-being. I had no time alone with him and as I left the room (deliberately in advance of Monica), Philip reached out to me in a passionate embrace. Deeply embarrassed, I froze under the hostile glare of Monica, who was sitting on the opposite side of the bed. Quite distraught at being unable to handle the situation, I extricated myself as quickly as I could. The following day, I took my father and French Goddaughter on a long planned holiday, and did not see Philip for three weeks.

By the time I returned, he was at home, looking pallid, haggard and frightened, even though he had not been told the blunt truth about his illness. He must have guessed it, but his particular dread of cancer made him terrified of acknowledging it. Ever since his father had died 37 years before, at the age of 63, Philip had been convinced that he too was destined to die of the same disorder, at the same age. It was now early August, and close to his 63rd birthday. In those days before blank cards, in which one writes one's own message, were so readily obtainable, I remember how careful I was to avoid a card with the message 'many happy returns', or any reference to the year ahead. By late August he had returned to the Library on a part-time basis, but it was more a gesture than a commitment to work. He was clearly apathetic, fretful and unable to concentrate. He made a pretence of resuming his normal activities, but clearly life held little purpose or pleasure. In spite of the constant companionship of Monica Jones and others who were closer to him than I then was, he seemed lonely, possibly because he was unable to articulate his fears. He confessed that he would have liked to go away for a few days but Monica was not well enough to go with him.

His behaviour was inconsistent: he went for short drives alone but was unwilling to go to Evensong unaccompanied. I felt helpless and fearful of intruding; sad too that we were unable, as we once were, to impart our innermost thoughts and feelings at such a critical time. He was quite clearly full of foreboding which he could not communicate and I dared not voice.

However, he seemed to enjoy a brief resurgence of his old form, when, at the end of September he officiated at a colleague's retirement. Hinting at the retiree's well-known foibles, he recalled with gentle irony that the amorphous mass of labour history material which she had been appointed (on a three year contract), to organise remained to this day, seventeen years later, 'a wilderness of seditious literature!' [23] He explained that this was not entirely due to the nature of the material – pamphlets, leaflets, broadsheets, posters, notices, newspaper cuttings and other ephemera, the sort of thing the unwary would simply discard – but might also be attributed to her well-intentioned, but imprudent, tendency to be all too readily diverted to other, albeit admirable, projects. Notwithstanding, he continued, we should miss her for her candour, ebullience, warmth and

[23] In an essay in *Philip Larkin: The Man and his Work*, ed. Dale Salwak (London: Macmillan, 1989), I wrote 'wasteland of seditious literature'. My colleague Bob Smeaton assures me that 'wilderness' was the word used.

good humour. In fact, he concluded, 'Every library should have a Sally Boston. But only one!' In spite of the prevailing despondency about his health, it was clear that neither his wit nor his charm had deserted him. The official photographs of this event show him wistful but smiling; they are a fitting record of the last Library gathering at which he was present.

My own retirement party should have taken place at the same time but Philip, who had been dreading the occasion, asked if I would mind deferring it until he felt stronger. For myself, I should have preferred to forego the celebration altogether rather than add to his anxieties, but he insisted on fixing a date and 21 November was agreed. One week before, however, I received a sad little note, explaining that he would not, after all, be able to be present as 'Some new alarming symptoms' had developed and his doctor had signed him off work for another two weeks. He urged on me the necessity to go through with the ceremony: 'Despite your feelings & mine, the show must go on. It will be a very big occasion' (*SL* 757). The irony of this development was not lost on me or my colleagues. I had worked with Philip longer than anyone else, and work had played a significant part in our personal relationship, yet mine was the only retirement party at which he did not preside; a fact which he described as 'titanically ironic'.

More than a decade later, I see that had Philip officiated at my retire-ment, the poignancy of the circumstances would have heightened an already emotive situation which would have been harrowing for both of us, and deeply distressing for everyone else. His voice on the tape on which he dictated his tribute, to be read out by the Chairman of the Library Committee, betrays the anguish he felt in performing this last duty. At the end of September, immediately after I retired, I went to stay with friends on the French Riviera. During my absence Philip had been in hospital yet again for more tests and when I next saw him his deterioration was very marked. We last met on 30 October when he was extremely agitated about important interviews for the post of deputy librarian he was due to conduct on 4 November. He confessed that he was out of touch with current professional concerns and consequently felt unable to frame pertinent questions for the candidates. As it hap-pened, I was working on a new *Year's Work in ...* series for the UK Serials Group and my designated responsibility was an overview of current developments in librarianship in general, and in periodical literature in particular. Consequently, it was easy for me to draw up a list of topics on which Philip could base questions to put to the interviewees. Sadly, my efforts, although appreciated, were superfluous since over the weekend he developed what he described as ''flu-like symptoms' and the interviews were cancelled.

From then onwards his decline was rapid, but as I did not see him – I dared not ask permission to visit him – I was not aware just how fast he was deteriorating. He kept in touch by 'phone until 20 November, the day before my retirement party. He knew that I was apprehensive about the occasion, not least on account of his inability to be there, and rang to wish me luck, and give me some practical advice about voice projection and control. He concluded by saying he was going into hospital the following day for further tests, and although he promised to telephone as soon as he could, we never spoke again. Monica rang instead and said that, although back at home, Philip had retired to bed feeling very unwell. Within a week he was back in hospital and died 48 hours later, in the early hours of 2 December 1985. Monica 'phoned with the news at 7.30 am. She asked me to notify the Library and former senior colleagues, now in chief posts, such as Brenda Moon at Edinburgh University, Peter Hoare at Nottingham and others, before the information was released to the media.

I was quite unprepared for the news. Like Philip, I had buried my head in the sand, refusing to believe that death was imminent, in spite of all the indications. I was confused; I had hoped to see him again. In the last six months we had seemed to draw close again and then retreated, leaving me uncertain whether I was intimate friend, or mere colleague of long standing. A friend – with whom I was not in regular touch – writing on 19.xii.85 uncannily perceived my dilemma: 'There was a lot of confusion, it seemed to me, that must have added to your difficulties. And I suppose there is a kind of confusion at the end from your point of view ... No confusion now for him, remember'. I am glad I did not know then what still greater confusion lay in store for me.

7

Afterwards

The sure extinction that we travel to
And shall be lost in always. (*CP* 208)

So dazed was I by the news of Philip's death that Monday morning that
some time later my father had to remind me of my undertaking to notify
Brenda Moon and other former colleagues whom Monica Jones had
asked me to contact, not least the Library itself. Once the news was made
public, it seemed my telephone never stopped ringing. Largely, it was
close friends or colleagues calling to offer their condolences. Most, rea-
lising that I was probably in deep shock, were solicitous for my welfare
and this touched me. The following days cards and letters of sympathy
began to arrive. Their number surprised me and I was moved by friends'
perception of my sense of loss in spite of the moderation of my rela-
tionship with Philip in recent years. The first note, and in many ways
the most comforting, was from a friend and colleague who wrote: 'This
card is inadequate but it is to hand and I want to send you quickly a
word of condolence on a very great loss. Many people will feel the pangs
of parting from Philip Larkin, but you more than most' (Jean Curtis
2.xii.85). Another close friend wrote: 'All I can say is that at the end of
his life you were brought back and recognised as part of it. This must
comfort you ... Be glad and proud that you shared in part of his life'
(Frances Curnock-Newton 3.xii.85).

One letter from a friend at Queen's Library, Belfast, was particularly
poignant. She herself was dying of cancer and, like Philip, she too had
had part of her oesophagus removed and, only recently, some glands in
her neck. She knew she had very little time left. When, two months later,
her sister informed me of her death, she told me that although Audrey's
strength had been at a particularly low ebb at the time of Philip's death,
nothing would deflect her from writing to me. Another colleague from
our early years in the Library explained: 'I have been trying since Tuesday
to write this letter. Philip's death shocked and saddened me and I wanted

to send my sympathy to some-one; but who? You, I believe, were probably the closest to him of any of us and I therefore thought to write to you' (Pat Hurst 8.xii.85). Charles Monteith, speaking on television, made this same point, explaining that Faber and Faber had received many letters of condolence from members of the public who likewise had not known whom to contact.

Brenda Moon's sympathy was all-embracing:

> How people will be grieving all over the country – even people who never knew him. But those of us who were privileged to know even a small part of him feel a special loss because he was so much more than he appeared in his publications.

On a more personal level she continued: 'I grieve for you in particular because you were so close to him and he to you, and I am sure you will miss him in an every-day way in which those of us who have been living away for some time are spared' (2.xii.85). A director of Blackwell's whom I had come to know very well over many years of business association surmised: 'A colleague and friend for so many years, I suspect you must be one of the few people who ever really got to know him ... So now the University Library will move into an entirely different era, and I am sure that you are glad that you have withdrawn from the scene' (John Merriman 3.xii.85).

The day after Philip's death I went to the Library to pick up some inter-library loan material I had requested. Everyone there seemed as stunned as I was. The atmosphere was eerily quiet and staff and readers alike appeared subdued as if, as another friend put it, 'haunted by the knowledge that we will not see Philip walking round [the Library] again' (Joyce Bellamy 7.xii.85). Most of my former colleagues felt too diffident to approach me, nor was I anxious to engage in conversation myself. In any case I was bound for early evening Mass at the Catholic Chaplaincy and on the way met Professor Eddie Dawes, Chairman of the Library Committee, who less than a fortnight before had officiated at my retire-ment party. We talked for some time about Philip's death and its effect on the Library, and on us personally.

Now late for Mass, I arrived as the priest, the Rev. David Watson, was saying the Bidding prayers, which to my surprise, he was offering for Philip. He was the first, and indeed one of the very few people, to dwell on the importance of Larkin's contribution to the University, and the Library in particular, which, he said, inevitably meant more to those of us who had worked with him than the more publicised recognition of his literary work. After Mass the Chaplain detained me. He said he had only met Philip once – at an Anglican Chaplaincy housewarming. I recalled privately that Philip had told me that he had made a contribution to the refurbishment of a smaller house which the Chaplaincy had moved into a year or two previously. I did not know David Watson well at that time, and in fact had been surprised to see him at my retirement party. He said that on that occasion he had realised, from the tributes Philip and I paid each other in our respective speeches, that there had been a special affinity between us. I was grateful for his sensitive perception and particularly appreciated his recognition of Philip's contribution to the life of the University.

It was a long, sad week as I waited for information about the timing and location of the funeral. Although his home in Newland Park was close to a large municipal cemetery in Hull, it was rumoured that he was to be buried in Cottingham where, by coincidence, the cemetery is no more than 200 yards from my own home. (I did not know then that he had bought a plot there.) This was confirmed in due course and the funeral took place on 9 December in Cottingham's medieval parish church of St. Mary the Virgin which, by tradition, is also the University's church. It was made clear that while all were welcome at the church, the interment was to be strictly private. Great therefore was my surprise when Monica telephoned on the eve of the funeral to say that if I would like to join the *cortège* at the graveside, I was to feel free to do so, adding that she thought Philip would wish me to be there. I was touched and grateful to be thus acknowledged as a close friend.

The large church was packed to capacity. Most of the Library staff were there, as well as many former staff, including Brenda Moon who travelled down from Edinburgh and stayed at my home overnight, the officers of the University, teaching colleagues, national and other university librarians, as well as members of the public. The rector, the Rev. Terence Grigg, assisted by the Rev. Francis Bown, priest-in-charge of St. Stephen's, Hull, conducted the service. Philip had attended Evensong in both their churches in the recent past. Each acknowledged his agnosticism but sensed his striving for integrity and truth, adding that Christian burial was therefore appropriate. I don't know who chose the hymns, 'Abide with Me', 'Lead Kindly Light' and 'The day Thou gavest, Lord, is ended'. The second is my favourite, while the third causes me to digress, even if inappropriately, as it reminded me sharply of a witty exchange which had taken place at a Library Committee meeting a year or so previously.

Faced with further cutbacks in the Library grant, teaching departments had been asked to submit lists of periodicals, ascribed to their subject interest, in descending order of importance, placing at the top of the list those titles with which they could most easily dispense in a forthcoming programme of cancellations. The closing date for this exercise happened to coincide with a Library Committee meeting. It was the first substantive item on the agenda which Philip introduced with the opening line of the hymn, 'The day Thou gavest, Lord, is ended'. This was immediately capped by a recalcitrant professor whose department had failed to submit its list. 'But Mr Chairman' he retorted, carefully studying his watch, 'at 14.10 hours the day the Lord gavest is by no means yet ended', much to the amusement of everyone present. I, who was at the meeting to report on the cancellation strategy, did not then anticipate that I would next be reminded of this incident at Philip's funeral service.

The late Sir Kingsley Amis, Philip's friend (and rival) since the early 1940s, gave the funeral address. He emphasised Philip's personal qualities: 'his impeccable attentive courtesy', his humour, his honesty, 'more total in his case than in any other I've known, that gave his poetry such power' which, combined with his realistic approach to the fundamental truths of life and death, made his views not pessimistic but challenging. Above all, he concluded, his poetry reveals 'fragments of poignancy and humour in everyday things, ... moments of illumination and beauty we should never have seen or known but for Philip.' It was a simple though dignified service in the best Anglican tradition which ended with the beautiful words of the *Nunc Dimittis*, 'Lord, now lettest thou thy servant depart in peace, according to thy word'.

Outside, the grey, cold day intensified my misery as I waited at the cemetery gates for the *cortège* of not more than a dozen mourners, amongst them Philip's sister, Kitty, and her daughter Rosemary, Kingsley and his former wife, Lady Kilmarnock, Andrew and Jan Motion, Charles Monteith, representing Faber and Faber; but not Monica. She had been advised by her doctor that morning not to attend the funeral. Betty Mackereth joined me as we followed the other mourners to the graveside. Afterwards, while examining the floral tributes, I spoke to Kitty, and Rosemary, to some friends of Monica's who were concerned by her absence, and to Andrew Motion who was leaning heavily on an ebony stick after a severe attack of arthritis. I don't think I spoke to the Amises or Monteith, other than to exchange formal civilities. As we left the open grave, the last line of 'Here' came into my mind: 'Facing the sun, untalkative, out of reach'. Although no shaft of light penetrated the gloom of that December day, the words struck me as a fitting epitaph for their author.

And as I walked the short distance back to my home, I reflected on what Philip had meant to me. I had known him for more than half my life and for the past twenty five years he had influenced me more than anyone else. During that time we had been attracted to one another by an irresistible force from which we never entirely broke free. In spite of its ultimate inconclusiveness, and notwithstanding the revelations yet to come of his duplicity, this friendship, with its unworldly dimension, was the most enriching experience of my life. I thought then, and still consider, how privileged I was to have shared the spiritual side of Philip Larkin's disposition.

The death of a colleague in office is a disturbing event. The sudden absence, forever, of someone one was used to seeing daily leaves a wide vacuum, and the sense of loss is vivid and painful. Moreover in Philip's case, many of us had worked with him for a long time. A few were not far short of the thirty years I had worked with him, and several others had been on the staff for twenty years. We had known him when the university was much smaller; we had grown with the Library he created, and were proud of his achievements, and ours. By the time he died, he was in charge of a large organisation, a responsibility he never shirked; we looked to him for leadership and were never disappointed. Last, but not least, we were aware of his large physical presence which, though unobtrusive, was ubiquitous. Little escaped his eagle eye, but his vigilance commanded our respect. On these grounds alone we were bound to miss his proximity and influence. As a friend who had moved to Queen's, Belfast, but who had worked at Hull for ten years, put it in a letter to me: 'Everybody in Hull will miss him very much, and I find it difficult to imagine the Library, or the University, without him. I have never worked with anybody who was so well liked and respected by his staff and colleagues. He was a gentleman, and I'm afraid there are not many of them left any longer' (Ann McKeown 15.xii.85).

Over and above these personal considerations, there was the question of his successor and the inevitable changes a newcomer would make. And how long would the Library be leaderless – the post of deputy librarian which had been vacated in August had been frozen – and who was to be in charge in the meantime? One enormous body blow required immediate action. Shortly after the funeral, the University Administration, under pressure to expand student numbers and services, and to maximise the use of existing accommodation, announced its intention to purloin the entire east wing of the Library (basically Stage I) for other purposes. Apparently the plan had been gestating for some months, but out of consideration for Larkin's uncertain health, it had been kept from him. The Library staff and others, not knowing this, were outraged by the public announcement of the proposal so soon after his death, and a campaign to save the east wing was hastily mounted. Someone designed a badge with the slogan 'I love Larkin's Library' which proved very popular. Posters with the same message appeared everywhere; there were impassioned pleas to keep the Library intact. Unfortunately these strategies only won a temporary reprieve and a year later most, though not all, of the east building was converted to other uses.

In the meantime, the 1985 Library Christmas party was cancelled as a mark of respect; no-one was in the mood for it anyway. When Philip and I had gone to the previous year's party together, I certainly had no thought that this would be the last Christmas ritual we would attend together. Philip, however, had then said something which struck me as strange. Thinking of my retirement party in nine months' time, he sighed deeply before saying, as if with some subconscious premonition: 'I do wish you had had your retirement send-off this September [1984] when your full-time contract terminated.' I don't remember my reply but the possibility that terminal illness would prevent him from officiating when my part-time re-engagement came to an end certainly did not occur to me, let alone the reality that by Christmas 1985 I would be fretting about writing his obituary.

I was taken by surprise when the editor of *BJL News* asked me to write an appreciation of Philip's life and work for the next issue of the Library's termly bulletin. My immediate response was: 'But you can't ask me; I'm no longer a member of staff; you must ask someone who is.' The editor's reply was short and emphatic: 'There is no-one else.' She pointed out that no-one else in the University had known him for as long, or as well, as I had. I protested that Philip's long-time secretary, Betty Mackereth, or Brenda Moon, neither of whom, admittedly, were now on the staff, might have a better insight. But the editor was adamant, and so I agreed. Although honoured by this candid trust in me, I was overawed by the responsibility, never having written an obituary before, and it added to my sadness over Christmas.

Colleagues other than those in the Library were also affected by Philip's death and wanted to do something to commemorate both his poetic talent and his contribution to the life of the University. Consequently, in January 1986 the Vice-Chancellor, Sir William Taylor, asked pro Vice-Chancellor John Chapple to appoint a committee to consider and initiate suitable tributes. At the same time, Barry Bloomfield, a Director of the British Library (and incidentally Philip's bibliographer) approached the University with a proposal to promote a nation-wide memorial appeal fund. It was agreed that 14 February was a suitable date to pursue this idea when interested individuals would be in London for the Memorial Service in Westminster Abbey. Consequently, John Chapple asked me to accompany him to a meeting at Barry Bloomfield's office in Store Street along with Brenda Moon who had also been invited. We formed the core committee which was subsequently joined by Charles Monteith and Anthony Thwaite. We worked out a strategy for launching the Philip Larkin Memorial Appeal Fund in September 1986. Its purpose was twofold: 1) to assist libraries in the UK and Ireland to purchase modern literary manuscripts and 2) to assist the University of Hull to furbish a room in the Brynmor Jones Library which would bear his name and accommodate the Philip Larkin Collection of books and other memorabilia relating to him.

The nation had, of course, paid its most dignified tribute at Westminster Abbey earlier in the day. Although he had tried, Philip had not found consolation in religion, 'That vast moth-eaten musical brocade / Created to pretend we never die', and so would not have felt he merited a Memorial Service in such august surroundings. Had he known he would be honoured in such fashion, I suspect his ambivalence would have given way to mingled pride and humility in the face of this solemn compliment accorded by Church and State. At first I had no thought of attending the Service but my friend and former colleague, Charles Brook, persuaded me that I should go and volunteered to accompany me. By now the shock, which had numbed and to some extent protected me in December, had worn off, thus aggravating my sense of loss. As a result, I found this event even more distressing than the funeral itself. We had seats in the choir stalls amongst friends, colleagues, and national figures. Norman St. John Stevas, now Lord St. John of Fawsley, sat directly behind me. The Abbey, its capacity several times greater than that of the parish church in Cottingham, was full. Between the prayers and hymns, which again included 'Lead Kindly Light' and 'Abide with me', Ted Hughes, the Poet Laureate, read the Lesson from 'Ecclesiasticus' 44, beginning 'Let us now praise famous men and our fathers that begat us'. Jill Balcon, the widow of an earlier Poet Laureate, Cecil Day-Lewis, before reciting 'Love Songs in Age', 'Church Going' and 'An Arundel Tomb' read an excerpt from the Preface to *All What Jazz*.

This was the signal for a jazz group, an alien presence in those surroundings, to strike up Sidney Bechet's 'Blue Horizon'. Permission to introduce this innovation in recognition of Philip's passion for jazz, which he had once described to Jim Sutton as their generation's substitute for religion, had been negotiated with the Sub-Dean by Mike Bowen, a close Hull friend of the last decade. Philip, always a traditionalist in such matters, would have been astonished by this novelty but gratified that this particular personal taste should be thus accommodated. Even to my unappreciative ears, the jazz pieces did not strike a discordant note. On the contrary, Alan Elsdon's trumpet interpretation of 'A Closer Walk with Thee', as the service drew to a close, sounded a singularly pure, uplifting note.

This time Monica was present, supported by Mike Bowen, as well as Charles Monteith, Kingsley Amis and other members of the London literary scene. Kitty and Rosemary spoke to me as we left the Abbey and I felt sorry that they, though Philip's closest relatives, seemed to have been excluded from the hospitality arrangements made by Charles Monteith for his literary friends. Charles Brook and I met up with a large crowd of former colleagues for a simple and singularly cheerless lunch in a dreary milk-bar, the only place we could readily find as all of us were constrained by early afternoon appointments, or train times, or both. It marked one of the most melancholy days of my life.

On 2 June, exactly six months after Larkin's death, the first of the University's official tributes, an exhibition called *Philip Larkin: His Life and Work*, opened in the Library and ran until 12 July. In the Foreword to the exhibition's catalogue, Professor E. A. Dawes explained that it was 'designed to present a balanced view of his [Larkin's] manifold contributions both as an eminent literary figure and as an Officer of the University of Hull.' It focused attention on his writings, on his librarianship, and on the honours he had received. Chiefly organised by the University Archivist, Brian Dyson, the emphasis was on the thirty years Larkin spent in Hull. As well as first editions and critical studies, exhibits included a wide range of manuscripts and typescripts of published and unpublished poems. Related items illuminated individual poems such as the programme of the concert which inspired 'Broadcast', accompanied by the whimsical cartoon drawing of Larkin listening to the broadcast, which he drew in my copy of the first published version of the poem in the *Listener*. George Hartley lent a valuable archive relating to the publication and subsequent recording of *The Less Deceived*. Much of the section under the heading 'THE TOAD WORK' dealt with the planning and construction of the two stages of the Library between 1955 and 1970. The jazz interest was represented by photographs of jazz players lent by fellow enthusiast, Mike Bowen, while more personal letters and post-cards revealed a more mercurial and esoteric side of Larkin's character.

The exhibition attracted national as well as local media attention. Blake Morrison, writing in the *Times Literary Supplement* for 4 July 1986 hailed it as 'this rapidly assembled but superbly organised exhibition'. John Ezard described it in the *Guardian* as 'an exhibition which is a learned, fond memorial to the art, life and professional care of a "vital spirit"', bringing together 'a treasure-trove of items which may never be seen in public again' (2.vi.86). Above all it reversed the image of Larkin as a gloomy misanthropist, for 'what is revealed here is a man with a wide acquaint-anceship who revelled in the company of his friends and colleagues and they in him' (Michael Hickling, *Yorkshire Post* 9.vi.86). Reports of the exhibition even reached California – although just after the closing date – where Janice Rossen was working on her book, *Philip Larkin: His Life's Work*. Undaunted, she telephoned Brian Dyson to enquire if it would nevertheless still be possible to see the material. I was with him when her call came through late one Friday afternoon in mid-July; we were astounded that news of our home-spun tribute – for I had also been involved in its organisation – had travelled so far. By Monday she was in Hull, acknowledging that the exhibits had greatly increased her understanding of Larkin. In November the exhibition was loaned to University College, London, for a month, where it was opened by Anthony Thwaite. His Foreword in the new catalogue expanded Hickling's insight of Philip as 'a deeply serious, very funny, totally endearing and wholly individual person. And that is what is so acutely captured in this exhibition.'

The University's next formal tribute was staged on 30 June 1986 in the Middleton Hall, the campus's all-purpose venue for public lectures, con-certs, theatrical productions and mid-year degree congregations. Billed as *Philip Larkin: A Thanksgiving* it was an affectionate presentation of recollections and readings by friends and colleagues. The inspiration was that of Donald Roy, Head of Drama, and John Osborne, lecturer in American Studies, and although my name appears alongside theirs on the programme, I can claim no credit for its excellent invention. My role was largely to suggest and engage likely contributors. One of the most rewarding approaches I made at this time was to Jean Hartley of whom I had seen little since she and George parted company in 1968. Before then I had often accompanied Philip to their home in Hessle where they ran the Marvell Press. When I telephoned her in February 1986 to ask if she would take part in the tribute we were planning, a spontaneous bond of sympathy was re-kindled and has resulted in a firm, enriching friendship ever since.

I reminded her of the first time we met, at Christmas 1961 when, to my astonishment, Philip shyly produced dolls for her daughters, Laurien (10) and Alison (nearly 8). The thought of Philip going into a shop to buy dolls had struck me as faintly absurd but at the same time endearing, and I cannot remember now where he said he bought them in answer to my eager question on the way home. In spite of the divorce, Jean remained in touch with Philip for the rest of his life. During our conversation in February 1986 she volunteered that over the years she had been the recipient of Philip's confidences. Before she had even met me, she told me, he had confessed to her that he had fallen deeply in love with a Catholic, a concern which posed as serious a dilemma for him as did his long-standing commitment to Monica Jones. From time to time he addressed both worries to Jean without either asking or expecting any response. He simply wanted a sympathetic ear.

Jean's contribution to the Thanksgiving programme was a short talk about the Marvell Press and the publication of *The Less Deceived* six months after Philip's arrival in Hull. Encouraged by the reception of her talk, which was generally acknowledged as the evening's best feature, Jean was stimulated to write her much acclaimed autobiography, *Philip Larkin, the Marvell Press and Me* (1989).

Other contributors shed light on very diverse, often unsuspected, aspects of Philip's personality. Some were serious, others witty and amusing; many were touching. One of the wittiest contributions of the evening was the account given by Anthony Hedges, Reader in Composition at the University, of his collaboration with Philip in the mid-1970s on the cantata, 'Bridge for the Living' which I have summarised in an earlier chapter. I was already familiar with the difficulties Philip had experienced when writing the poem, and his lack of enthusiasm for the bridge itself. Listening to the composer's story for the first time, I was fascinated. Listening to it on tape subsequently reduces me, every time, to helpless laughter as he dramatically built up the narrative, step by step, with a wit that rivalled Philip's own.

Donald Campbell gave an amusing glimpse of Philip's interest in the opposite sex. As Director of Works, he had worked closely with Philip on Stages I and II of the Library. Their deliberations usually took place in the Librarian's room which, prior to the move in 1959, had the most commanding position of any office in the University. It occupied a corner site on the ground floor of what was then known as the Science block.

Everyone who entered the quadrangle which led not only to the science teaching departments and laboratories, but also to the Library, staff refectory, Senior Common Room and Assembly Hall, passed in front of Philip's windows. Donald described how, whenever a pretty girl came into view, Philip produced a spy glass from his desk, the better to see the 'honeys' as he called those girls who thus took his eye! Considering the strategic position of his office, this must have frequently interfered with his concentration.

After the Library moved to its new site, Philip's room did not have such an advantageous position, so there was less opportunity for this kind of distraction. Instead he would interrupt their business deliberations with impromptu nonsense verse, two examples of which Donald recited. A change of architects between Stages I and II prompted the following witticism:

> Castle, Park, Dean and Hook
> Gave the Universities a look.
> What a racket to take part in,
> All my eye and Leslie Martin.

Frustration with the funding restraints of the University Grants Committee (or UGC) evoked this little parody:

> In Xanadu did Kubla Khan
> A stately pleasure dome decree
> He would have had to change his plan
> If subject to the UGC.

I very nearly missed the evening. The funeral of a favourite uncle had taken place earlier that day in Southport. There was no question of simply leaving after the service as there was a formal lunch for family and close friends after which it was arranged that we should bring my aunt back to Yorkshire with us. We hit the Manchester orbit of the M62 at rush hour which meant irksome delays in blistering heat. Fortunately, because of the nature of my contribution, I was billed to appear last on the programme, so there was no undue alarm when I missed the photocall. I arrived just as the presentation had started. I told my ambulance anecdotes, which I have already related and recalled the pre-publication rehearsal of 'Aubade'. The evening was a very moving medley which represented the many facets of Philip's mercurial personality as reflected by each of the seventeen contributors. A full recording of the evening's programme is held in the Archives of the Brynmor Jones Library.

Inevitably, publications formed part of the University's commemorative programme for its longest serving librarian, and in January 1987 the Hull University Press published the first of the Philip Larkin Memorial Series, 'A Lifted Study-Storehouse'. This was a re-issue of Larkin's The Brynmor Jones Library, 1929–1979, a short account, written to mark the Library's golden jubilee, with an additional chapter to the end of his tenure of office and an evaluation of his achievements which I was very happy to be asked to write. Two further pamphlets have been issued in this series: The Labour Archive at the University of Hull by John Saville (1989), a collection Larkin did much to encourage in spite of his opposing political views; and Philip Larkin's Hull and East Yorkshire by Jean Hartley (1995).

This last pamphlet was written to coincide with the launch of the Philip Larkin Society on the tenth anniversary of his death. The following year responsibility for the series was transferred to the Society under whose auspices Trevor Tolley's study of the work books, Larkin at Work, appeared in 1997, followed in 1999 by Reference Back: Philip Larkin's Uncollected Jazz Writings, edited by Richard Palmer and John White. In the meantime the Library Association published in 1989 The Modern Academic Library: Essays in memory of Philip Larkin, edited by Brian Dyson. With the exception of Barry Bloomfield, Philip's bibliographer and himself a national librarian, all the other contributors had worked at one time or other in the Brynmor Jones Library with Philip. Four of them, including Brenda Moon, had already taken office at other university libraries and another had changed his career to that of publisher. My contribution, the biographical sketch, introduced me to Ruth Siverns (née Bowman) and Jim Sutton who both gave me hitherto unknown information about Philip's early life. Royalties from this book have been donated to the national Memorial Appeal Fund set up in 1986.

The Fund's first commitment was to provide cash for the refurbishment of a room in the Brynmor Jones Library, to be dedicated to Larkin's memory. The Poetry Room, a feature promoted by Philip and incorporated in an interim extension in 1967, was a suitable choice for the purpose. Its original use had declined while the growing use of archival material, and not least the increasing interest in Larkinalia, meant there was a pressing need for a reading room where archives' readers could be adequately supervised. Consequently, through the auspices of the Appeal Fund, the Pilgrim Trust and Blackwell's of Oxford made direct grants to the Library for the refurbishment of the Poetry Room as an Archives Reading Room. In addition, the new room provided accommodation for the expanding Philip Larkin collection (started in 1973) of first editions, audio and videotapes, records and criticism, alongside the Brynmor Jones collection of first editions of academic and literary landmarks published between 1890 and 1940. Re-named the Larkin Suite, the official opening, took place on 2 December 1987, thus completing the series of tributes planned by the University in January 1986.

Following Larkin's death the Library became the natural focus for scholars researching his work but as yet it had no major archive to establish it as an indisputable centre of excellence. The acquisition of the Sutton Letters in 1988, outlined in the Introduction to this Memoir, filled this need, and so, this unique record of the young Philip Larkin came to the Library in which he had spent so much of his subsequent life. The purchase of these letters was a tremendous boost for the Library in its aim to be the centre for Larkin research, and subsequently attracted other important records, including a valuable archive deposited by the Trustees of Larkin's Estate in 1993 and, a year or so later, an equally rich deposit of family papers, entrusted to the Library by his niece.

Also in 1988 the Library hosted the joint launch of the *Collected Poems* edited by Anthony Thwaite, and *Philip Larkin: The Man and his Work* edited by Dale Salwak. Four years later, Thwaite again chose to launch the *Selected Letters* in the Library, an event complemented by a second noteworthy exhibition, *Philip Larkin: Letter Writer* (2.xi–12.xii.92). I missed the second event and the opportunity to meet Win Dawson (*née* Winifred Arnott). By coincidence, I had gone to stay with Ruth Siverns (*née* Bowman), whom I first met in 1987. I left Win a note explaining my absence and on her return home she got in touch with both of us. A few months later we all three met at Ruth's, and ever since this three-way friendship has flourished.

In the spring of 1995, the Vice-Chancellor, Professor David Dilks, invited proposals to mark the tenth anniversary of Larkin's death in December. The unanimous response was the creation of a society to promote awareness of his life and work. Anthony Thwaite agreed to be its President. The Ferens Education Trust, the University's charitable foundation, provided a generous grant to promote the Society which was launched at the Hull Literature Festival on 11 November 1995 in the impressive setting of the city's Guildhall. The Society's inaugural event took place in the Brynmor Jones Library on 2 December, exactly ten years after Larkin's death, when approximately 100 members and well-wishers enjoyed a wine and buffet luncheon, followed by an informal talk given by Alan Plater, one of the Society's vice-presidents.

In its first five years, the Society has enlisted nearly 300 members.

Regular meetings, catering for a variety of subject interests, are held in Hull, and in addition meetings have been held in London and Oxford. Birthday walks, led by Don Lee, have become an annual event, having taken place in Coventry (1997 and 1998), in Wellington, where Larkin started his professional career (1999), and in Oxford (2000). *About Larkin* is the Society's twice yearly newsletter. It contains substantive articles and is considerably more than a news bulletin. So far, however, the Society's most ambitious and successful achievement was the organisation of the first Larkin international conference, 'New Larkins for Old', at the University of Hull from 27–29 June 1997, the brainchild of two members of the Committee, James Booth and John Osborne. Papers were submitted by authors from a wide spectrum of disciplines, extending from Hull to Harvard, from British Columbia to Sydney, from New Zealand to Hungary and back to the UK. Delegates were drawn from several other countries including Germany, Luxembourg, Romania, Japan and Korea.

There was a felicitous mix of academic and non-academic – many 'ordinary' members of the Society attended; of literary critics and specialists in other fields – two geographers, a lecturer in Irish Cultural Studies, another in Interdisciplinary Humanist Studies, a novelist, and an environmental campaigner. Likewise, there was a wide age range of young and old – and in between; of Larkin's friends and colleagues, drawn from different phases of his life – Leicester, Belfast, Hull; and inevitably, the majority who only knew him through his poetry but were eager to hear what those who had known him personally had to say.

I don't know what Philip would have made of it. Three days of intensive analysis of his writing when he repeatedly said both in private and in public: 'there's not much to say about my work. When you've read a poem, that's it, it's all quite clear what it means' (*RW* 54). And again: 'If sometimes I have failed, no marginal annotation will help now' (*RW* 83). He believed that poetry was to be read for pleasure, not analysed under microscope. 'Oh, for Christ's sake, one doesn't study poets! You read them' (*RW* 62). He was even more robust about modern art, whether painting, music or literature, and the industry of modern critical theory which has grown up around it: 'the term "modern" when applied to art ... denotes a quality of irresponsibility peculiar to this century, known sometimes as modernism' (*RW* 293). In private conversation he was equally dismissive about post-modernism and post-structuralism.

He would, however, have been charmed by the Alice-in-Wonderland touch which brought the weekend to a close. On a very wet Monday morning, five of us joined Don Lee's unscheduled trail of Larkin's haunts in Cottingham, appropriately finishing at the graveside. Walking for one and a half hours in incessant rain had more than dampened our clothes, and to some extent our spirits, which nevertheless leapt when, at our approach, a large brown rabbit appeared from behind the headstone and bounded over the grave. It would please Philip to know that the scourge of myxomatosis has abated and that rabbits once more play freely in this quiet place.

Contemplating his grave in the rain, it struck me how much Larkin's image had changed since his death. When he died the obituaries endowed him with near sainthood: 'He stood high above his contemporaries' (*Daily Telegraph*); 'One of the most distinctive sensibilities of the age' (*Spectator*); 'Pre-eminent among Britain's post-war poets' (*The Times*) Then, with the publication of the *Selected Letters* in 1992 and Andrew Motion's biography in 1993, opinion changed sharply. Larkin had become a racist, a misogynist, foul-mouthed, addicted to pornography, a politically incorrect misanthropist who belittled his closest friends. Moreover, even his poetry was discredited.

Although the political correctness debate was still raging fiercely in political and academic circles when the *Selected Letters* and *A Writer's Life* were published, its ideology was already being discredited elsewhere. 'By the early nineties, use of the term political correctness was almost always pejorative while ... to be non-p. c. is frequently considered as a positive attribute' (*Oxford Dictionary of New Words*, new edn 1997). However, in spite of this, its protagonists launched a vicious attack, not only on Larkin the man, but also on his poetry, in the light of disclosures in the *Letters* and the *Life*. The argument was that his politically incorrect views largely corrupted his poetry. 'The Britishness of Larkin's poetry carries a baggage of attitudes which the *Selected Letters* now make explicit' wrote Lisa Jardine in the *Guardian* (3.xii.92). Continuing the debate she later wrote that at Queen Mary and Westfield College, London, where she holds a Chair in English, the decision had been made to 'contextualise him in a specialist second year course on "Fifties British poetry"', thereby effectively 'edg[ing] Larkin from the centre to the margins' (Dunant 111). Reviewing the biography in the *Independent* (18.iii.93) Brian Appleyard wrote that although many writers 'have adopted a personal pose of extreme pessimism and loathing of the world ... none has done so with quite such a grinding focus on littleness and triviality as Larkin the man.' A pseudonymous columnist writing in the *Library Association Record* went so far as to suggest, after reading the *Selected Letters*, that Larkin's books should be banned from UK libraries! (*LAR* v.95.2, 1993).

Counteracting this barrage of criticism, Andrew Motion, in a lecture 'Philip Larkin: Sex and Political Correctness', delivered at the University of Hull on 22.iv.93, declared that contrary to the beliefs of his critics, Larkin was by no means unique among writers, nor indeed among his generation, class and sex in holding right-wing prejudices: 'His political thinking, his opinions in their broadest application, his form of patriotism, even his pornography are all in their way typical of his type and times.' Similarly, he added, Wordsworth, Dickens, Woolf, Eliot, Pound and Lawrence would all have failed to meet the criteria of political correctness by which academics and literary critics were currently judging Larkin.

In fact Larkin was not a political animal and shrank from heated arguments on subjects which either held little interest for him or which he found painful. I have known him either retreat behind an entrenched position, as in the case of domestic politics, thereby effectively stifling further discussion; or he would adroitly change a conversation – on say the nuclear debate – steering it towards topics which he found more acceptable.

As one of Larkin's generation I would go even further and maintain that up to the late 1960s, most people in Britain, of whatever class, were guilty of holding and voicing opinions now regarded as offensive. Racism, for instance, was equally commonplace amongst the working classes, fearful of black immigrants undercutting them in the labour market, as it was amongst the middle and upper classes, contemptuous of the supposed social and intellectual inferiority of non-whites. Anti-Semitism was not the prerogative of Nazi Germany: Jews were not readily assimilated into British post-war society for many years; indeed the process still has some way to go. It was taken for granted that the age-old antagonism between workers and employers, popularly characterised by the 'them and us' syndrome was incapable of resolution. The slow breakdown of class barriers in the last thirty years has obscured our acknowledgement of how ingrained and admissible such attitudes formerly were. I do not seek to excuse mine and earlier generations for their lack of political correctness: it was simply something we never thought of. Britain's imperialist past and two world wars had made us indifferent, insular and insensitive to those who, for one reason or another, were outside our normal experience.

I don't think I heard the term 'political correctness' until the early 1990s although the ideology of p.c. had permeated society since the mid-1970s and it had become *de rigueur* with most thinking people to be more guarded when expressing their prejudices. Initially born out of the feminist movement's bid for equality, 'political correctness' gained momentum as the feminists in turn championed the rights of ethnic and social minority groups. Its principles were given political clout under Ken Livingstone's chairmanship of the Greater London Council (1981–86). Inevitably, the serious intentions of p.c. gave rise to some absurd guidelines which came in for a good deal of ridicule and undermined their validity. Such excesses included the banning of the *Little Black Sambo* books from libraries and bookshops, and golliwogs from toyshops and nurseries, not to speak of derisive euphemisms like 'physically challenged' and 'follicularly challenged'. As recently as the summer of 1998 I heard on Radio 4's *Today* programme that Gloucestershire County Council was in the process of replacing all its 'Accident Black Spot!' signs with 'Accident Hot Spot!' notices, evidence that, as the commentator scathingly observed, political correctness is still alive and well. One recommendation that particularly irritated Larkin was the use of the non-sexist word 'Chair' instead of 'Chairman' or 'Chairwoman. When, in some departmental minutes I was once described as the 'Chair', he said 'You don't look much like a chair to me.' To him such terminology was unnatural and affected and therefore he overreacted by ridiculing the principles of p.c. – not that I think he would have recognised the phrase. At the same time it may surprise Larkin's critics to know that he actually handled management tensions effectively and sensitively. His spontaneous repartee in private belied his hatred of open confrontation, and before addressing any professional crisis he prepared his ground meticulously and judiciously.

In spite of its 20-year gestation, the term 'political correctness' did not, according to the *Oxford Dictionary of New Words*, come into popular usage until 1986/87, first in the United States, and not until the turn of the decade in the United Kingdom, five or more years after Larkin's death. So, although we discussed some of the issues raised by p.c. we were not familiar with the phrase or its acronym. It seems all the more ironic, therefore, that by the time the argument was turned against Larkin with such ferocity, not only was he censured for a shortcoming of which he had almost certainly never heard – political incorrectness – but also that by 1993 to be non-p.c. had come to be considered, by some at least, more of a virtue than the reverse.

Had Larkin had the chance to enter the debate, he would have wholeheartedly endorsed the opinion of television personality, Anna Ford: 'We have such political correctness in this country – it drives me potty and makes me want to take off my clothes and swear very loudly in public' (interview with Andrew Duncan, *Radio Times*, 25–31.vii.98, 15). He would no doubt have added, with at least a two-finger gesture, something to the effect that this was censorship of the most vicious kind which violated the principles of freedom of speech, thereby negating the very ideology it intended to promote.

In spite of this, however, eleven and a half years after his death, one weekend in June 1997, one hundred delegates from all over the world had gathered to discuss his work, evidence enough that his literary reputation at least continues to stimulate scholars, young and old alike. Larkin's timeless poetic preoccupations seemed to interest the young particularly, and I was surprised that more than one delegate engaged me in conversation about his pursuit of the transcendental, to reach beyond 'The sun-comprehending glass' to 'the deep blue air that shows / Nothing, and is nowhere, and is endless' (*CP* 165).

So while his literary standing is recovering, his personal reputation remains in question. When he died I described him as 'a well-loved colleague, ... a charismatic figure', whose outstanding qualities were 'dignity, courtesy, compassion and honesty (with himself and with others)' (*BJL News*, 15, 1986). Then between 1988 and 1993 I was confronted with some unpalatable truths which profoundly shook my faith in him, the most distressing of which was his duplicity in the final phase of our friendship. My self-esteem was shattered as I imagined how often my *naïveté*, and what he probably regarded as my prudishness, must have irritated him. As I grappled with these doubts during this period, reason ultimately told me these reservations completely belied his marked forbearance in our relationship, and anyway if I had exasperated him to the extent which I now suspected, why had he allowed it to continue for so long? He could, after all, have terminated it whenever it suited him for he was under no moral obligation to me.

The fact was that initially, and over a sustained period of time, my ingenuousness, like my religion and my restraint, was what appealed to him. Quite late in our relationship – I made a note of the occasion – he said: 'Part of your charm is a certain child-like quality you have' (4.vi.76). Then, after his death, I learnt that he had confided his regard for me to others; both the Hartleys had volunteered their separate versions of his disclosures. What is more, Philip himself had claimed on numerous occasions that I was the one person he knew with whom he believed marriage could work. Indeed, the more I thought about his failings, the more I became convinced that his decision to conceal them from me, especially his affair with Betty, was right. Rather than shady duplicity I came to see it by degrees as a genuine desire to protect me from what he knew would have been a shattering discovery. Philip, more than anyone, knew the blows life had dealt me in the months leading up to the severance of our eighteen-year intimacy, beginning with my mother's death in May 1977, and ending with the break up of our affair the following March.

However, I am very glad I remained ignorant of its underlying cause until after his death, and although angered by his betrayal for a time, I am now convinced that his economy with the truth was intended, and was in fact, in my best interests. His taste for pornography and foul language was equally disappointing. But I should have been more disillusioned had *he* revealed these tendencies to me. There was always a certain elegance in his manner towards me which instinctively excluded anything offensive. So in the end – ironically because he kept them from me – I came to terms with these flaws without being blind to those I was aware of in his lifetime, thus endorsing one of his best known lines: 'What will survive of us is love'. In an interview, Philip said a friend once asked him if he knew a poem ending with this line, adding: 'I was delighted ... It suggested the poem was making its way without me. I like them to do that' (Haffenden 125). That was a long time ago, but I was that friend!

When asked in the same interview if he felt sceptical about this image of fidelity preserved in stone, Larkin replied: 'No, I was very moved by it. Of course it was years ago. I think what survives of us *is* love, whether in the simple biological sense or just in responding to life, making it happier, even if it's only making a joke.' Twenty years before he made this observation, when I had asked a similar question, his answer was pretty much the same.

Obviously, the man we, his friends and colleagues, knew was a far cry from the general public's view of him. Ten years after my encounter with the woman from the University bookshop who had been so outspoken about her dislike of Larkin, I was at a concert with my friend, Hilary Nowell, who introduced me to a woman of her acquaintance. In the course of the polite exchanges that followed, she asked how and when my friend and I had first met. We replied that we had known each other ever since we worked together in the University Library in the early 1950s; whereupon the stranger looked at us incredulously and ejaculated 'You don't mean to say you worked for that ABOMINABLE man!' Now, unlike the woman in the bookshop, this woman had never met Philip and her view of him had been gleaned solely from the media. Hilary and I were both completely taken aback by the vehemence of the remark but she had the presence of mind to retort 'Well, that wasn't the way we saw him.' Flawed, yes, albeit endearing; but never abominable.

Which assessment of Larkin is the correct one: the public image or the private view of friends and colleagues? Or was he simply the embodiment of his own poetry which Clive James defines on the sleeve of the recording of *High Windows*, as 'the expression of a wrecked personality in a ruined world ... arguing with its own beauty against the anguish it professes'? [24] I don't know. These conflicting opinions only strengthened my resolve to write down my recollections of the man I knew and relate events as I experienced them, at the same time re-affirming my pride in his friendship. This memoir is a celebration of our association.

[24] *British Poets of Our Time: Philip Larkin: High Windows; Poems read by the author* (London: Decca Record Company: Argo Division, 1974).

8

Twelve painful months

To the left, behind Philip's grave are interred the ashes of David Bassett, the friend who in 1979 succeeded Philip in my affections. David died suddenly of a heart attack in August 1989, aged 58. He was a historian and specialist in the history of South-East Asia, and it was this expertise that brought him to Hull in 1965. It is my belief that David provided the stimulus for Philip to finish 'Love Again' in 1979, although he was not the original target of his jealousy when he began the poem in 1975. David was certainly the most magnanimous man I have ever met and offered a very broad shoulder to cry on, particularly after Philip's death. His own death, three and a half years later, deprived me of a most supportive and loyal friend.

My father's death, three and a half years after this, on 28 March 1993 at the age of 93, coincided with the publication of Andrew Motion's biography, which I had been very anxious to keep from him. Throughout the month speculation had mounted in the media, following its seriali-sation in the *Independent on Sunday* (*Sunday Review*, 14, 21, 28.iii.93). As my father remained in command of his faculties until the last day of his life, newspapers had to be censored before being passed to him, and all who came into the house were asked to refrain from comment about the biography. This included doctors, nurses, the priest, as well as friends and family. He would have been appalled to see one of his daughters figure so prominently in the book, and her name bandied about the newspapers, not to speak of his disenchantment with its subject. He had told me some years before that he had been disillusioned when Philip introduced four-letter words into his poetry.

Fortunately, I did not have to explain my dilemma to either the priest or the doctor. Father Anthony Storey had been resident Catholic chaplain at the University throughout the 1960s and had been our parish priest since 1980. He was well aware of my liaison with Philip while he was University chaplain and knew Philip quite well in the way that everyone knew everyone else on campus in those days. He had even looked in on Philip while doing chaplain duty at the Hull Royal Infirmary in June

1985. Mark Hancocks, my G.P., on the other hand, learnt of my relationship with Philip just a few months before my father died, when, he told me that, at a party, talk had focused on the forthcoming biography, revealing, to his astonishment, my rôle in the story.

Although we managed to keep news of the biography from him, my father obviously sensed that something concerning a member of the family was seriously wrong. One afternoon, three or four days before he died, I was sitting in the room below him when suddenly I heard a heavy thud which suggested that he had fallen out of bed. I rushed upstairs to find him in a state of delirium, with all the bedclothes flung aside: what I had heard was the sound of a hot-water-bottle falling to the floor. As I approached him, he started raving: 'Haven't you heard of the terrible disgrace that has befallen the family? It's going to be in all the papers tomorrow. We'll never live it down.' When I asked what disgrace, convinced he must have some inkling of the truth, and who had brought it on the family, he replied: 'Surely you've heard; everyone is talking about it. You must know it's Edward [one of my nephews]. Oh what shame he has brought on us. I'll never get over it.' He didn't say what the unsuspecting Edward had done and eventually became quiet and fell asleep. He did not refer to the incident again.

A nightmare; or more likely a case of extra-sensory perception, a faculty more usually found in mothers than in fathers. My mother always sensed when things were not going right, but I had never before experienced it with my father. I found the episode very disturbing and though relieved that attention had been deflected from me, I was sorry that the stigma had fallen on Edward. Anyway, when Edward and his sister, Claire, came to say goodbye to their grandfather a few hours before he died, he showed no sign of disapproval of Edward. In fact, although by now almost completely unconscious, my father clearly responded to their young voices in a way he had ceased to be aware of the rest of us. It was obvious that Edward's presence caused him no distress.

In the evening of the day of my father's disconcerting premonition, two visitors arrived simultaneously. One was the consultant surgeon, Ian Galloway, who had performed a palliative operation on my father three or four weeks earlier. He confirmed that the patient's condition was fast deteriorating and that little more could be done other than to keep him as comfortable as possible. The second visitor was our cousin, Margaret McNally, known in the family as Peg. For the past ten years she had come up from her home in Bath three or four times a year to keep house for my father while I got a break. For this alone, I was much in her debt.

Furthermore, she had always promised that she would be with me when he died. She and her younger sister had been boarders at the Ursuline Convent in Sligo where my sister, Moira, and I had been enrolled in June 1940. In 1954, with her husband and two children, Peg left Ireland to live in London. From this time until she was widowed in 1978 we lost touch with her, although we had news of her from time to time through her family in Ireland.

On her arrival on this late March day in 1993, I reported the afternoon's disturbing incident, my interpretation of which she grasped immediately for she was well aware of my apprehension regarding the imminent publication of Andrew Motion's biography. She knew how distressed I had been a year earlier by the penultimate draft which Motion had sent me for comment. I was shocked by its more distasteful revelations, and in particular by the overall portrayal of Philip, and the misinterpretation of our relationship. To add to my difficulties, Motion stipulated that the book's contents should not be shown to, or discussed with, anyone. I scrupulously obeyed this exhortation, conveyed my reservations to him as best I could, and hoped that by letting him see Philip's letters to me, the distortion would be adjusted.

Two months later a revised version arrived which addressed some of my objections but contained new, equally distressing elements. This time, I resolved that for my own peace of mind – by now I was extremely demoralised – I would take Peg into my confidence. She was due to arrive shortly to spend Easter (1992) with us and I could rely on her not to gossip. Still feeling guilty about abusing the author's trust, I compromised by only showing her the 16 to 20 (non-consecutive) pages which troubled me most. With a more dispassionate eye than mine, she quickly understood my objections and with remarkable dexterity suggested how certain sections could be rephrased to correct wrong interpretations or present facts in a more accurate light. Needless to say, our deliberations had to be carried out without my father's knowledge. Initially, we repaired to a pub with the offending sheets and subsequently worked on them after he had gone to bed! Had he seen the drafts, or known of my worries, he would have sent for his solicitor immediately. As it was, I'm happy to say Andrew Motion accepted our joint recommendations, but alone I lacked the confidence to be completely candid about my reservations. My gratitude to Peg in this instance was enormous. Now, a year later, here she was again to support me, not only as the book was published, but more importantly through my father's final days. That Easter, following his death, Peg and I went up to the North York Moors to escape the oppression of recent events, and to put a distance between us and friends or neighbours who may have watched the *Book Mark* programmes marking the publication of the biography, shown on BBC2 on Good Friday and Easter Saturday. We watched them in the seclusion of our hotel room. I doubt if I should have had the courage to watch them alone at home.

The qualities I most admired in my father were his lively mind, his fierce independence of spirit and his ready wit. Simultaneously these characteristics had their down side which at times made him strong-willed, obstinate and possessive, and I found it particularly hard to re-adjust to living with him after my mother's death. But as he grew older, he mellowed considerably and came to appreciate fully his long life and comfortable old age. Even when confined to his bedroom in the last week of his life, he was cheerful, grateful, co-operative, and retained his sense of humour. Twenty-four hours before he died, I went out in search of liquid morphine which the doctor had prescribed that evening, leaving my father with Peg (Margaret) and a nurse, Maureen, who had been attending my father almost daily for eighteen months. By the time I returned the night nurse, whose name was Mavis, had arrived. All three were in the bedroom as I entered with the medicine. My father was sitting up in bed having his supper, and with a broad grin he said: 'Here comes another bossy "M". Good God, what have I done to be at the mercy of so many bossy women whose names all begin with "M"!' A highly intelligent and articulate man, it was consoling that he retained his faculties until he began to lose consciousness the following day. I still miss his invigorating mind, his wisdom, his wit, and last but not least his steadfast loyalty and affection. He was, after all, my most abiding and staunchest ally.

Needless to say in the days and weeks following my father's death I was too pre-occupied with practical arrangements to give much thought to the forthcoming publication of Motion's biography (5 April). Articles and comments had been appearing since early March. But, apart from those in the papers which we took – the *Yorkshire Post*, *Independent on Sunday* and the *Tablet*, together with a stray *Daily Express* thrust upon me by a well-wisher on 22 March, I managed to insulate myself from the torrent of publicity for several weeks. Jean Hartley and another friend, John Farrell, had put on one side all the reviews they had collected, but thoughtfully did not hand over until I was in a better emotional frame of mind to deal with them. In that it cushioned me from the worst impact of the media backlash, my father's death was a timely blessing. I had not, of course, escaped the earlier features like 'Mr Nice tackles Mr Nasty' in the *Independent on Sunday* (7 March) and the more seductive headline of the *Daily Express* review: 'Larkin the secret lover. Hidden affairs of a woman-hating poet' complete with photographs of four of his 'conquests', including me (22.iii.93).

Six weeks later it was no less distressing to read captions like: 'The Dreary laureate of our Provincialism' (*Independent* 18.iii.93), 'Hull life, low life' (*Sunday Telegraph* 28.iii.93), 'Portrait of a sumptuous old misery' (*Weekend Telegraph* 3.iv.93). It was still more painful to see Philip described as 'a foul-mouthed bigot [who] made a small talent go a very long way indeed' (P. Ackroyd, *The Times* 1.iv.93) and again as 'Socially reclusive, emotionally recessive' (P. Conrad, *Observer* 28.iii.93), not to mention A. N. Wilson who, in an article entitled: 'Larkin: the old friend I never liked', and therefore claiming to speak from personal acquaintance, dismissed his erstwhile friend as 'by far the meanest man I have ever met – a kind of petty-bourgeois fascist.' He found it difficult, he continued, to imagine poems like 'An Arundel Tomb' and 'The Whitsun Weddings' 'coming out of the really rather nasty, prematurely aged man whom I knew' (*Evening Standard* 11.iii.93).

But the review I found most distasteful of all was Alan Bennett's 'Alas! Deceived', not least because of its cheap personal jibes directed, not only at Philip, but also at his (still living) women friends. Fortunately, I did not come across it until it was reprinted in *Writing Home*, a year or more after its appearance in the *London Review of Books* (25.iii.93). I cannot think what I should have felt had I read it as my father lay dying: I should probably have wanted his grave to swallow me up also. Fourteen months later my reaction was considerably more robust, though nonetheless shocked.

The tone of 'Alas! Deceived' was not in the least what I had expected. I had always enjoyed Bennett's monologues on television and admired his dry humour and the amiable teddy-bear image he projects. Alas! How sadly undeceived I was when I read the review. It is not like those other reviews whose authors reacted in anger, revulsion or genuine dismay to the man portrayed in *A Writer's Life*. It is rather an extension of Motion's book, with a good deal of Bennett's independent interpretation of events and facts, written in a facetious, cynical, even at times, malign style. It is full of snide asides ('propriety seems to have been maintained and there was no slipping down to the stacks for a spot of beef jerky') and sly innuendoes ('he [Larkin] bears more than a passing resemblance to Reginald Halliday Christie. Haunting his cemeteries and churchyards he could be on the verge of exposing himself, and whether it's to a grim, head-scarved wife from Hessle[25] or in a slim volume from Faber and Faber seems a bit of a toss-up', *Writing Home* 371). I find it alarming that an esteemed writer should liken Larkin – or anyone else – to Christie, one of the worst serial murderers in British history. Why weren't the champions of political correctness up in arms about this? Possibly some readers find this kind of writing witty but many must find it, as I do, more appropriate to a music hall revue than a literary review. At the same time I am surprised that the academic and literary worlds approved of it sufficiently to include it in a collection of *bona fide* critical essays.[26]

Claiming that 'Much of Motion's story is about sex', Bennett concentrates on this angle with scant reference to any other beyond admitting that Larkin did his job as Librarian 'exceptionally well' (*Writing Home* 360). And naturally since sex is Bennett's main preoccupation, he turns the spotlight on the women in Larkin's life, claiming that 'one's sympathies, as always in Larkin's affairs, go to the woman' (361). He reserves his deepest sympathy for me. Not only is he sorry for me because he perceives me as having had the rawest deal, but also because our eighteen-year relationship, 'romantic and innocent' on my part, 'companionable and protective' on Philip's, must have been so 'dull' (372). This conclusion rather suggests the writer himself has no conception of romantic love. Furthermore, in my view it is deeply offensive to mock another's religion ('A fervent Catholic (trust his luck), Maeve took a long time before she would sleep with him …'). In particular, I resent the flippancy of: 'as soon as she does start to sleep with him on a regular basis her days are numbered' (372). How does he know? I didn't tell him; Motion doesn't say so. In fact more than once Motion stated my views on pre-marital sex, a principle I did not abandon 'without grave violation to my conscience', so there was no 'regular basis' about it (*Life* 336, 447, 451). Why do journalists make wild statements without verifying them? Another quip, equally untrue, though perhaps not unkindly meant, was made by a *Guardian* writer, who claimed that after Philip's death I turned my bed round so that it lay in the same direction as his grave! Admittedly my home is no more than 200 yards, as the crow flies, from the cemetery, but my bed is in the same position in which it has always been since I moved into the house in 1977. The size of my bedroom, together with

---

[25] Bennett has confused Hessle Road, the working-class area of Hull where trawlermen have traditionally lived, with the leafy village of Hessle, just outside Hull.

[26] Stephen Regan (ed.), *New Casebooks. Philip Larkin* (London: Macmillan, 1997).

the disposition of fitted and free-standing furniture, leaves no room for such a fanciful manoeuvre!

As I came to write this section, I realised that quite unconsciously I have already refuted, throughout this memoir, other fallacies in Bennett's review. Examples are: 'he seems never to have taken much pleasure in the look of things – furniture, pictures and so on ... he kept his flat like a dentist's waiting room'; 'beyond the jokes was a sphere of gloom, fear and self-pity that nothing and no-one touched'. Nor did he get it right about women who have shared the same lover never getting together to compare notes. Although not the trio Bennett would have preferred (though I do meet Betty Mackereth socially) I have elsewhere outlined how a close friendship has grown up between Ruth Siverns (*née* Bowman) and me since 1987, with Win Dawson (*née* Arnott) joining us in 1993. I think our conversation might disappoint him since it by no means focuses exclusively on Philip and never included comparisons of the kind Bennett envisages. As Win stated in an interview: 'Perhaps the fact that we all get on so well might be due to what a psychologist friend of mine tells me is "assortative mating", the selection of a series of mates who have a strong resemblance to each other' (*About Larkin* No. 1, April 1996, 15).

Then again Bennett condemns Larkin for wanting 'to keep women at a distance, fend off family life, because he felt that writing poetry depended on it' (373). Well, Philip never made a secret of putting his art first and acknowledged this would be an obstacle to marriage. He was always honest about it, so why berate him for deliberately avoiding a situation which he believed would have disastrous consequences not only for himself, but for everyone else concerned?

And last but not least, I never saw my relationship with Philip as 'a line to posterity' (374). Unlike Philip, it seems that Bennett does not understand the female psyche, or

> How separate and unearthly love is,
> Or women are, or what they do,
> Or in our young unreal wishes
> Seem to be ... (*CP* 135)

At least, however, Bennett concedes that the poetry transcends the life.

9

⑨✕⑨

Recollections

Apart from the reviewers' comments, the negative picture of Larkin which succeeded the publication of the *Selected Letters* and Andrew Motion's biography was very painful to me. Could the authoritarian, ill-mannered and lustful Larkin I read about in the Sunday supplements be the same person I had known? As part of my preparation for writing this memoir I therefore approached, in 1996 and 1997, as many of his colleagues as possible, to see if their recollections matched mine.[27]

I found that, for the most part, time had not diminished their favourable impressions although only one commented on his standing as a poet and the effect of his poetry on them. 'Staff were proud of him as an outstanding literary figure. There was a definite glow, a pride, an aura if you worked with Philip Larkin' observed Geoff Weston, Associate Director of Academic Services. Many colleagues had been disturbed by the biographical disclosures of the early 1990s and were anxious to counterbalance the unflattering view thereby generated. Alan Marshall (University Photographer 1959–87) robustly refuted this image, noting that: 'Many words have been written and TV programmes produced about the life of Philip Larkin but frankly I do not recognise him as portrayed in them.' As was to be expected, those who had known him over a long period and looked on him not only as a boss, but also as a friend, held fonder memories than those who knew him later when deafness, age and increased staff numbers placed him at a distance. Women too, as a rule, remember him more affectionately. As Sally Boston (Assistant Librarian 1967–85) put it: 'He had an aura of "Little Boy Lost" about him which appealed to women.'

Wendy Mann, who worked with him from 1956, was not alone in singling out the easy accord he had with staff he had known longest. In 1961 she had been one of those who qualified for the 'Library Invalids

---

[27] Some colleagues gave me their impressions in writing; others I spoke to and made notes from what they said and some gave me edited or recorded versions of questionnaires they had completed in 1996–97 for archival purposes.

Club' which Philip had proposed from his London Hospital bed at the same time as she was undergoing various exploratory tests in Hull. In addition to consideration for his staff's personal well-being, Wendy judged that 'one of his outstanding qualities was his care for their professional welfare and his concomitant ability to pick out their strengths and weaknesses'.

Freda Carroll, who joined the staff in 1973, made the same point: 'He knew a great deal more about staff than most of us realised', she said. 'He was good at weighing people up and was quick to spot not only their ability but also their shortcomings. Consequently he never made excessive demands on colleagues, but gently nudged them in the direction he wanted them to go, at the same time believing it to be in their best interests.' In Wendy Mann's case, in particular, Larkin envisaged an entirely new career for her in the 1950s. He intended to create a post of photographic technician in the new Library, and, having Wendy in mind for this appointment, persuaded her to exchange classes in librarian-ship for a course in photography. However, when the time came, the Library Committee resolved that an experienced photographer with wider responsibilities should be appointed, and Alan Marshall, who had several years' experience with the local evening paper, secured the post.

One of his first assignments was to make a photographic record of the move to the new Library in September 1959. He remembers Larkin as 'a kindly, courteous and quickly-understanding Head of Department ... meetings with him were business-like but full of good humour, and I often left his room chuckling at his dry and potent wit.' At the same time: 'He was not a man to be trifled with'; small failings irritated him – 'I recall him having a notice put up in the staff room on how to spell "supersede".' Finally, Alan remembers him 'as a quiet man, supportive, but expecting loyalty from us also'.

Alan subsequently told me an engaging story illustrating the trouble Larkin took to gain the confidence of a porter whose nervous manner made him appear somewhat slow. Philip discovered that not only had Tony had an unusual war record, working on Russian naval convoys, but also that he was well-read. Intrigued, Philip used to draw Tony about his wartime experiences or discuss with him the latest book he was reading. This rapport between the Librarian and a shy, hesitant member of staff would seem inconceivable to outsiders, but it was typical of Philip's many unseen acts of kindness.

Larkin in fact made it his business to find out the spare-time interests of each member of staff – usually at their interview of appointment; this gave him a subsequent talking point. Bob Smeaton recalls his interview for the post of Assistant Librarian in 1979. 'I particularly remember his questions regarding my jazz interests. "I suppose you don't listen to anything before Charlie Parker?" I replied that I did indeed like ... a range of pre-Parker jazz ... He seemed impressed that I at least knew the names of some of the right people.' Apparently not all later exchanges on their mutual hobby were cordial. One time, having remarked that he enjoyed playing transcriptions of Oscar Peterson, Bob observed that Philip 'seemed to sense that I wasn't being entirely genuine, and said rather unkindly: "You can't play like Oscar Peterson."'

Another member of staff, Peter Crowther (Sub-Librarian 1972–89), who often sat on interviewing committees with Philip, noted his courtesy and sensitivity towards others, especially 'when he was interviewing (some-times nervous) candidates ... He had great personal charm and was adept at putting people at their ease', even if he 'tended to over-esteem candi-dates who had extrovert, self-confident personalities, possibly because he admired in them those qualities which he ... felt he lacked in himself.' Brian Dyson also recalls that at his interview for the post of Senior Library Assistant in December 1980, Larkin at that time 'struck me as an avuncular figure – wise and kindly, with a sense of humour: there was a surprising amount of laughter.'

Anne Holbrook, appointed as a library assistant in 1973, recalled his thoughtfulness and politeness to all grades of staff. 'The first impression he made was one of grave courtesy. He was never impolite or rude to his juniors and treated us all with respect.' She remembers his readiness to express appreciation and gratitude to individuals, not only for special services, but also for work well done. Long after his death', she added, 'one of my junior colleagues talking of him said to me "He was a gentleman to us, wasn't he?" And this, I think, sums up what we all felt about him.'

Pauline Dennison (Assistant Librarian 1963–95) corroborated this view: 'He always liaised and consulted; he was fair-minded and willing to listen. Above all, he never failed to express appreciation and give encouragement. In short, he was a gentleman; courteous, polite, perceptive and interested in the welfare of his staff.' John Morris (Assistant Librarian 1966–2000) reflected: 'Larkin always supported staff and attempted to get the best possible conditions for them. And because he allowed staff to get on with their work without undue interference, he succeeded in building an open, friendly, non-threatening relationship between staff.' However, not every-one related to him so readily, John observed: 'Some found him aloof and distant and consequently difficult to approach.' He added that while diffidence and hardness of hearing no doubt played their part, Larkin too 'found it difficult to talk to many people and got his information about what was going on from too narrow a range of staff.'

Another member of staff extended this view: 'He had good relationships with those he had known longest: it was probably a matter of trust, confidence, and I think a generational thing. So newer, younger staff ... didn't really come within his orbit or mindset. My experience was that he could be very remote and very arrogant without perhaps intending to be.' I have to admit myself that, even in the early years, I had noted Philip's tendency, on occasion, to take irrational dislikes to individuals. Sometimes, I saw it was a matter of incompetence or work-shyness; at other times, simply a clash of temperament. It is true that as he got older and his deafness increased, he was easily disconcerted by anyone he found difficulty in hearing, or whose accent (particularly if foreign) he could not follow. Whatever the cause, his seeming intolerance erected a barrier which he found hard to overcome and at the same time left the victim perplexed.

Not without justification, Larkin has been criticised for his resistance to new professional developments. John Morris noted: 'He was particularly resistant to IT ... and refused to countenance online searching until he discovered ... that Hull was the only university not to offer it. When finally convinced, however, he always found the resources for the best.' Lynne Wallace (Systems Librarian 1980–87) considered that Larkin was never really reconciled to automation, and regarded the computer 'with outright hostility. During the last few months of his time as Librarian' she continued, 'his customary greeting to the Systems Librarian was a jocular enquiry about "the beast in the basement" and its current state of health' (*MAL* 81). On completion of the building programme Larkin increasingly delegated the forward planning of the Library to Brenda Moon, who was anxious to introduce automation. As Geoff Weston explained, Larkin was 'not an innovator as regards librarianship. This was the reason Hull was so late in having an automated issue system. However, the turnkey system, independent of the University's mainframe, which he finally approved, was a very radical step, chosen very much under Brenda's influence, and put Hull once again at the forefront [of the Library world].'

As long as I had known Philip he had been out of sympathy with automation for library procedures; electronic handling of information was alien to his way of thinking. He found it preposterous, boring, even menacing. Ever since March 1961, when we attended a lecture together in Leeds on developments in library automation, during which Philip fell asleep, but then, on waking, rashly asked the first question, I have seen him mentally switch off whenever the subject was under discussion. This talk was also my first introduction to automation and it left me no more enthusiastic than he was. In 1961 it was completely beyond my comprehension or imagination. Twenty years later I had to grapple with the practical steps of preparing the Library's book stock for computerisation, still without experience of the end result, which made it extremely difficult for me to grasp the technical problems encountered on the way. Philip, however, neither needed nor wanted to concern himself with such details. Consequently, while I graduated from ignorance to apprehension of the operation, he remained completely detached from it.

We neither of us made the leap from the mould of traditional librarian in which we had both been nurtured to the completely different cast of late twentieth-century information networking. At Hull, Larkin's professional energies had been concentrated on planning and building a large library which he then proceeded to stock judiciously and administer efficiently. I think he saw automation as a threat to the prestigious collections he had developed, and even to the printed word itself. Whenever I go into the Library now, it strikes me forcibly that books are no longer very obvious in the public areas, and certainly no-one is reading them. Instead, miles of wall space, it seems, are lined with VDUs to which the contemporary student is glued as the electronic reproduction of his reading matter dances before his eyes, causing me to wonder idly if today's students ever *read* books.

It is easy to conjure up the unforgettable cartoon sketch or mimic turn this scenario would have elicited from Philip, featuring a boss-eyed VDU user, receiving frenetic messages, accompanied by an absurdly witty caption. For his sense of humour was ever ready to spring into action, whether at work or away from it. Just as the private jokes in his letters never fail to delight me, colleagues' recollections of his ability to enliven the atmosphere at work provide similar entertainment.

Peter Crowther remembers '. . . the very many occasions on which he made dull staff committee meetings bearable by his hilarious wit and his ability to mimic people ... He was genuinely funny and able to make people laugh.' One of his funniest acts of mimicry will only be remembered by those staff who worked in the old library in the 1950s. Assistants on the Issue Desk there sat behind a high glass partition with a hatch in the middle through which readers placed the books they were returning. A certain lecturer had the absurd habit of not only putting his books through the hatch, but also his head. Of tall build, with a long neck, dark horn-rimmed glasses and balding, in looks he was not unlike Philip. Aware of this, the latter frequently entertained us with his hilarious imitation of this man, bending and wriggling his head through the aperture, and then straightening up once it was on the other side. Philip described this contorted action as a maggot crawling out of an apple! At the time, no-one in the University had any difficulty in recognising the object of this caricature.

Later on, Pauline Dennison, who was in charge of the Issue Desk and was therefore the Library's front line woman, said that whenever she made an appointment to see the Librarian, he would mutter audibly in a Yorkshire accent as she entered his office: 'Oh! Here comes trouble at t'mill!', a West Riding expression directed at a West Riding person. Pauline also reminded me of a long-forgotten incident at a staff committee meeting when Philip suddenly said: 'I hear a noise like the mewing of kittens in a basket. Was that you, Brenda?' The question was addressed to Brenda Moon, whose thin, high voice, issuing from a tiny frame, belied her tremendous energy and force of intellect.

John Hooton (Sub-Librarian 1965–96) recalls Larkin's opening gambit, delivered with a mock grimace, on his weekly visits to his office: 'Just dropping in for a bit of a gloom'. Geoff Weston added: 'His remarks, even when politically incorrect, did not cause offence because he was so funny.' Nor, in the early days, was he averse to playing practical jokes. The assistant in charge of Inter-Library Loans was the object of a long-running prank which caused all of us, including her, much amusement. A very attractive young woman, she had gone out of her way to help a lecturer on secondment from a university in the Middle East to track down a bibliographical reference. So appreciative was he of this small service, so the story ran, that when he next bumped into Philip he was fulsome in his praise of the assistant. Philip lost no time in relaying this conversation, heavily embroidered, to the young woman concerned, revealing that the lecturer, anxious to install her in his harem back home, had offered Larkin a camel in exchange for her! Shortly afterwards, a small replica of a camel appeared on the assistant's desk, joined at intervals by similar figures so that eventually a cavalcade of the beasts trailed across her desk. When I wrote for confirmation of this incident, the now not-so-young woman replied: 'Your request for details of the "camel episode" does indeed come as a surprise; I thought it a forgotten incident ... I must admit to being highly entertained and flattered at the time' (PH 14.viii.96).

He once sent me a *billet-doux* in Russian, purporting to come from a lecturer in that department whom Philip suspected was sweet on me. I don't know to this day who prompted the text because he knew no Russian. On the other hand, I don't know how grammatically correct it was! In fact, mock jealousy featured prominently in his letters to me which I still find hilarious. One on-going saga involved a hypothetical admirer who, for the crime of 'fancying' me, was to be forced to resign his teaching post which in turn would mean selling his house because he would have no salary with which to pay the mortgage. However, rather than see him on the streets, Philip thought the University would probably give my now disgraced admirer a job as a gardener and allow him to live in 'a little hut behind the boiler house ... It's a bit damp in winter because it hasn't a very good roof but not bad really. Newlove [the University's Catering Officer] will probably let him sort through the dustbins every day for food too. I'm sure everyone will be co-operative and considerate, & not hold it against him, being such a rotten swine' (25.vii.65).

A holiday post-card from a couple who at the time lived in the flat below him in Pearson Park provoked a rumbustious outburst. When at home, Philip was enraged by their inability to close doors quietly, therefore he conjured up a picture of them holidaying in the former Yugoslavia, 'no doubt defending their European door-banging title – perhaps in preparation for Tokyo, where they are certain to win a gold medal for Great Britain in the Senseless Domestic Noise division' (PAL to MMB 2.ix.64). On one occasion he wrote to me: 'There was a letter for me this morning bearing a House of Commons crest. I thought it was Mr. Wilson [Prime Minister] asking if I'd accept the laureateship but in fact it was Kevin MacNamara [MP for North Hull] renewing his reader's ticket' (20.ix.67).

Once he went to Salcombe for a holiday, a place where I had stayed a few years earlier. On arrival he needed to buy toothpaste, and was thwarted by the apparent absence of shops. Aware of my addiction to them, he mused in a letter to me: 'I suppose I thought "Anywhere Maeve has been to must be a cracking good shopping centre" but this looks the worst yet.' In the same letter continued a day or two later he thanked me for my birthday card which I had apparently felt diffident about sending. However, he found it 'delightful ... – really very typical ... and not at all incriminating'. He continued: 'I thought it was some fearfully improper "comic" one, from the caution you implied it had to be treated with – something like I'D LIKE TO SLEEP WITH YOU on the front, and BRUSHING THE FLIES AWAY FROM ME inside, or something like that' (7–9.viii.67).

Sometimes the humour concerned professional matters. Commenting on a new library guide I had just prepared, he teased: 'I see you've chosen green for the cover of your Periodicals booklet – I've gone the whole hog and asked for green paper as well. A free harp will be given away with every tenth copy, and sham, or even real, rocks glued on the last page and back inside cover. I hope you'll like it' (16.ix.71). Another time he reported: 'Brenda [Moon] is still happily assembling her "beside the seaside" exhibition: I've lent her a stick of Brighton rock. No doubt it will stay in her memory like her first banana' (23.vii.75). I was once attending a conference in Oxford and Philip fantasised about the exciting time I was sure to be having, 'popping out of giant Easter eggs at the climax of banquets, & having champagne drunk out of your slippers' (25.iii.77). All innocuous, private jokes which make me explode with laughter as I re-read them, twenty, thirty and more years after they were written.

Talking of banquets, Charles Brook (Sub-Librarian 1971–81) recalled Philip's generosity in taking senior staff out to dinner annually at his own expense. We numbered 20 or more and the bill amounted to several hundred pounds. Philip said it was his way of acknowledging staff support during the previous year. Such generosity is offset by other stories of his meanness, illustrating the extraordinary complexity of his personality.

10

⌇

'What will survive of us is love'

It was in the relative calm between Larkin's death and the appearance of Anthony Thwaite's *Selected Letters* in 1992, and Andrew Motion's biography in 1993, that I read Philip's letters to Jim Sutton. As well as being fascinated by their frank and detailed self-portrait of Larkin's formative years, I was relieved to recognise in them much of the man I had known: his idealism, romanticism, lyricism, benevolence and candid good humour. At the same time, the harsher traits I had not known – the cynicism, boredom, malice and studied philistinism – were also plain to see. Nor was I the only person to be distressed by the darker image which the *Letters* and the biography uncovered. So were others who had known him well and likewise had not perceived the dichotomy in his personality during his lifetime.

Larkin himself was aware of it and at the age of seventeen put it to Sutton in a graphic simile: 'I am one of those dishonest serpents, with one coil touching the stars, another through some dung, and another crushing a rose and making it slimy. Symbolism!' ([Sept. 1939?]). Sutton also discerned it, possibly even earlier than Larkin himself. Writing of him as a schoolboy on the verge of his teens, Sutton described his friend as 'superbly intolerant and crushing of any stupidities wherever he found them,' adding 'It was only later that the kinder side of his nature became apparent to me.' Continuing with the first line of thought, Sutton explained: 'His expression of views was very emphatic & fierce, very well expressed & quotable & often highly amusing. In fact, he was largely the Philip we all knew ... from his very early years' (JBS to MMB 5.iv.87).

'The Philip we all knew'! Since his death I have oscillated between the arrogant assumption that I knew him very well and the insidious mis-giving that I had completely failed to understand him. More than a decade later, I realise that I knew one side of him very well: the side that responded to similar qualities in me. Consequently there was that affinity between us which brought out the best in each of us. But this was a skill Larkin admitted he knew how to exploit better than most, and used to advantage with most of his friends. So that it was not only in letters that 'he divided his private life ... into compartments', but also in the company of friends and acquaintances alike, with the result that he revealed to each of them 'the face he knew would please them most' (*Life* 332). To very few did he expose all – or even most of – the faces of his multi-faceted personality. Sutton, however, was one friend with whom he felt he could be frank, at least most of the time. He therefore poured out his deepest feelings unrestrainedly in these early letters, without any thought to what posterity might make of them. Consequently, this very candour leaves Larkin open to misinterpretation by today's readers, especially critics, biographers and journalists.

Interpreting the dichotomy, however, is more difficult than recognising it. But it unquestionably had its origin in Larkin's long-held belief which he summed up laconically in an interview in later years as 'Deprivation is for me what daffodils were for Wordsworth'. Developing this idea, he continued: 'it's unhappiness that provokes a poem. Being happy doesn't provoke a poem. As Montherlant says somewhere, happiness writes white' (*RW* 47). Sadness and a sense of privation underlie most of Larkin's poetry. Sometimes the melancholy springs from personal experience: 'Beyond the light stand failure and remorse' (*CP* 181–2); at others it is prompted by its universal relevance: 'nothing contravenes/ The coming dark, though crowds each evening try/ With wasteful, weak, propitiatory flowers' (*CP* 191–3). Ray Brett explores this dual sense of privation and its expression in poems as diverse as 'Ambulances', 'Dockery and Son' and 'MCMXIV': 'whose deprivation did he have in mind – his own or other people's? The answer must be both. For we are all brought together in a unity of suffering' (Brett 105).

Larkin's conviction that unhappiness stimulated and heightened his artistic expression had long been the basis of his philosophy. This he formulated repeatedly from schooldays (JBS to MMB 18.vi.87) and subsequently in letters to Sutton from his early twenties:

> outbursts of creative activity are always preceded by periods of intense depression which seems to precipitate the poetry. Consequently, nearly all my poems are sad ones, which is wrong. (15.i.45)

And since 'the writing of a poem is something I put far beyond everything' (20.viii.44), it was as if his muse demanded that he be in a state of constant privation in order to write. Basing his philosophy on Blake, he elucidated: 'Joy impregnates, sorrow brings forth; perhaps that is the explanation' (15.i.45). A month later, he put it another way, stressing that his deepest belief was that 'life, personally is unhappy: impersonally it is happy' (23.ii.45).

Still grappling with this wisdom eighteen months later, he tried to express it in verse:

> I have just finished a poem – a long one for me, a hundred-odd (very odd) lines – and am feeling the backwash of unachievement. In the poem I tried to express something of an attitude ... The attitude is that sorrow is personal & temporal, joy impersonal & eternal. (*SL* 127)

In the poem, 'Many famous feet have trod', included in the aborted collection, *In the Grip of Light*, Larkin attempted to trace the 'Lineage of sorrow: lineage of joy' (*CP* 15) within the parameters of total knowledge; a complex philosophy to compress into verse. Hardly surprisingly, it was not to his satisfaction, as he admitted to Sutton. When it came to applying these theories to life, he confessed:

> The real trouble with me is my relations with illusion & reality. Illusion is poetry, art, love, belief, confidence and is what you are enthusiastic about. Reality is daily work, illness, death, money, sex, one's actions independent of one's beliefs or fancies, and is impossible to be enthusiastic about. (3.vii.50)

It is significant that Larkin distinguishes between love and sex, classifying love as illusion and sex as reality. This is surely the key to his romanticism. At a personal level it explains his approach to our relationship; why he separated love from sex and why, when illusion became reality, the affair eventually came to grief. Similarly James Booth analyses the love poems under the separate headings of sex, sexual politics and love. He explores in them 'the gulf between dream and reality' (131) which inevitably ends with Larkin reflecting bitterly or sadly on 'the pathetic fallacies by which we live and the inevitability of their disappointment' (119). In short, illusion represented impersonal joy for Larkin, and reality personal sorrow. But illusion, though rewarding for a time, must eventually lead to disillusionment, and from there to cynicism and pessimism. And reality for Larkin always stood for misery and suffering.

Thus, it is entirely understandable that Larkin should be elated about abstract ideas, introduced elegant descriptive passages into his letters to Sutton, held romantic ideals, wrote lyrical poetry, was courteous, generous and compassionate. These qualities embodied the nobler side of his temperament (joy). At the same time, it is equally unsurprising that he should give vent to those attributes born out of personal sorrow – melancholy, depression, cynicism, malice, and disparagement of what he held dear – for these constituted the flaws in his personality. While it may have suited Larkin during his lifetime to intimate the darker side of his character to the world at large, since his death it has unfortunately become the public's entrenched view of him.

From the age of 23 his prospect of the world and his life – as set forth in the following excerpt – was singularly pessimistic and tragically prophetic:

> I sit enclosed in the insanitary darkness of my own soul ... I believe that the world is composed for the most part of people so unlike me that we think each other mad and wicked ... I believe that human beings can do nothing for one except provide amusement, which is pleasant but does not last. By amusement I include everything from an evening at the cinema to a love-affair. I believe that when I am old I shall bitterly regret having wasted my life, whatever I may have done. This is because I shall never attain the absolute – in other words, the *continual* ecstasy – because it doesn't exist. Therefore in addition to being afraid of death I shall feel cheated and angry. (14.vii.45)

Sadly this was his view at the end of his life and his last decade was one of increasing disillusionment. But in spite of the impression Larkin invariably gave, there was an interim period from the publication of *The Less Deceived* (1955) to *High Windows* (1974) when he enjoyed much personal happiness and satisfaction. These years represented immense literary achievement and recognition, with corresponding professional accomplishment. In fact Sutton identifies *XX Poems* (1951) as the decisive turning point in Larkin's literary career, when he had virtually abandoned his role as novelist and discovered his true vocation as a poet. (We also know from Motion's biography – chapters 26 to 30 – that during this period life took a happier turn for Larkin both personally and professionally.) Furthermore, Sutton believed that the impersonal joy/personal sorrow theory, which evolved from a pre-war belief that life fell into three distinct phases, can be directly related to Larkin's early literary achievements. The first of these phases Sutton defined as a state of innocence and joy which was lost or destroyed in the second stage. Then, the third state, which could only be attained – if at all – after a colossal struggle, would surpass the first phase in terms of happiness or achievement.

It is interesting that both Sutton and Brett identify Larkin's philosophy at different stages in his life with a subconscious yearning for a biblical state of innocence. Developing this particular theory, Sutton equated the three stages with 'the myth of the Garden of Eden:- 1) The state of innocence 2) The loss of innocence and expulsion and 3) Return to the

Garden of Eden' (JBS to MMB 18.vi.87). Brett, commenting on Larkin's much later concept of deprivation, likened its expression in 'I Remember, I Remember' and 'MCMXIV' to 'the sense of a lost Eden' (Brett 106).

In relating the theory to the early work, Sutton continued: '*Jill* is the first stage – innocence under attack to destruction. *A Girl in Winter* is the second stage – awful, almost hopeless barren destruction of the self. The poetry from *XX Poems* onwards is the third stage' into which the quintessence of the third failed novel was distilled, resulting in:

> these poems in which his concept of personal sorrow/impersonal joy comes through so strongly. The joy and sadness balance, joy in the perfection of expression, sadness in the reflection of life. Impersonal joy is the force that frees the ship or the soul in the frozen North, & life can go on ... There seems logic & inevitability that the poems take over when the novels stop, & go from strength to strength ... So Philip succeeded in his artistic aims. (JBS to MMB 18.vi.87)

Rossen makes a similar point. Thwarted by his inability to write another novel, and disappointed by the rejection of *In the Grip of Light*, she demonstrates how 'Larkin wrote himself out of failure and into an immediate, vivid poetic style, by tackling this problem in his writing' (Rossen 5). Ironically, as long ago as 1945, Larkin himself used the imagery of the poem 'The North Ship' to describe his strategy for a third novel which he intended as a natural sequel to *Jill* and *A Girl in Winter* (originally *The Kingdom of Winter*).

> *The Kingdom of Winter* is rather unimpressive compared with *Jill* ... it is a deathly book and has for theme the relinquishing of live response to life. The central character, Katherine, picks up where John left off and carries the story out into the frozen wastes – the kingdom of winter, to be exact. Now I am thinking of a third book in which the central character will pick up where Katherine left off and develop *logically* back to life again. In other words, the north ship will come back instead of being bogged up there in a glacier. Then I shall have finished this particular branch of soul-history (my own of course) ... But this third book will need colossal strength and application and I doubt if I can do it yet. (*SL* 109–10)

So strong was his resolve in 1945 to be a novelist that he could not envisage then that poetry, rather than prose, was to be the force that would set his creative talent free and complete 'this particular branch of [his] soul history'.

With the publication of *The Less Deceived* in 1955, the north ship was certainly set on its course for calmer waters and there it lay moored through the publication of *The Whitsun Weddings* (1964) and *High Windows* (1974). During this twenty-year span Larkin won increasing acclaim as one of England's best post-war poets, while at the same time the planning, building and judicious stocking of the Brynmor Jones Library, one of the country's first large post-war libraries, brought him substantial professional renown. Both these events gave him all the recognition and satisfaction he had craved in the years he was writing to Sutton, as well as much personal contentment.

My friendship with Larkin coincided with this happy phase, which largely accounts for my perception of him as an affectionate man of sanguine disposition, far distanced from the curmudgeonly misanthropist of later public image. In fact I found him a stimulating companion, witty, urbane, great fun to be with, prone to impulsive gestures – often guileless but endearing in their simplicity – and spontaneous acts of generosity; a man of good-natured humour, great tenderness and inspiring idealism. I was fortunate to have known him during this time of growing literary repute – for this was the mainspring of his happiness and joy (in spite of the caveat that it was 'impersonal and eternal') – if only because the rest – professional recognition and love – followed. Jean Hartley, who also knew him well, observed this growing contentment which she too ascribed to his steadily increasing reputation on both literary and professional levels: 'Philip seemed most light-hearted and fulfilled in the 1960s and early 1970s when, despite his habitual irony and self-deprecation he must have felt potent in two distinct spheres of his public life.' As a result, she concluded, 'his friends noticed that, in tune with the times, Philip became more expansive' (J. Hartley 136).

When the poetic muse deserted him in the last few years of his life, personal sorrow took over and his soul became once more trapped in the dark recesses of his own mind. By the mid-1970s, feeling that he had also given of his best professionally, even 'the toad *work*' no longer afforded the challenge and fulfilment it had once done. From 1977 onwards, the deaths of his mother and several contemporaries (including Patsy Murphy, Bruce Montgomery, Barbara Pym and later Sir John Betjeman) increased his melancholy, and as the age (63) at which he had long prophesied his own death drew nearer, he became more introverted and progressively turned his back on life. He snatched what happiness he could from his personal life but the constant reminder of 'the terrible neutralising effect' of a quarrel which he had witnessed between his parents 40 years before left him unable to trust himself to his emotions (PAL to JBS 12–14.iv.43). What he put into life, Jean Hartley observed, 'had always been carefully weighed against what he stood to lose. It saddened me to hear him voice his regret at having invariably allowed his head to rule his heart' (J. Hartley 174).

The friendship with Sutton terminated abruptly in January 1952. They never met again, although Sutton told me there was a desultory exchange of letters two or three years before Larkin died which are now in the Brynmor Jones Library. Such, however, was Larkin's charisma that eighteen months after his death Sutton wrote:

> he was the most absorbing person I ever met. Even though I lost touch with him in the early fifties he has spoiled me for deep relationships (excluding family) ever since ... & I still miss him & so can sympathise with you – though it is 35 years since I saw him last ... (JBS to MMB 19.vii.87)

It is ironic that Larkin, who belittled the popularity of 'What will survive of us is love', claiming to set more store by 'They fuck you up, your mum and dad', should be remembered with such warmth. However, each of these lines is equally representative and pithily illustrates the dichotomy of his personality, the idealism of the one offset by the cynicism of the other; probably

> Something to do with violence
> A long way back, and wrong rewards,
> And arrogant eternity. (*CP* 215)

Nevertheless, in spite of his scepticism about love, and his conviction about parents, I have no doubt which line Larkin would prefer as an epitaph.

Abbreviations and bibliography

Letters are referred to by the initials of sender and receiver, as follows:

MMB   Maeve Brennan
PAL   Philip Larkin
JBS   James Sutton

The following abbreviations are used for frequently-cited works:

CP   *Collected Poems*
Life   Motion, Andrew, *Philip Larkin: A Writer's Life*
MAL   Dyson, Brian (ed.), *The Modern Academic Library*
RW   *Required Writing*
SL   *Selected Letters*

Letters not included in the *Selected Letters* are cited by date.

Works by Larkin

Poetry

The North Ship (London: Fortune Press, 1945; Faber and Faber, 1966).

XX Poems (Belfast: Carswells, 1951).

The Less Deceived (Hessle: The Marvell Press, 1955).

The Whitsun Weddings (London: Faber and Faber, 1964).

High Windows (London: Faber and Faber, 1974).

Collected Poems, ed. Anthony Thwaite (London: The Marvell Press and Faber and Faber, 1988).

Edited anthology

The Oxford Book of Twentieth Century English Verse, chosen by Philip Larkin (Oxford: Clarendon Press, 1973).

Novels

Jill (London: Fortune Press, 1946; London: Faber and Faber, 1964).

A Girl in Winter (London: Faber and Faber, 1947; 1965).

Prose

All What Jazz: A Record Diary 1961–68 (London: Faber and Faber, 1970).

Required Writing: Miscellaneous Pieces 1955–82 (London: Faber and Faber, 1983).

'*A Lifted Study-Storehouse': The Brynmor Jones Library 1929–1979, updated to 1985 with an Appreciation of Philip Larkin as Librarian by Maeve Brennan* (Hull: Hull University Press, 1987).

Letters

Letters to James Ballard Sutton 1938–52. Brynmor Jones Library, University of Hull. MS DP/174/2/1–219.

Selected Letters 1940–1985, ed. Anthony Thwaite (London: Faber and Faber, 1992).

Secondary works

Bennett, Alan, *Writing Home* (London: Faber and Faber, 1994).

Booth, James, *Philip Larkin: Writer* (Hemel Hempstead: Harvester Wheatsheaf, 1992).

Brennan, Maeve, 'Philip Larkin: a biographical sketch', in Dyson 1989, 1–19.

Brett, Raymond, 'Philip Larkin in Hull', in George Hartley 1988, 100–14.

Dunant, Sarah (ed.), *The War of the Words: The Political Correctness Debate* (London: Virago Press, 1994).

Dyson, Brian (ed.), *The Modern Academic Library: Essays in Memory of Philip Larkin* (London: The Library Association, 1989).

Haffenden, John. 'Philip Larkin.' *Viewpoints: Poets in Conversation with John Haffenden* (London: Faber and Faber, 1981).

Hartley, George (ed.), *Philip Larkin 1922–1985: A Tribute* (London: The Marvell Press, 1988).

Hartley, Jean, *Philip Larkin, The Marvell Press and Me* (Manchester: Carcanet, 1989).

Hartley, Jean, *Philip Larkin's Hull and East Yorkshire*, ed. Brian Dyson (Hull: Brynmor Jones Library and Hutton Press, 1995).

Motion, Andrew, *Philip Larkin: A Writer's Life* (London: Faber and Faber, 1993).

Rossen, Janice, *Philip Larkin: His Life's Work* (Hemel Hempstead: Harvester Wheatsheaf, 1989).

Swarbrick, Andrew. *Out of Reach: The Poetry of Philip Larkin* (Basingstoke and London: Macmillan, 1995).

A selection of letters

Introduction

Philip and I exchanged over 400 letters in 25 years[1] which made picking out a judicious selection of 50 or so harder than I had anticipated. I wanted a representative mix of the interests which influenced our friendship: love, work, literature, our mutual and separate concerns, as well as occasional comments on wider events which happened to touch our lives. As my letters tended to be much longer than Philip's, especially when written from colourful holiday locations, I have deleted passages which had no direct bearing on our personal or professional relationship. On the other hand, I have only cut an occasional paragraph in Philip's letters where there are observations about people who are readily identifiable.

Until the spring of 1999 when I made this selection, I had not read my letters since the day they were written, a gap of 38 years in the case of the earliest ones. Being confronted with one's past in this way was a shock. It was sobering to see how immature and tentative the early correspondence was, and then, as I gained more confidence in Philip's regard for me, how frivolous, gossipy and light-hearted the tone became. At the same time I was surprised to note how funny I often was. Flippancy, in fact, was an antidote I cultivated in the early years to prevent what always threatened to be a doomed affair from becoming too serious. Attending the wedding of a close friend in Grenoble in April 1964, I wrote: 'nevertheless the immaturity' (an unfortunate choice of word; perhaps I meant 'frivolity'!) 'I bring to our relationship ... prevents it from becoming too serious and gives it its rather giddy gaiety at times'. Philip likewise diverted my tendency to flirt to absurd fantasy to prevent feelings getting out of hand. In the end these ploys failed and inevitably, as the affair matured and ultimately foundered, the letters took on a more sombre tone. But before matters came to this pass there was much love,

---

[1] A total hardly to be compared with the *c.* 1500 letters he wrote to Monica Jones, or the 2000 which he wrote to his mother.

laughter and fun, and for my part these letters of the early and mid-1960s were the happiest I ever wrote, exuberant, bubbling with sheer joy as the following passage, taken from a letter not included in the present selection, illustrates:

> I am missing *your* kisses (that's a bit malicious, but don't take it too seriously) and the rather delirious fun we have such a lot of the time. I do so hope we're not going to end in tears; I've never had so much pure pleasure from a friendship with anyone in my life.

And later in the same letter, anticipating the pleasure of a drive back to Hull from Woodstock (Oxon) where we planned to meet (I was returning from South Wales, Philip from Loughborough), I wrote:

> We'd probably not be able to drive home for laughing because we'd be sillier than ever. Do you remember how carried away you were in particular last August? That train journey back [from London], sitting opposite those older middle-aged stuffed shirts – after all we too are in middle-age – sad thought. (3.viii.64)

Of course, the spectre of 'ending in tears' was never far away and until I re-read the letters, I had forgotten that throughout the heady months of 1961 it was our intention to end our affair at Christmas in deference to our respective long-standing partners. Philip's gold chain and pearl gift that Christmas was intended as a parting present as the accompanying gift card indicated: 'For dear Maeve, herself a jewel, remembering 1961'. For a long time afterwards, I associated this gift with 'the throbbing intensity of an awakening love' (17.vi.65), its ecstasy not unmixed with pain.

However, as we planned to part, my long-standing boyfriend, also named Philip, piqued by my philandering with Larkin, met and fell in love with a colleague at a works Christmas party. Consequently, we severed our relationship on 1 April 1962. I can't remember if I saw much of Larkin outside the Library during this time; probably not, but he knew that I was irrationally distressed by this unexpected development in my affairs, and no doubt feeling he was greatly to blame, played the role of disinterested comforter. My feelings for him had, curiously, evaporated and until Christmas 1962 he remained in the background, supportive but detached.

Then suddenly our love was re-kindled and for the next fifteen years we remained emotionally enmeshed in spite of the ever-present threat posed by Philip's continuing relationship with Monica. It was a sword of Damocles which hung over our heads but, because Philip had quite simply fallen in love with me, and I with him, I saw no reason to back down. Barely six months after the renewal of our affair, an eve-of-holiday leave-taking was marred by a painful reminder of our predicament as our exchange of letters in July 1963 shows.

Over the years we tried hard to resolve the impasse. We frequently parted but except for a sixteen-month break in 1973/74 the partings were of brief duration. I usually instigated them. The intention was to allow Philip 'space' to sort out his feelings for Monica and for me, but seeing each other daily at work would have required a much stronger will to stay apart than either of us was willing to exercise. In the autumn of 1964, for instance, a cooling-off period had been declared when, on my birthday, an expensive pearl and marcasite brooch arrived through the post. (I was away on holiday.) Acknowledging it with obvious delight, I nevertheless reminded Philip of the truce: 'Anyway, don't lose sight of the fact that we're not supposed to be loving each other any more, and that being so, you shouldn't have sent me such an extravagant, beautiful present' (29–30.ix.64). A few days later, while still away from home, I received a formal, typed, unsigned letter along with plans for Stage II of the Library, on which, as usual, he required immediate comment. I enquired somewhat pertly if the lack of signature was 'deliberate so as not to embarrass us both further by signing so coldly *P. A. Larkin*? ... I was rather taken aback to receive a typed letter from you whilst on holiday: I thought it must be you really taking a firm line instead of me just talking about it' (3.x.64). Needless to say, even before I could reply, Philip's impersonal note was reversed by a much warmer letter.

Ten years later, halfway through the longest separation of our 18-year relationship, I was taken by surprise when Philip handed me a copy of *High Windows*, explaining that it was one of the six personal copies to which he, as the author, was entitled. I was therefore one of the earliest recipients of the new collection; hence the reason for my letter of acknowledgement (7.v.74). Furthermore it carried a simple but touching inscription: 'For Maeve, with affectionate gratitude for so much – Philip'. Surprised, for we had no thought then of resuming our intimacy, I asked him what the hidden significance of his words was. He replied: 'Oh Maeve! You have taught me so much about the breadth and depth of human emotions, and more about my own than anyone has ever done'. Still puzzled, but deeply moved, I resumed my life of separation without knowing whether he and Monica were any closer. I used to think with some bitterness that Monica, for her part, never gave Philip a similar breathing space, or if she did, I was never told of it.

Two quarrels on the subject – we hardly ever quarrelled about anything else – are well documented simply because in the first instance I departed on holiday immediately after the disagreement (1967) and on the second occasion Philip was on sabbatical leave in Oxford (1971). I have reproduced these exchanges in full. Even though these misunderstandings caused immense distress at the time, such was the emotional stranglehold we had on each other that the immediate reason for the tiff was quickly overlooked. But the underlying cause never went away, and finally defeated me. Strange to say, I cannot now recall what confidence I was supposed to have betrayed which caused Monica so much distress in 1971 (6–10.i.71). Clearly Philip conveyed the offending disclosure to me over the 'phone on 9 January but no amount of soul-searching has come up with the answer. Further proof, if it were needed, that whatever it was was so preposterous that I happily banished it from my mind without further thought: a classic example of a storm in a teacup.

I have included a perhaps disproportionate number of Philip's letters written while he was on sabbatical leave in 1970/71. His accounts of his daily routine and progress with the *Oxford Book of Twentieth Century English Verse*, not to speak of the literary figures who wined and dined him, are fresh, interesting and intimate. His last letter to me from Beechwood House is dated 16 January 1971 after which date an eight or nine week postal strike intervened. By the time it was over, Philip's leave was up and he had returned to Hull. In the meantime he made at least two return visits, one at the beginning of February for the funeral of Arthur Wood, the Deputy Librarian who had been in post since 1948, the other later in the month to make copies of his choices for the *Oxford Book* – at this stage pasted on sheets of paper – and to have them ring bound. I was surprised how frequently he returned to Hull; between September and Christmas he came back at least three times. The visits were usually quite short and on Library business, but just before Christmas, feeling deprived of the facilities and comforts of his flat, he returned for a week. This enabled us to go together to the Library Christmas party and the Senior Common Room Christmas dinner as usual, as well as spend some private time together.

Several letters are included to show how important a part work played in our lives. Apart from the two-way concern with floor plans during the building of Stage II, other work-related matters occupied us. For example, Philip's comments on my annual report for 1974/75, documenting Hull's first periodicals' cancellations exercise, are noteworthy as well as amusing – he thought it could be set to music in the manner of Wagner! (7.viii.75).

These exercises were repeated several times in the next decade as government cutbacks in university funding bit deeper, and marred the remainder of both our professional lives. For Philip in particular they accelerated his sense of disillusionment with the University's administration as the Library ceased to enjoy the special status it had enjoyed during the Vice-Chancellorship of Sir Brynmor Jones (1956–72). The latter had always given most generous moral and financial support to the Library but after B.J.'s retirement (he was always known as B.J.), Philip found the new administration less sympathetic. The truth was, however, that the lavish scale of funding of the past two decades was no longer possible and from now on economies had to be made by all departments.

Philip's short observations on the student riots of 1968 are of historic interest (11 & 12.vi.68). They had started in Paris and spread quickly to their counterparts across the Channel. The aim of the rioters was to procure greater student participation in the running of universities. Students at Hull were particularly vociferous in their demands, which, backed by their actions, made prominent news headlines. (As a result, Hull earned the reputation of being able to organise 'a good demo' for subsequent generations of students.) Just as the riots started I went to London on a fact-finding mission to learn how to acquire periodicals, government publications and other semi-official reports from South-East Asia. Most of them were elusive, many were regarded as ephemeral and they were not obtainable through the normal bookselling agencies. The student riots did not seem to affect the libraries I was visiting at the School of Oriental and African Studies, Senate House and the British Museum so Philip's short bulletins kept me in touch with the fraught situation at home.

Another historic event which I recorded the following year was the first lunar landing which I watched on French television while on holiday in Brittany (19.vii.69). My excitement was certainly not matched by Philip who was having an altogether different experience at home. 'So the day men landed on the moon I landed in the Nuffield [Hospital]' (23.vii.69).

What struck me most on a sustained re-reading of both sides of the correspondence, besides the tenderness and our mutual professional concerns, was the fun we had and the jokes we shared. One recurrent joke in particular intrigues and frustrates me because 35 years later I have no idea what gave rise to it. There are several brief allusions to it, focusing on 'six pairs of beady little eyes.' It was a refrain that slipped easily off the tongue and I remember we used to chant it with breathless haste, but even this fact fails to jog my memory as to its origin. Philip was the first to refer to it in a letter (23.vii.64). I replied: 'I'm glad you haven't forgotten the 6 beady little pairs of eyes: the image makes me laugh so, but the reality wouldn't, I assure you' (28.vii.64). Up to this point I assumed the 'eyes' belonged to birds or rabbits or other wild creatures, but a few days later, having spent a nerve-racking day with the children of friends, I declaimed: 'If that was a typical day in the life of an ordinary family, I could wish all the bright beady little pairs of eyes at the bottom of the sea' (Monday a.m. [10.viii.64]). Writing from Scotland later in the month Philip also associated the image with children when he complained that the early morning peace of the hotel in which he was staying was disturbed by 'Little beady eyed door bangers on the move now' (29.viii.64). Was this joke really a very uncharacteristic tease that we might end up with half a dozen children!? It's possible for the mid-1960s were heady years.

Philip's choice of nicknames was both colourful and appropriate, but I should be embarrassed to have to identify Professor Crudemind; fortunately I can't after this lapse of time. On the other hand, I have no such difficulty with the member of my staff whom he called 'The Lump with the Lamp' although I don't really know where the lamp came in. At the same time, he had a collective name for the younger Library staff whose hearty appetites never ceased to amaze him. He regarded them with envy as they demolished left-over party food – often brought in by party-givers for this purpose – or mid-morning snacks in quantities that never seemed to affect their trim figures, and nicknamed them the 'grinders' or the 'guzzlers'.

Not all our letters have survived. I was curiously careless, not to say disgracefully unprofessional, about Philip's and kept them only loosely held together in ribbons or rubber bands on the floor of a boxroom beside my bedroom in the Victorian house we inhabited in Hull. In this room was a small low door through which one could crawl under the eaves and gain access to other attic rooms by similar doors. Letters could easily have strayed or inadvertently been pushed under the boxroom door which gave access to the eaves. When we left the house in 1977, I'm afraid it did not occur to me to check this esoteric place for stray letters, or anything else for that matter. The only objects normally to be found there were dead birds.

When, at a later date, I re-assembled Philip's letters, it struck me as odd that there were so few for 1975–76 (five, compared with twelve written by me), just at the time our relationship had been so ardently re-awakened. Many years later I went back to the old house to enquire if any letters had been found, or might still be lying under the eaves, but was assured that there was no likelihood of this. I hadn't the audacity to ask if I might make a search myself. In any case, by this time there had been a change of ownership.

The history of my own letters is less careless but equally ill-considered. Shortly after Philip's death, Monica 'phoned me to ask what I wanted her to do with half-a-dozen letters I had written to Philip in the last six months of his life. She explained that he had left instructions in his will that letters should either be returned to their senders or destroyed unread. She added that as she had not found any earlier letters of mine, she assumed that Philip himself had destroyed them.

I had never before had to consider the implications or importance of friends' letters in the life of a public figure, and in any case it was inconceivable that mine could be of interest to anyone. To have re-claimed them, I reasoned, would have seemed presumptuous, and in any case, if there were no others, what would be the point of keeping these few? So I sanctioned their destruction. It was not long before I regretted this decision when I recalled that one of my last letters, written from Cannes where I was staying with a French friend immediately after I retired in October 1985, was an introspective and nostalgic account of my 33 years at the Library. In it I pointed out that for more than half that time my enthusiasm for work had been greatly stimulated by our close personal relationship, but once we parted my heart also went out of my job and when therefore the opportunity arose, I opted for early retirement. This letter would have been particularly appropriate to include in this selection, setting out as it did the extent to which both my personal happiness and professional fulfilment had been dependent on Philip. A still later letter listed the current issues in librarianship which I had offered to highlight as a possible foundation for discussion at the interviews for the vacancy of Deputy Librarian. These were due to be held on 4 November but in fact were cancelled because of Philip's rapidly failing health (see Chapter 6).

Six months after Philip's death, when Anthony Thwaite told me that he had discovered a large cache of my letters in Philip's boxroom, I regretted all the more that I had let those few last letters go. Unlike my boxroom, Philip's was shelved. I had admired its orderliness when he showed it to me once. He kept his correspondents' letters in shoe boxes, also tied in yearly bundles; most of mine were fastened with silver string or pink ribbon. His to me lay unprotected amongst gum boots, gas masks and other detritus from the war, as well as later household discards. Perhaps the miracle is that so many survived.

145

One of my favourite letters in this selection is that written by Philip on 29 July 1965. It encompasses so many aspects of his daily life: at work; at home; the juggle with dates to fit in visits to his Mother, Monica, friends, and at the same time leave a space for me; social commitments; social obligations, even his poetic aspirations: 'I should really like to write a *winter* poem about you ... (You'll be thinking I only like you in winter but that's not so: it isn't quite *liking*, it's seeing you poetically.)' In my romantic literature-fed schooldays, it would have been inconceivable that I should one day be the addressee of such a romantic passage, penned by one of England's most distinguished poets of the second half of the twentieth century. It wasn't just a matter of being in the right place at the right time; it was rather a mutual openness to romantic principles and an intuitive pursuit of similar ideals as so elegantly expressed in Philip's 'Moment of Ecstasy' letter.

Letters

Dear Maeve,

Knowing all the work you have done, I am sure that wishing you luck is quite unnecessary. But, as you know, you have my very best wishes, and everybody else's too.

Looking forward to hearing about it – dare I ring up on Wednesday night?

Yours sincerely

Philip Larkin

☙

578, Beverley High Road,
Hull

6th March 1961

My dear Philip,

This is the third attempt I have made to write this letter, so perhaps I shall be lucky this time and be able to finish!

I don't know what to say. When I heard early this evening that you were in hospital, the bottom dropped out of part of my world (I mustn't exaggerate and say the 'whole' of my world!) and I immediately went over our conversation at lunch-time today, word for word. I *was* worried about how you looked and mentioned the fact to one or two people including my Mother before hearing the later news about you. I am so sorry Philip, for so many reasons. I know how you will hate being in hospital because you like your privacy so much. But try not to be too impatient because I'm sure you will have much better treatment where you are than in a private nursing home. I didn't know how near to the truth my words, jestingly spoken, this morning were, that you needed 3 weeks' rest in a dark room to rid you of your eye-strain! Which brings me to another reason, purely selfish, why I am so sorry. The library won't be the same without you; I had been enjoying your little trips down to the workroom so much lately and looked forward to our flippant, flirtatious chats! [...]

Underneath my flippant exterior, I understand how worried you must

147

be. We are all worried for you, but I'm sure this is all the result of severe strain over many months [...] In the meantime – promise not to laugh at me because it's the only way I can help you just now – I will say a few prayers for you – I have great faith in my prayers (they have got me through a few exams, you know!)

I shan't be very happy Philip dear until I have seen you. I hope to come along and see you pretty soon but I expect when I do come you will have a constant stream of visitors. You will be astonished how popular you are!

Be sure and let me know if there is anything I can do for you or get for you. I have nothing to send you now except my sincerest wishes for your speedy recovery, and affection of an unadulterated nature!

I'm very glad to have a copy of *The Less Deceived*, so nicely inscribed too; it is another 'mémoire chérie'! I started to re-read the poems this afternoon (instead of getting on with my essay) and my favourite is still, I think, 'Born Yesterday'.

You must be tired of my rambling. I do hope I shall see you soon – perhaps you may even drop me a line when you are feeling better – I should like that. Don't worry, everything will be all right.

Yours affectionately,

Maeve

☙❦☙

Ward 5 Kingston General Hotel,
Beverley Road,
Hull
7 March 1961

Maeve dear,

Your very kind letter was in my hands by about 12.15 today, so I had it with my lunch.

I don't really know what's wrong with me except that I fainted, & had a headache & have a temperature. I gather that they are keeping me a little longer to look at, though nothing obvious is wrong. As you'll imagine, I felt awful when I was talking to you & I suppose if I'd had any sense I'd have called the meeting off. I hardly remember anything after about then. Certainly none of the Committee.

Betty & John came as you know, & Brett & Charlton & the Coveneys, & today Monica arrived from Leics for a night or even two. Very kind of her & the others.

Probably what I want is more readable books & the others taken away. It's boring here, & the other patients are a trifle *terre à terre* (Betty wd love them), but all the staff are kindness itself. Some of the nurses live at 34 Pearson Park. I loved your letter because it had the warmth & kindness I was still glowing with from Saturday, plus the very kind thought about your prayers. Do add me on to them: it may bring my temperature down. Perhaps I picked up a germ in the Griddle Car/Coach?!

This isn't a good letter, dear Maeve, but it carries my tender gratitude for yours. Do come in when you can – perhaps Thurs. or Fri. I've had my Horlicks – 9 p.m.

Loving good wishes

Philip

෨෨

[from Kingston General Hospital]
Sunday morning
12 March 1961

Maeve dear,

None the less here is a note for you, the first of the very pretty batch to be used. Thank you very much for them. They are a charming excuse for not writing very much – and to be quite honest I don't want to write very much at present. I don't feel in good enough spirits: I should only moan. Not that I have anything much to moan about – I'm still much the same this morning as I was yesterday – but with all this time to spare, & without getting better, I have not been able to keep myself from worrying rather. I dare say I looked a bit blue last night. Still, my visitors cheered me up.

I hope I didn't embarrass you by my demonstration of affection when you went. You were looking so pretty & I was feeling so lonely that I found it hard to resist temptation. I promise not to do it again if you prefer not.

Yours affectionately

Philip

Needler Hall
[Cottingham]
20 March 1961

Maeve dear,

I wanted to thank you again for coming and cheering me up last night. You were so very sweet and loving I couldn't help losing some of the anxiety that has been riding me lately, and felt *much* happier as a result.

You'll wonder what the enclosed cheque is for! Once upon a time I said to Betty I'd like to help pay for the drinks at Mary's dinner. I only remembered it this morning. I don't know how much you drink (you in particular) but this should give you a start. I hope you all have a jolly good evening and commemorate Mary's departure as it should be commemorated.[2]

– Dr Raines came just then: he is going to investigate the London position, I expect I shall end up by going, oh dear. Shan't I be lonely.

I hope when we meet again the atmosphere will be happier & less panicky (on my part!), but it couldn't have been kinder and more understanding on yours. I'll keep you in touch with what happens.

Affectionately

Philip

∞

Fielden House,
Stepney Way,
E.1.
13 April 1961

Maeve dear,

Twenty five to ten, & we are supposed to be going to bed. Sounds funny, doesn't it. But we're roused early enough to make ten seem a pretty late hour. Well, today has been a day without tests: all the evidence is in the can, or bag, awaiting Sir Russell to come & look at it, wch he won't do till Monday I'm told, so I have four whole days to build up anxiety.

Don't take all this too seriously, but it is quite a strain not knowing what the great Brain will pronounce. It may of course simply be that he wants more tests in wch case I shd be v. loth to stay in further: I'd sooner have them as an outpatient. Well, we shall see.

---

[2] Mary Judd, a retiring member of staff.

This writing looks very large & childish. I must try to reduce it. How have you found everything at Hull? All well, I hope – & Betty tells me Wendy didn't have appendicitis after all, wch is good news if they have cured whatever she had got. The Library seems very far away at the moment as I haven't seen it for nearly six weeks! But I'm sure all is going well. And you? I think of you often & wonder what you are doing. I hope nobody is demanding great lists of gaps or wanting odd parts you've impounded for binding. Have you any new clothes?

I'd better close now, for the time being. Stephen Spender is supposed to be visiting me tomorrow, but I doubt if he'll find the hospital. Poets are so vague, you know!

Friday When I 'settled down' it was to find my right ear hurt so much that I couldn't lie on it. So I didn't, but rewoke at about 1.30 to find it hurting more. After 1½ hours I rang for the nurses, who gave me some codeine, & I slept again till 6:40 (very late for me!). Today it still hurts, & I expect the doctor will look at it. Must do something to while away the time until sentence is delivered. Don't think I imagine you will find this interesting! but it's the only thing that's happened since I stopped writing.

A letter from Wendy this morning, saying she isn't in hospital any longer but is still in bed. We should form a club of Library invalids. Qualification: hospital residence. Tie or brooch: a book on crutches. Object: to stay well. Means: Regular drinking parties. I can't at the moment think of who wd qualify: Myself, WM, MC, JF, & who else? Not exactly a bacchanalian rout. Perhaps they will be added to. How do you feel yourself, dear?

They have just tried to make me have a bath, wch I refused on the grounds I have had one already today. At 7.15, when you are still asleep, I am daily lying in a rather grim bath, in an overheated bathroom, the water scented with Morny sandalwood in a vain effort to pretend all is well. It is a luxury I like, a morning bath, & there's nothing to stop me always having one except that it means getting up at 7.15!

Saturday I was hoping for something from you this morning, & felt very grateful you didn't disappoint me. The book mark is charming & I'll certainly use it – if I ever read any more books, for I am now *ill*, damn & blast it, or rather *them*, those hamfisted unhygienic swine in the Ear Dept – I have infection & inflammation in *both* ears, *fearfully* painful, temperature, shots of penicillin in the backside, feeling absolutely rotten, confined to bed, *ill*, which I haven't been before & *wasn't when I came in*, sweating, feeble, no appetite, etc etc etc. So now I am *not* cheerful, but in a great mood of fury & irritation & wishing I'd never set foot in this lazar house. God knows when I shall get out – 1984 perhaps?

God knows When I shall get out – 1984 perhaps? But honestly to be made ill by a hospital is so maddening I can hardly keep my language decent.

But honestly to be *made* ill by a hospital is so maddening I can hardly keep my language decent. My ears ache, my eyes ache, my teeth ache, my face aches. God how I pity me, as Harold Ross used to say.

Pigeons of various sorts coo infuriatingly outside. The weather is fine, demonstrating that the world goes on all right. My poem about *Ambulances* will be on the Third Monday night, about 11 pm. But perhaps you don't stay up that late! Or if you do, it's not to listen to the wireless.

Sunday Both ears singing away like merry Hell. Fury, agony, rage.

With gentle affection

Philip

578 Beverley High Road,
Hull
14th April 1961

Philip dear,

No doubt this is conclusive evidence of my madness that I start a letter to you at this time of night, almost 11.45 pm! So I've propped my pillows up behind me and have switched my blanket on so I shall be able to write under reasonably comfortable conditions. At any rate the reason for post-poning writing until now is a very valid one – I have been working (at library science) this evening, the first opportunity I have had since I returned home [...]

Your last letter, which was altogether cheerful, pleased me very much, and made me laugh too! Especially the bits about the menus and God being fond of me! Concerning the former point, I'm glad they give you some value for your money, and thinking of Newlove, he has twice asked me particularly to give you his good wishes 'if and when I should be in touch with you'. I have had the menu-holders done now very much to his satisfaction, so he thinks the sun shines out of me just now. (Of course he has yet to hear your more critical views on the matter!) It has struck me once or twice, that as you gave me your telephone number, do you have a 'phone in your room, or at least can one speak to patients direct? Not that I seriously contemplated ringing you,[3] but it would be interesting to know if your room really does resemble a suite at Claridge's – the view at any rate doesn't sound as if it does. You certainly seem to be getting the works as regards tests and graphs and grams. It must all be very tiring, and then the suspense of waiting for the results, but at least you must feel that they're not wasting your time.

I think your suggestion that God has, or rather might have, inflicted this on you in order to arrest any interesting developments between you and me, infers that He has taken rather drastic measures to dampen our enthusiasm.[4] And any way, I can't see that a very effective stop has been put to it yet [...] One thought which has struck me several times is that a year ago, I was religiously writing you essays on classification; now I'm covering almost as much paper and spending as much time writing you letters! I can't decide which is the pleasanter task, because I can think of

[3] Not until the 1970s or 1980s did the telephone become the social medium it is today. Long-distance calls in particular were expensive and therefore kept to a minimum, with conversations brisk and brief.

[4] See Chapter 5, pp. 74–5.

many better circumstances for letter-writing than the present ones, but shall I say you are more interesting personally to me now than you were at that time. Perhaps it's as well it's this way round or I shouldn't have got that exam!

What strange premonition prompted you to write 'Ambulances' so shortly before you were to have experience of one? And what do you really know about confessionals, I wonder? That's a weird experience which I'll tell you about sometime – you certainly have to apply your mental powers more in there than one normally can when riding in an ambulance. I also liked 'Talking in bed', cynical, but I suppose unfortunately true (I'm a very romantic soul at heart and it's always a shock to me that other people aren't!) I'm certainly in no position to discuss your poetry, dear; indeed it's something I never *dare* mention to you until very recently. You know how I had this 'thing' about talking to you, how I thought, and indeed still think, you exist on a very different plane from me, literary, artistic, intellectual and every other wise [...]

You were wrong in thinking I should be at my class on Tuesday. The class came up to the University that day and Joyce and I showed them round and took them to the SCR for coffee afterwards. They were all duly impressed and envious of our happy lot. The following evening it was our turn to be shown the intricacies of public librarianship, and Joyce, Mary F. and I spent a very profitable 2½ hrs there (not library time, please note!). I wondered when we were there if I might have induced you to come, under normal circumstances, because it was most interesting and informative. I still can't get over the magic of Telex, although I'd had plenty of lectures on it from Philip whose firm is linked with *continental* telex operators, I think. After the session at the P.L. I went to see Wendy, whose latest news you now know, because I posted her letter to you. She looks jaded and not at all herself, and like you, is worried about what they might find wrong with her. I think it has got to the position (what clumsy English) in the Library now where we look round at one another and think well, whose turn next?

Saturday – early evening. It has been a glorious day today, very warm and sunny, and all the bright young things have brought out their summer dresses. I went to the town straight from the Library, had lunch with my Mother and her cronies and then went round the shops, hoping to be inspired by some spring and/or summer clothes. But I wasn't, and the town was depressing – I hate towns on sunny afternoons: everything acquires a bright, cheap and tawdry air which it doesn't have in the morning light [...]

Saturday – much later – it's a good job I don't have to write to you daily: I should never be any good at that, and what an irksome love task it must become in a very short time.

I enjoyed *Glass of Blessings* but not as much as *Less than Angels*: I thought Catherine such a warm(!) character and I was so sorry she didn't have Tom in the end. His death was rather an unexpected turn, although I realize he had to be got out of the way in order to accommodate Alaric & Digby, but they needn't have been brought into prominence so; and I thought Catherine & Alaric would be a most unsuitable alliance. Yesterday I bought the 2 best-sellers of the year, *Lady C's Lover* and the new translation of the *New Testament*! I think some-one in evidence at the trial compared the two in fact, perhaps whoever referred to the 'puritanical' tradition in which the novel was written. That was Hoggart, wasn't it? He was in the Library, by the way, today.

This letter seems badly written, but perhaps the lateness of the hour excuses me. It is now after midnight, and that reminds me it is 4 weeks today since I saw you. I am sleepy for once (at bedtime) and I shan't have to be too late up in the morning. I usually go to 9 o'clock Mass when I shall remember to ask for your well-being, my dear. I do hope your next letter will have good news – I shall be anxious (and apprehensive) to know what ails you. – *Sunday morning* and it promises to be another lovely day. We've just come back from church and I'm wanting to finish this so that Dermot can post it for me at the G.P.O. when he goes to his orchestral class in half an hour or so. This way, you should get it first post in the morning. Write soon, even if you are depressed – I like to receive your letters – but I hope you won't have cause to be. Hope you'll be back soon, dear. Very best wishes for the results – I'm keeping my fingers crossed.

V. affectionately,

Maeve

P.S. I'm a little surprised you don't care for 'shop window dressing' in churches. I shdn't have thought your approach to religion (it's somewhat surprising you have any approach!) wd. be wholly intellectual.

Fielden House,
Stepney Way
London E1.

18 April 1961

Maeve dear,

I'm afraid this may not be as long a letter as some, as I hope they are fixing a test for me tomorrow wch will require me to rest for the rest of the day, or so they tell me! If so, I shan't get around to adding anything to it till Thursday(!)

Yes, I have a telephone by my bed, & just by ringing Bishopgate 8223 you can get through easily. (If you were thinking of doing so, however, I should recommend avoiding the visiting hours, 11–12, 3–5, 8–9.) There's not much luxury here, though. It's nice to be alone & have one's own wardrobe & washbowl, but *as a room* it's like a very poor hotel. Nothing on the floor but lino. Decorations pretty shoddy. Anyhow, people do ring up quite a lot, from London I mean.

It was lovely to have your letter & good wishes, & to know what you've been doing. I do see how hard it is to have to write me letters *&* write essays for the other cove on what to do if snowed up in a mobile library, as opposed to writing only essays on intention and extension last year, but I do hope it won't last much longer, and the letters are dearly appreciated.

Just as I had sent off my letter on Sunday, Sir R. B. came in. He really said very little, just that there were more X-rays he wanted. The investigation was 'proceeding nicely', I think he said, but what that means I don't know. Yesterday to my surprise I was taken off for another EEG, much longer & under a sort of drug wch left me feeling a bit grim. The 'x-ray' will be I expect this thing tomorrow, which involves sending a bubble of air up my spine & round my brain so that they can photograph it. It will apparently give me a headache, & I don't wonder. I am worrying rather whether this week's tests are because last week's showed something wrong, or whether they are just more tests. Nobody tells you things like that. However, my ears are nearly better, wch is one comfort.

John Betjeman called to see me last evening, wch was kind of him. He didn't stay long as he was just off to Ireland. He was much gentler & quieter than I'd expected.

Later Quite late at night, really – I'm waiting for the fight broadcast. I'm glad I sound cheerful – I'm not always, & not particularly so now.

Bit scared about this show tomorrow, after having had to sign a form about it. And a bit scared in general: nobody tells you whether your successive tests are getting you out of the wood or deeper into it, that's the real worry. I just sit turning it over in my mind & getting more depressed. Still, this thing, this 'air-encephalogram', is a fairly routine procedure, or so they say, so I suppose it will go off all right.

Kingsley & his wife were in today for about an hour. K. looked pretty shagged but I envied them as they walked away into the evening sunshine.

Well, dear, I'd better close for tonight. I might add some more in the morning – I'm not to have any breakfast, so I shall have plenty of time. Dope at 9.30, test at 10.30. All over by 11.30 (I hope). Then they say I shall have a headache for the rest of the day. Sounds grim, doesn't it? I hope it isn't too bad a headache. Well, we shall see. Good night!

Friday Just after being got up, 7 a.m. God! They certainly didn't over-exaggerate the thing I had: it was hell. I was pretty well corpsed for two days with a bad, sometimes very bad, headache. It was really like a sort of operation – terrific atmosphere of tension as they punctured my spine, sister pouncing on my pulse all the time, & ½-hour blood pressure checks afterwards. I'll tell you all about it one day.

Anyway, RB came in soon afterwards & said it & all the other tests had been successful, & I could be discharged 'not later than Monday'. He will I hope come in today & tell me exactly what he thinks about the whole thing, past and future. Maybe it *is* an unerupted wisdom tooth after all. So I am once more greatly relieved.

It was enormously encouraging yesterday morning to get your letter & I felt rather contrite at not keeping you better informed. What I *expect* I shall do is go home for a few days (21 York Road Loughborough Leics), & then return to Hull to take up treatment under Raines. It depends very much on what RB says I should do. But I expect I shall see you again soon, dear, & then you can stop thinking about me, as you have so kindly been doing. It has meant a great deal to me to have your sympathetic letters. I don't connect them with flirtation or my taking advantage of you or you making yourself cheap or any other cliché of human relations: they were just one person showing kindness to and concern for another. And this is a jolly rare thing in my experience. Thank you, dear, thank you with all my heart.

I won't try to fill this sheet as they are bringing breakfast & I want to get it off. There is a dear little girl in one of the rooms I should like to make soup of. But O, to get out! Out! Out!

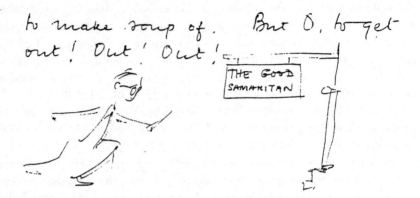

I'll send you a card when I get to wherever I go.

Goodbye, dear, till we meet again wch won't be long I hope.

Hugs & kisses,

Philip

ͽϗϿ

> 32 Pearson Park
> Hull
> 11 July 1963
> or is it 12 by now!

My dear,

It's silly to write to you when you will see me sooner than you will get this, especially as I can write only what I shall say: that I am wretched that tonight ended so unhappily. I don't at all want to leave you on that note. I love making you *happy* – as you make me – and the thought of upsetting you just as I am going away is quite awful.

Do please remember how glad I always am to be with you, something I *couldn't* conceal if I tried.

Love

Philip

12 July (proper) This looks even less worth sending in daylight, but you say you don't get many letters, so I'll send it. I am still sad at spoiling such a lovely evening – it was, really, wasn't it?

578, Beverley High Road,
Hull

15th July, 1 a.m. 1963

My dear Philip,

Even though it is so late I want to start a letter to you whilst I am still so touched by your note of Thurs/Fri. night. Who, but you, would have made such a thoughtful gesture? It did a great deal to relieve the upset, which I've more or less got over now. On reflection, it wasn't really so dreadful, no more than the common-sense considerations of the situation [...] plus the internal complications within you and the external ones which surround me (Catholicism), all of which I had been losing sight of lately. I didn't like being brought back to earth with such a jolt, but even so the memory of Thurs. evening still remains pleasant: I too just like being with you. Thank you for the letter: it meant such a lot.

I've been very busy since you went away with all manner of things. Work at the Library not the least but of course I haven't made much headway there yet. It was nice to be able to concentrate on real work after the distractions of the last fortnight. My parents have gone away, so there is plenty of housework, with no-one to share the washing, ironing, drying etc. But I don't mind. I listened to a very good play whilst ironing this evening, *The servants of the Lord* by a Norwegian; it wasn't unlike Walpole's *The Cathedral* which stands out as the best book I've read in recent years [...]

How about you? You must have plenty of news. The weather has improved a bit since your departure and it has certainly been warmer, quite stuffy in fact, but today we seem to be reverting to the same heavy, short showers. I keep thinking about you and trying to envisage your routine, wondering if it is warm enough to bathe and nice enough to lounge about all day. No doubt you'll tell me on a p. c. at least. I'll add a bit more tomorrow. Goodnight.

(*Wed.*, small hours) It always seems to be so late when I get round to adding a bit more to my letter that there's little wonder I'm not much in the mood for writing. Another busy day and a visit to Mrs. —— this evening whom I'd promised [...] I would visit [...] She's quite loveable really, a bit crabby, but her own worst enemy. I thought I'd go lashed up, so wore my psychological puzzle shift (the pink & grey one, not the deck-chair) and had it on at the Library this afternoon. It was a great success; even A—— couldn't refrain from passing comment, and it's many years since he passed personal remarks to me!

Betty et alia were away for the day on the Boston Spa jaunt; all the power was cut off or blown up in the staff-room today so tea etc. had to be brewed in Alan's department. It's fantastic the lengths we go to to ensure those drinks at break-times; people who quite happily forego their lunch in order to shop or have hair-dos will not forfeit tea & coffee [...]

I had a very warm letter of welcome from Michèle yesterday who will be at home during the whole of my visit. This is an unexpected pleasure as she usually spends all the summer abroad. She is 9 years younger than me, but we have always been great friends (i.e. for 13 years) and she's great fun and very beautiful and elegant in the best well-to-do French tradition. I must finish for tonight dear or I shall never be able to wake up in the morning [...] I like writing to you; it's a (poor) substitute for talking to you, i.e. unburdening myself of all the little things that happen or occur to me, but it is one: not a wholly altruistic motive, you see.

Wednesday. Another v. full day. I am working very hard but not seeing a great deal for my efforts. It has been particularly soul-destroying today as I spent the whole day putting things right (not my mistakes) and when I left at 6.40 I was precisely half an hour or so advanced in productive work where I left off last night. I'm sorry, you don't want to hear all this, and it's very unfair of me to mention it [...] I am looking for someone to accompany me to the Science Fair at the Coll. of Technology this week. I think I might find it beneficial now that I spend quite a bit of time in science depts. amongst science books! If I can't persuade a botanist or a chemist, perhaps Alan might be going – I think I wd. be completely at sea to go on my own – he takes great interest in this sort of thing.

I ought to finish off tonight & put this letter in the post tomorrow. I don't think I shall write again whilst you are at Sark, but if I thought it wd. interest you, I might compile a little diary of events for your return. I don't promise, and if I don't it will be out of consideration for your feelings. I look for a card with every post, but nothing yet, perhaps tomorrow. I do want to hear from you: I keep thinking of all the enjoyable times we always have, even if they're sometimes tinged with sadness. Tomorrow I go to see my old lady again and after her, to see R who has taken to confiding in me! Have a good holiday, I'm thinking about you, but not really missing you. I've so much to keep me occupied!

Love

Maeve

Veere, Island of Volkeren

6th August 1963

My dear Philip,

When you get out my letters to re-read in a few years, you will think to yourself, 'well at least that girl wrote to me from some exotic addresses' and you'll think how adventurous I was compared with you, [...] I'm missing you, dear, which sets me wondering how well or unwell we'd get along on holiday, because I never cease to marvel how relaxed and completely at ease I am with you at home. You have a more soothing effect on me than anyone has ever had, but this isn't news to you [...] because it's not the first time I've said it. I don't know why I'm saying all this, but it does seem a long time since I saw you properly, even since last Tues. and I *am* looking forward to receiving a letter from you at Grenoble: I hope I shan't be disappointed.

I hope your birthday card doesn't arrive too long after your birthday. If I had posted it from some big town today it would undoubtedly have arrived on the day, but I posted it here, which is the equivalent of a tiny village on one of the Channel Islands, although Volkeren is bigger than Sark, 32 miles round the island, and about 6 or 8 across, I would say at a guess. There are a number of small villages, and 3 sizeable towns, Middleburg, Flushing and Domberg. The former two were very badly bombed during the war and most of the historic (14th century) buildings were heavily damaged; they also got another bad battering in the disastrous floods of 1952/3. Everything has been rebuilt or restored in the original style and although it looks well, you can't get away from the fact that it's fake and hasn't weathered yet. Veere is a very quaint little place, reminds me in some ways of Salcombe with all the fishing and sailing. It is not on the open sea, which has been cut off now by the dams and great polderworks which are being built between all the Zeeland islands to form a barrier against the inroads of the sea. But there is plenty of water all round, nonetheless, and of course on the north coasts of the island there is the sea and beautiful sandy beaches.

There is only one hotel at Veere which we couldn't get into but the manager very kindly found us accommodation in a private house which is all right as we have running water in our room. We eat out at the hotel [...]: the food is excellent. The hotel itself is an old fortress and there are two dining rooms in the turret part with the windows looking out over the sound [...] the view across the water for all the world like Salcombe creek [...]

Quite a lot of the last page has been written today, 7th August. Just now we're sitting on a lovely white, uncrowded beach on the lake-side up near the dam: it's much more sheltered this side than on the sea side and all kinds of water sports and pastimes take part [*sic*] here. It is really very picturesque. We had a boat trip from Veere up to the dam and the chappie in charge was very kind and translated his little piece into English just for [us]. He said that in 1953, 1850 people lost their lives in the floods in this string of islands (Zeeland). The dam isn't so very high, but I suppose it's the way it's built which fends the sea off. You can walk along the top of it.

We climbed the tower of the great ugly church at Veere this morning, but I was a bit of a coward and funked it when it came to a narrow slat ladder for the last lap, high up in the belfry. The setting was for all the world like that oft-repeated scene in Hitchcock's *Vertigo* and half way up I thought of this and realised I should really panic about the descent, so I came down [...] The church, by the way, isn't in use (as a church anyway) and hasn't been since Napoleon's time when his armies used it for stabling their horses. Today there were several wagons inside as if the stage were all set for *Wells Fargo* or *Wagon Trail*: perhaps Hollywood have got a studio there after all!

It is quite hot enough and sunny enough for swimming, but I [...] wouldn't find it much fun to do on my own. There are lots of yachts skimming peacefully around: I'd love to go sailing. I wish you could see some of these foreign places with me. I think I ought to have pressed you more about Denmark!

I wonder what sort of birthday you will have: probably not very exciting unless Monica comes down. What are you doing for the rest of your holiday, and have you fixed up your University bookshop tour? I hope you won't be away when I arrive back, but that's quite a long way off yet!

I haven't really explained that we've decided to spend only one night in Belgium now: it's much more restful to be in a place like this than tearing about on autobahns and always wet with perspiration. Still we shall have to push off tomorrow, otherwise it would be rather difficult for me to get to Brussels. I'm not really looking forward to the journey to Grenoble, but it'll be lovely when I get there. It's a long journey and I have to cross Paris and probably have a stand-up fight with a Parisian taxi-driver who wants to charge me twice as much as he ought to. I hate being *done* even if I am extravagant about other things.

I brought *A Kind of Loving* along to read and am impressed by its grim realism. The thought processes are well done if a bit crude [...]

The library seems a long way off, and all its worries, or rather my worries appertaining to it. Even though I work myself to the point of exhaustion before coming away, I always manage to put it at the back of my mind once out of sight! I haven't heard from my Mother since coming away: of course it wasn't worth while her writing before we left The Hague and so I can't hear from her before I reach Grenoble, but I've rarely been away for so long a period before hearing from home. And I miss it, I mean news from home and contact with them. I've led a sheltered life, haven't I?

Did I tell you we spent Sunday in Amsterdam? I can't give you much of an impression of it because it's too vast to take in in just a few hours. We didn't have time to go to the Rijks Museum which contains some very famous works including a lot of Rembrandts. We did visit a little museum, the Amsterdam Historical Museum of which the Jewish section was the most interesting, and naturally most opulent. We walked, by accident down the oldest and most notorious street, i.e. the red light district and actually saw the girls sitting in the windows looking on to the street, with flowing hair and the come-hither-looks, but to me they seemed rather frowsy and blousy. We had a tour of the canals which are very charming and picturesque, and then after a drink and something to eat, it was pretty well time to go home.

Well my dear, I want to close this letter now so that I can post it tomorrow before we leave for Bruges. [...] I do miss you dear and wish so much you were here at times. Can you guess what would give me immense pleasure on my return to England D.V.? But I'm not even daring to hope that you could be in London, I still mean what we agreed before about not wanting it to be awkward for you Library-wise or conscience-wise.

I'll write again when I'm settled at Grenoble when I hope I shall have heard from you. Goodbye dear,

With much love and affection,

Maeve XXX

☙❧

[32 Pearson Park,
Hull]

17 August 63

Maeve dear,

This is really just to see if a letter posted on Sat. *will* reach you before you go, at your new anonymous address – how terrible France sounds, all no post and thunderbolts. I had your letter this morning – many thanks – & am just sitting in the *foyer* (out of the frying pan into the foyer) of the White House after a dull but inoffensive lunch. Oh dear, if you thought my first letter was distant, what will you think of my second – written for the most part in a trough of fedupness & insulated isolation. Never mind, dear. I think of you hourly. I think I am just a naturally distant correspondent. I wish I could write letters full of passion & compliments – I don't I know – never have done.

I thought your train companions sounded cows of the first water – *just the sort that go abroad* – I'm sure I shouldn't have liked them, not if you'd been there, anyway. I bet you didn't sleep – it's hardly worth having a sleeper, is it, except to lie down. I haven't got your letter with me – I brought the previous one by mistake – but of course I'm surprised and pleased, not that it's any of my business, to hear of Dermot's engagement. What a shock for you all, superficially anyway. What does your mother feel about it? I still feel I owe him a proper enlargement.

I wonder if you'll write again, dear, & drop some precious word like I am arriving at Cromwell Rd at 1.10 a. m. please sit up. I don't think you ever shouted very loud & clear at me when your plane got in, did you? I ought to have paid closer attention. Anyway, at the very worst we shall meet at breakfast. I wonder what you feel like about getting home. I ought to be back by Wednesday night – but we could have a lunch somewhere.

I was alarmed to hear of the accident to your 'plane – still, lightning never strikes twice in the same place. How funny, hearing I 'go out with' an Assistant Libn. – sounds so teenagey – I expect you thought I spent more time trying to go in with, didn't you, dear? [5]

Must go and shop. The ratty women are eyeing me! A safe journey, dear, & I look forward to seeing you.

Love

Philip

xxx

---

[5] I had written to Philip on 11 August: 'Your name is known in Grenoble, apart from *The Telegraph*; mine too it seems. One of *our* students has been Assistant d'Anglais in the same school as Michèle during the past year. She teaches English too, so naturally they have discussed contemporary English writers and so even more naturally your name came up, and of course this student was able to give some inside information (mostly literary) about le poète bibliothècaire and he concluded by saying, 'he goes out with one of the assistant librarians'. Whereupon Michèle said 'I must ask Maeve when she comes who it is, what she's like, etc!!!''

578, Beverley High Road,
Hull

26th March 1964

My dear Philip,

I must try and keep this letter reasonably short for the simple reason that if I don't I shan't have it ready to put in the box before going out tomorrow, and I'm doubtful anyway if you'll get it by Saturday, but I just haven't had any time earlier to write.

Here are the promised statistics, not nicely presented I'm afraid, but it had to be a rush job and took quite a lot of time and wit. The totals don't surprise me so I suppose they must be about correct. We did the job fairly precisely and literally counted the approx. no. of vols and shelves taken up by each section. The detailed figures, given class by class represent bound volumes actually on the shelves: we didn't take into account volumes on loan, or in other locations, e.g. R. Room, Ref. or Law Room – presumably they would not be relegated in the new building to a basement stack anyway, and I haven't considered expansion at all. However the total figures come to something like 29,495 so I made it into the round figure to take care of volumes at binding and on loan. I did not keep details of the proportion of quarto shelving but I'm sure that would not exceed 12 stacks: I wonder if that can be right, that's rather a high proportion, perhaps it would be more like 8.

I think I would be in favour of the idea, although I daresay it would mean putting a good many runs of the titles of undergraduate interest into the Reading Room. Then this would bring up the question of duplication of current issues, because I think you would have to have the corresponding unbound parts under the same roof so to speak as the bound volumes housed in the R.R. Still, I'm quite sure that by that time there will be the need for duplication of a good many periodical titles. It would certainly be easier from the administrative point of view to keep all the titles now confined to the Library for 5, 10 or 20 years in the R.R. (in the new, i.e. reorganised R.R.)

There will be snags too, e.g. large runs of periodicals issued by Societies interested in say Shakespeare, Goethe, Schiller etc: are these to be divorced from the 'text book' material? Then there are the prolific societies which delve into authors or texts of a certain period – e.g. E.E.T.S.[6] and Svensk Forfatarre (Swedish Authors Society, which publishes definitive editions

---

[6] Early English Text Society.

of individual authors' works) and many similar things which we classify as periodicals, but I doubt if anyone else does. This line of thought might extend to all society publications of a monograph nature, which receive separate catal. treatment. I daresay a decision to shelve periodicals separately will raise many problems and cause many headaches, but by degrees I suppose they could be overcome. Brenda and I are in favour of much closer classification for periodicals than has hitherto been the practice, but the majority of our journal material is still at the beginning of each subject class.

I don't really venture to guess how the readers would view the division. I suppose we can educate them to whatever we want so long as there are adequate guides & catalogues. A catalogue in the Periodicals Room is going to be essential anyway [...]

I hope you have sufficient information, statistics and comments to keep you going until after Easter anyway. I should be disappointed if these careful workings out were not exactly what you wanted, but I suppose you'll be far too polite and thoughtful to tell me so.

Now let's get on to other topics [...] The shopping expedition I had after leaving you didn't help to cheer me up either.[7] Lynn Turner showed me the most ordinary selection of suits & three pieces and I wondered how I was going to extricate myself without a row – I was determined I wasn't going to be persuaded into having something I didn't really want, and I'd tried half the shop on: however during a lull of unearthing even duller things, I quickly got dressed and made my exit as quickly as possible. Having spent an hour there and not seen anything remotely suitable, I decided that I obviously just didn't suit this year's fashions. However I thought I'd make just one more effort and at Noel's in Paragon St. picked out 3 suits straight away, all of which were 'me' more than any one of the previous 50 I had tried on. The one I chose is rather a darker navy than I wanted, but very chic, good looking and a perfect fit (and sensible for later wear). So I'll have to brighten it up with quite giddy accessories. I also bought a delightfully frivolous dress, white with a large black spot, in terylene lawn (a material like organza) very close fitting and neat, with a high frilly neckline, back & front, long sleeves with very broad cuffs and frills: the Jane Eyre touch, demure-seeming, covering up a sexy cut, always assuming you've got that sort of figure!

Well, after that exhausting and finance-draining escapade I floundered

---

[7] I was buying outfits for the wedding of my French friend, Michèle Roullet, at which I was to be a chief witness.

from the trolley bus terminus to the bus station only to find crowds of people at both points and no buses in sight for hours it seemed. I eventually returned to the Library at 4.10 to find D expecting to be given tea. After his departure, S. J. Morrison from Operational Studies came to see me, then Clive rang up for half an hour (all about back sets of maths. periodicals). Then Betty came to see what I'd bought, having been tipped off by Pat, and so I finally settled to some real work at 5.50. I was fit to drop when I got home just before you rang, feeling ill and depressed with the pains in my head. It was lovely to hear you dear. I kept thinking about you at intervals during the harassing afternoon and wondering where you'd reached and how much you were disliking it. I think you made marvellous time and in spite of your facade, I think you were secretly quite pleased with your exploit.[8] I don't worry about you because I don't trust you or don't think you capable, you realise that don't you my dear? I'm just anxious because you are inexperienced and the hazards are so often unforeseen. Still you can't become experienced without exposing yourself to all sorts of conditions on the open road and I'll worry less each time you complete a journey without incident. Anyway congratulations on your competence on your first long trip.

I took the enclosed cuttings from today's *Yorkshire Post*. They are very timely with the column about *Jill* and I like the photograph. This appeared in their 'People' feature but on the same page as the book reviews – so *The Whitsun Weddings* review was on the right hand side and *Jill* on the other. Nothing particularly original in the review, but I'm sure you'll be pleased that they've singled out 'Faith Healing' for quotation: I know it has always been a favourite of yours. You ought to try the difference yourself it could make loving others, or rather an other!

I'm not really in a good letter-writing mood and when I read this over I'll no doubt feel like scrapping it. But it will have to do, I'm afraid. I don't know whether I'll have the opportunity to write again; I'll try, but the weekend is pretty fully planned [...] so there won't be any spare time for getting into mischief! Forgive the bad style of this particular letter and love me a bit, as I do you, well more than a bit. Je t'embrasse de tout coeur, mon cher,

Maeve

---

[8] Philip's first long drive, to his Mother's in Loughborough. He had only had a car for one month.

21 York Road
Loughborough
Leics.
28 March 1964

Maeve dear,

What a wonderful envelope arrived this morning – a *long* letter, lots of efficient stuff about work, & the cuttings into the bargain. I felt remorseful that I'd sent only a short note when I wrote, but I had wanted to get it off in good time on Thursday. Thank you very much. I had of course hoped I should hear from you, but had expected no more than a page.

This is being an awfully dreary Easter as far as weather goes – solid coffin-grey skies yesterday & today, and cold too. Yesterday I drove over to Sutton B. before lunch & was lucky enough to catch David & E in – they were leaving later in the day. They were surprised to see me, & much impressed by the car: both looked well, & produced sherry, wch I sipped as gingerly as you. They think they are going to live in West Kirby, wherever that is. They asked after you (or E did, probably nosy) & I said that if you knew I was seeing them you'd want to be remembered [...] I said that you expected to have relations in Wallasey soon (didn't say who with ogh ogh ogh), so you may be hearing from them. E is going to do some kind of work, but she didn't say what.

Looking over the figures, for which many, many thanks, I am surprised at the proportion of our stock wch is bound periodicals – 30,000 out of (say) 190,000 or 16% approx. This is a lot! It suggests that out of 1m. books 160,000 vols wd be periodicals. As regards how much space they take, the grand total averages 6 vols a ft, but the Q average is just under 5 vols a ft. (We reckon 7 per ft as a kind of working formula). QR & T make up 31% of the whole, wch suggests we ought to take 5 as an average.

But I wonder how practical the whole idea is. Periodicals are certainly not suitable for closed access – they would need to be shelved ordinarily, and would need a lot of seats nearby. What the architects are thinking of is a mass of closed storage underground. A periodical stack underground wd be possible, but I don't know that it wd help much. I agree it would have its problems, administratively. I wonder how many seats 160,000 vols of periodicals require?

Later Have been studying the plans, but doubt if there's enough room below ground for this kind of accommodation. And how good an idea is it, anyway, considering the shape of the building? Suppose German books were on floor 10, & German periodicals in the basement? Would it be convenient? I doubt it. There'll be enough hoohah about the division between reading room stock (in old building) & stack stock (in new building). The more I think about it the less confident I become. What do you think? It might save the scientists a climb, of course, but I doubt if the artists would like it.

I bought my jumper today – brown, rather uninteresting. I've also bought 2 pairs of cufflinks, both fairly cheap, one pretty vulgar, so I shall keep the laundry well supplied. The vulgar ones have all 12 signs of the zodiac on!

Not surprised to hear that —— is hanging round. Next time he calls for tea I'll make him a brew that will scald and viper through him until his ears fall off like figs, his toes grow big and black as balloons, and steam comes screaming out of his navel – can you guess what I'm quoting? I liked hearing about your clothes, though I can't imagine the dress. Anything less like Jane Eyre wd be hard to devise.

Thank you very much for *Y. Post* cuttings. All these reviews are funny, aren't they, making me out to be so 'nice' & good & all that. Yes, that's the first time 'Faith Healing' has been mentioned, much to my surprise. I think the end of it, part of wch he quotes, one of the best things in the book. Well, in reply to your crack, I do know the difference it makes being idiotically & helplessly enmeshed by someone, to the extent of *learning to drive* –

No, I really didn't like my journey: I think I went too fast for my experience, and once or twice was just *terrified*. Coming back I shall go more slowly. I doubt if it makes much difference really. I feel a long way from being a proper motorist, but there, I dare say I *am*. I haven't had the wretched thing a month yet. Anyway (*Sunday*) thank you, dear, for your kind & sympathetic encouragement – you're right in saying I must practise in order to learn.

Nice unexpected notice of *Jill* in *The Obs.* this morning – now I am waiting for the Critics ...

Later – Well, not too bad, though no mention of your favourite poem, was there. Pity!

[...] I must say, I hope your weather is better than ours here – it is dreadfully cold & grey, and with an occasional drizzle. My sister & co have gone to Portmeirion as always at Easter, but I should think it would be hell. We haven't been out at all, & I doubt if we shall, unless the weather improves – or if we go to Church this evening. I don't know a single person in Loughborough: marvellous holidays I have, don't I.

As you know, I hope to drive back on Wednesday after lunch, getting in before dark. I do hope it'll be possible for us to meet sometime during the evening – perhaps you'd like to come round about 9.30 pm? I'll run you home at 1 a. m. if you want an early night. Anyhow, be that as it may, many thanks for your lovely long letter. I send you lots of kisses for your unique mouth, tender ones & not so tender ones. I hope you have had a restoring holiday, & I look forward to seeing your clothes, and you.

With much love as always,

Philip

⤳

32 Pearson Park
Hull
23 July 1964

Maeve dear,

Writing in bed ought to be easiest ... It's just midnight & I am scribbling a note to you because if I don't heaven knows when I shall. Of course if the G.P.O. persists in its strike you won't get it, but still! I've had a pretty tiresome time since you went: yesterday was all the architect, morning & afternoon, and in the evening the Phillips dinner, that went on (not the dinner) till about 12.45! *very* tiring, lots of brandy & coffee and you wouldn't have enjoyed the conversation wch was full of classical music & stuff, & dominated by Mrs —— who didn't amuse me. I could hardly think of anything to say. They all seemed *better class* than I, too. Aawgh.

Today has been a very empty day until the evening, when I had to go to Hessle, collect the Hartleys & their recording apparatus, & take them up to the Library. When we got there we found a fuse had gone, and by the time I had got the electrician over the evening was wasted. Very tiresome. I took them to the Haworth for some drinks & drove them back, & myself back – a totally wasted evening.

The Library has seemed empty without you, dear, today (I hadn't time to notice yesterday), and I have often wondered how you were liking it at Moulton. Helen will have got much bigger, I expect. I haven't taken any trips up to your room! Today I appointed another junior, a June Scott (I think) from Estcourt – a sensible girl of 17, half Austrian. Then there are all the candidates for the clerical job, coming next week.

In Alan's room today I found Jill's pictures of the City Hall on degree day, & could just pick you out on the back row looking very dark & pretty.

I go up to Hexham tomorrow as you know – I hope I survive the journey. I always feel scared of long car journeys! I shall hope to be agreeable to Monica & not make the visit a disappointment, but one can never be sure how one will behave.

I really feel awfully sleepy – my eyes are heavy with being late last night, and I had better end this trivial note. I looked at your house tonight – the car was outside. Do you know, I seem to have lost my raincoat? I can't think where it is: I wonder if it has been stolen. Most annoying. Please don't treat this letter as anything but 'better than nothing' – I'll write more consideredly as soon as I can. In the meantime, much love – I remember the lovely times we have had recently, & the six pairs of beady eyes. Take care of yourself & *who you get talking to.*

Love,

Philip

⊙⋈⊙

Broughton,
Glams.

5th August 1964

Philip dear,

I'm just starting what I intend shall only be a short note to include with your birthday cards. I'm sending you two because you may well feel that THE one is not fit for display. Were your Mother to see it, she would fully understand your emotional instability! But after recent conversations & leg-pullings, it seemed to stand out in the shop with a little tag 'specially designed for Maeve to send to PAL'.

Well, I thought I should have all the time in the world on this holiday for letter-writing, annual reports about departmental libraries, Russian homework (I've got my slim paperback of short stories with me) etc. but the time is just flying and I average 2 letters per day; only since I've been here, mind you. Only the thought of having you at the very end of my holiday prevents me from wishing I could stay down here, with the present weather conditions, for several more weeks. Frances' mother and I spent the day on the beach today and I thought how much you would love it. When we arrived there the tide was still well out, and sand and rocks & coves stretched for miles with hardly a soul in sight. That's not quite true, there might have been up to 50 people, but dispersed over so huge an area that it was possible to be quite private. Until the incoming tide washed us off the ledge of rock we were sitting on, I was eating & writing & drinking with my feet dangling in a lovely warm pool. I should have liked to bathe, but didn't have a swimsuit with me and as I said before, it doesn't altogether appeal when I'm on my own. So I should have liked you here for that too. I'd like to fool about with you in the sea or in a swimming pool.

The tide comes in rather quickly and then cuts off the more private coves and ledges of rock, so then you are forced to be more communal. Even so, it's pretty good to find a beach in the British Isles which is difficult of access and has no tea stalls, ice-cream booths or any of the mod. cons. of 20th century seaside resorts. As a result of today's roasting, I doubt if you'll be able to recognise me, I'm such a glorious technicolour hue. I suppose I shall be a mass of peeling blisters by then, shooting up like a jack-in-a-box each time you breathe on me. I always manage to have some built-in protection device, don't I?

[...] I'm looking tremendously forward to seeing you. I hope you are to seeing me, and if so, I wonder how long we'll go on looking *so* forward to our reunions [...]

I hope I shall be able to find you something original for your birthday which you will like. I imagine I shall be giving you it when we meet. So in the meantime, I just underline the wishes expressed in the cards, and a particularly happy year ahead. Goodnight dear.

Much love and a special birthday kiss,

Maeve

x

[...]

Hull

17th June 1965

My dear Philip

I've just realised it's quite a tall order to arrange that you get a letter for your arrival home on Sunday, since it means posting tomorrow lunch-time at the latest. Not that it isn't the mightiest nerve to want there to be a letter waiting from me directly you leave the arms of another! And then you have the audacity to frown on my flirtations [...]

I had this morning off: bed until 8.30 then I had to prepare for Mass (feast of Corpus Christi) after which I dashed round the town for an hour, still looking for sandals which I still can't find to my liking. After which I had beer and buns in the bar with Haydn & Derrick, followed by the S.C.R. meeting which went on for more than an hour. Donald was elected Chairman, someone called Coupland Secretary, Treasurer & Hon. Treasurer to remain the same. And do you know I'm on that damned committee again? I had made it clear at the last committee meeting that I didn't want to stand again, but Prof. Crudemind got up and spouted at length about Miss Brennan's value on the Committee and how nice it was to have her on it, therefore propose she is re-elected etc. etc. Whereupon I sat up and re-iterated that I didn't want to stand for re-election & Cedric muttered from the Chair, when someone (un-identified) in the opposite corner of the room asked had the proposal been seconded, if not he did so, so what could I do? I think next time we'll have to have an edict from the Librarian forbidding Miss Brennan to go on again – too much time wasted [...]

I am beginning to miss you now: I love it when you come to my room at lunch-time or in the evening and we hold hands so feelingly. I've been wearing and thinking a lot more about my pearl, and about your remarks as to how you could better it as a gift. I don't think you could you know, because I don't believe we could ever quite recapture the mood we were both then in – at the same time wonderful and intense, but painful – and it is the magic of that mood that the pearl recalls, almost every time I wear it. I don't mean to say I don't feel for you as deeply now, but it's a different emotion, not without its magic hours too! But I never forget the throbbing intensity of an awakening love and I'm very grateful to have something to remember that time by, something which also happens to be very much to my taste and simple enough to wear always if I choose. Do you think it will wear out? 'A thing of beauty is a joy forever'.

Friday a. m.

[...] How are you getting on? The scene from Lords was being televised yesterday whilst I was in the bar but they only showed the spectators as a blurred mass – fortunately. The weather here remains very warm, but v. strong winds none the less. Have you seen Kingsley and/or Bob and their spouses? (it should be spice, like mice) [...]

I am at the hairdressers now and have been waiting 15 mins. without attention yet, so I shall be late getting back. I am working pretty hard trying to clear up as much as possible before stocktaking: I seem to have a great deal of correspondence just at the moment and I haven't done a thing yet with last week's orders, I mean the things we discussed at the balance meeting. And when I put them through, Lorna won't have time to type them. Oh the joys of stocktaking and the troubles left in its train!

I must finish dear. This is a very one-sided, silly letter, but at least it lets you know I'm thinking fondly of you. We didn't discuss the Needler film festival next week – do you want to go to anything?

I hope I shall have a word from you tomorrow, perhaps as you're so long, it may be a letter: post-cards are so brief and business-like. I hope you find your Mother in reasonable health and spirits: remember me kindly to her, or give her my love, if you like.

Looking forward to your return on Monday,
With much love

From Maeve
XXX

Loughborough
20 June 1965

Maeve dear,

However silly it is to write you anything to arrive on Tuesday when I, God willing will be back on Monday, I do want to thank you for sending such a nice letter to wait for me here – typical of your sweet nature, as ever, dear! I'm afraid my postcard can't compare with it – there was really no time to write in, as it turned out, & I had to content myself with hoping you would guess that you were often in my thoughts.

I arrived back about five pretty exhausted on a terribly hot afternoon – no taxis of course: I left my big case at the station – and it was comforting to have your letter, & also to relax in the silence & coolness of home. The roses in the garden were just coming out. After tea I took mother out for a short walk and we had a drink at the local hotel. Not that I wanted one! There was cold chicken & ham for supper, again more than I wanted. Mother looked at the medal & says what she always says, that she wishes Father could know (it always touches me): I think I shall leave it here for a while.

It always gives me a thrill to see you wearing the pearl – also that you like it so. I was really *very* pleased that you thought to put it on one side on a certainly [sic] recent Friday – not that you haven't a perfect right to wear it whenever you like, but I was touched you should think of it like that. You have a wonderful sense of occasion that makes so many happy memories, like the illfated St Christopher, that'll never lose their power over me.

Well, by the time you read this I expect it'll seem superfluous, but very special thanks & a big hug.

Much love dear

Philip

⤜⤛

32 Pearson Park
Hull
July 29 1965

Maeve dear,

I do hope my letter caught you at Bristol. I thought you might prefer a letter when you were more on your own to one at Mary's. It didn't occur to me that, the G.P.O. being what it is, it might be delayed. Anyway, it *is* there, for what it's worth.

Well, dear, everything jogs on much the same here – building mess, cloudy skies, people going off & coming back. One big jolt is that the new Library appears to come under the government's definition of buildings to be held up for six months! Of course, this will give the architects a chance to finish the drawings. Still, it's a blow.

A much worse blow last night was that I took it into my head to try to get a suspected grease spot out of the jacket of my dogtooth suit with a piece of blotting paper & a hot iron. When I took the iron away I found I had scorched the jacket badly: it's quite unwearable! Isn't that ghastly! I've written to Simpson's to see if they can sell me another jacket.

I was very pleased to have your letter (this *paper*!): it made me wish you were here, and stirred all the semi-dormant imaginings I have about you & your personality, not to mention your person ... I'm so glad you finished work feeling better than last year – I really don't like it when you are overworked & stay late, not only because I want your Company, either [...]

This afternoon I had ACW & PS & BEM in to settle one or two points. Wood produced a perfectly fatuous scheme for the two SLAs wch was hooted down. I told them about my desire for increased discipline & they all looked very blue. It's rather nice having them without any NCO's: I can be much franker about their shortcomings. I shall bring it up again at the next staff meeting. I was thinking that never in my time have we had people leaving except either to go to another library or to get married. Can you think of any? I think it's a great step down. This isn't anything to do with discipline, unless a sharp word earlier might have made them buck up. Of course (no gap there, just tired of driving my fountain pen over this paper), ——— is a soft ass who needs quietly putting down: he couldn't make a kangaroo jump to it.

I'm so amused that you liked the Jennings. I laughed much more than I expected, though I forget wch ones I liked – one about doctors, I know, and telephones, & the B. Potter one, naturally. The things I don't think are funny are his rhymes. Well, I expect we shall have you enlivening our days with humour of the when-is-a-door-not-a-door variety, if you go on like this [...]

Friday It's odd to be in my flat at 4.20 pm & writing to you. The fact is, what with having to go to Toad's tonight & with my cousins lousing tomorrow up, I thought I would take today off. In the end I haven't taken it all off, as my cleaner elected to come today, hence I was driven out. Also the Kipling funeral was this afternoon, 2.30 at the Unitarian Church in Park Street.[9] I went. It was a shock to be handed a service paper with *John Jervis Kipling* on it, & an even bigger shock to see the coffin on a sort of tubular-metal bier. The coffin was odd: it was wrapped tightly in a kind of mummy cloth & sealed with little crucifixes, like pins – stuck in like pins, I mean. I wondered if [it] was a Russian coffin! The church was tall, sinking badly on one side, fairly bare: no altar or anything like that. An organ. I went alone & was joined by Drinkwater. There were

---

[9] Dr J. J. Kipling, a lecturer in the Chemistry Department, died of a heart attack while attending a conference in Moscow in July 1965. Peter Henry was Head of Russian Studies. Larkin's implication of a shady plot was merely a joke.

quite a lot of university people there – the oddest being *Henry*, who *got up & went* about 2/3rds through. I expect he had to go & radio Moscow that no one suspected anything & they can use the method again. Derrick (as he spells it) was there. There was an address saying what a good chap Kipling was – it all seemed meaningless, really, even though, of course, he was a good chap. I listened as well as I could, but nothing I heard conjured up that characterful beaky face & speckled black hair. Mrs Kipling & the children & a horde of relatives were in the seats at the front [...] No B.J. If Chapman was there, I didn't see him. It took only about 45 mins, & we emerged into drizzle. I can't say I had any strong feelings during the service, except how depressing death is & how awful to be at the funeral of someone you loved. Yet when I think back on my father's funeral I know I'd been so raked with emotion for three months I was quite anaesthetised.

Well, this isn't a very bright letter! Earlier today I went to town & bought some shoes. They look expensive & *are* expensive: actually I got two pairs, brown ones, one a Barker, the other a Trench. Only trouble is, they don't seem perfectly comfortable. However, they aren't York-type, so have no fear.

Problems of weekends continue to plague me. My mother returns to L'boro' about midday on Aug 9th & I ought to do likewise. This means I couldn't start from Hexham, unless I broke the journey on Sunday night here. On the other hand, I'd have to say if I were going anywhere else for that weekend, & I don't suppose it wd go down too well. Also I should have to go up to Hexham on 21 August or some time like that, wch I honestly don't want to do, it's too near the holiday. Almost I feel inclined to go there next weekend [...] I am trying to preserve weekends in Hull when you'll be here, but at the same time pay Monica a visit in Hexham. Her first lot of visitors had a car mishap & didn't come after she'd laid in all the food, wasn't it a nuisance! And the husband of her second lot has got the shakes & can't come – so that's two lots not coming. It wd have been nice to come down to Cheltenham on Thursday, but I should have had to go on to the Egertons for the weekend, and go to Hexham on 21 August. Dear, this is all very tedious for you: last year you were writing so excitedly from where you are now, asking what I wanted to do after dinner at Woodstock ('not in too much detail'). Do you remember the very stiff few minutes in the lounge – well, you wouldn't, but I had about half an hour of the old bag breathing down my neck when I was waiting for you. What a romantic encounter! I shall never forget the Edith Piaf record we heard during breakfast the following day: at least, I couldn't sing it, but I can always recognise it. Am I doing right, not coming to Cheltenham in the hope that it will preserve a weekend later on? I feel I am. (Anyway, what are you doing in Cheltenham? Who lives in Cheltenham?) Dear Maeve, I should really like to write a *winter* poem about you – not a Christmas one, exactly, but certainly the time between autumn & winter. When fires start, and winter programmes of things, & dances – I do cherish the hope of one day getting over some of this, even with a bit of 'The Dance' in it. And dramatic societies (Moira, perhaps) beginning to rehearse. I know you like this time of year – I don't associate you with tennis rackets & bathing suits – perhaps because we first got going in winter, perhaps because I associate you so strongly with dinners & things by artificial light, & your winter clothes (that little fur collar) are so nice, and, well, you are a cosy winter fireside sort of person. (Then, again, you're a summery hayfield kind of person too! You'll be thinking I only like you in winter, but that's not so: it isn't quite *liking*, it's seeing you poetically).

Sunday – at that point I noticed the time, & had to rush for Toad's,[10] so now it is Sunday, after an exhausting time between. Do you know, I didn't get back till close on 3 a. m.! Toad kept me talking after his guests had gone, & finally started bringing out records, oh dear. I am so terribly weak about this kind of thing – I shouldn't have minded, but I had these cousins coming on Saturday & there was much to be done. They duly came & stayed all day: we lunched at The White House & looked round the town: 'tea' at the flat, pretty crude it was too: I shall have some cake for the grinders at the Library. The visit was no worse than I expected, but no better either: as you know, I find people not so much boring as tiring, particularly when I am doing the entertaining. Anyway, they're gone now, & I have a lovely lonely day ahead.

There was some discussion in the *TLS* on Friday (or is it Thursday) of 'Talking in Bed' – they had a poetry article about the sixties. I expect this will lead to reproaches. You ought to write one called 'Writing in Bed'! The life & letters of Maeve Brennan. It's such a pleasure to have your gossipy communications anyway, and the fact that some of them are written in bed give an added fascination, as if in some metaphysical way I was joining you in that retreat – not that you'd write much if I did. I do remember the day you mention, but what an odd day to be so fond of! As I recall, all we did was walk along main well-frequented roads, with one ill judged excursion up a lane that didn't lead anywhere, where

---

[10] Philip's nickname for John Norton Smith, a lecturer in the English Department, whose elegant home in the East Riding Philip called Toad Hall.

I took the photographs. Still, any day with you is a delight. Do you remember the Wuthering Heights, beyond-Driffield day? I almost think the Sancton day was the nicest pre-car outing.

Well, I am all anyhow today – it's about ten past two, and I haven't thought about lunch yet. Just at present I have lost 3 lbs!! Pray they don't find me again, though I expect it'll be awfully hard to diet at home. It tends to be looked on as *foolishness*.

Well, dear, Hull is empty without you, but everywhere reminds me of you. The Beatles film is on next week. Shall I save it for you? It sounds a bit crazy, but I expect we can put up with it. A long, long kiss, dear, with my tongue against yours for what always seems the first time.

With love as ever

Philip

෨෴෩

578, Beverley High Road,
Hull.

10th September 1965

My dear Philip,

I will start a letter to you this evening, but intend to add to it when I can during the next few days. You know I think I oughtn't to write frequently under the present circumstances, so I'll try to make up for it by writing at some length.

There has been more excitement in the form of my cabinet which arrived on Tuesday morning. Fortunately my parents, who are still on holiday this week, had not gone out, otherwise I don't know how we'd have managed (about the delivery, I mean). Well it's really lovely and looks most elegant in the alcove beside the fire-place. It looks like a beautiful piece of 18th century furniture in mint condition, not a bit brash or harshly new. It's most aristocratic and dignified looking, and your anemones are standing on it in one corner and look very pretty against the wall-paper. Of course I've spent a lot of time fiddling with my things and arranging them in the cupboards and drawer. There is accommodation for about 100 records, and all my glasses, including the water glasses and the salad bowl which were your present last Christmas, have easily found a safer and more accessible home. In the bottle compartment, there is one forlorn looking specimen containing about ¼ inch of sweet madeira. I have some table wine, but don't really want to house it there. I shall just have to stock up again on my return from holiday, when I see what the state of my bank balance is. No-one except my parents and the dogs have seen the cabinet, so I'm anxious to get the first viewer's reactions, and in particular I shall want to have your opinion, although I know that you couldn't look upon a piece of furniture as 'a thing of beauty [which] is a joy forever'. But I can.

... This week is seeming quite long, perhaps it's your absence, although I hasten to add I'm not consciously pining for you! I've been having verbal scenes with you-know-who, who had been able to surmise that you must be away since your car wasn't about since Monday ... I'm afraid there are times when he doesn't bring out the best in me: your virtue is that you do and this I suppose is why I find your company so restful and free from strain and inhibition of any kind – which I like to think is my natural state, but it can't be when I think of all the people who seem to rub me up the wrong way! I must be the most irritable of people and this picture of myself is just a fond, Freudian dream framed in my long lost youth!

Well it's now Sunday and I haven't been able to add to your letter for one reason or another since I started it on Thurs. I seem to have been very busy with domestic chores and Friday evening, what was left of it when I was ready to sit down at 9.30 for the first time, I spent writing business letters of one kind & another (my business, not the Library's) and making out cheques! Then last night my aunt & uncle from Southport arrived for a week and as I was the only person at home, I had to do them the honours until my parents returned. I had Sat. morning off & went to town where I bought an anorak at C & A's a ghastly, cheap shop, if you don't know it, but I got just what I wanted at the price I wished to pay – i.e. v. little. I'm sure you can't imagine me wearing one, and you're not really meant to, but these country holidays I go on call for one very much, especially S. Wales [...] One other noteworthy purchase was a too cheerful house-coat in wool & courtelle in red; very cosy and inviting! But brighter than I had thought it in the shop.

I am listening to V. Williams 5th symphony and so thinking of you. I haven't played it for quite a long time. It is very nostalgic & yearning and beautiful. Listening to records I think is the next most relaxing thing after being with you!

Moira is due back from Austria tomorrow – she has had appalling weather and in fact quite alarmed us at one time by writing to say it seemed unlikely she would be able to get back on time as the main road leading to the village where she was staying had been washed away by floods! And it would take at least a week to put down a temporary surface, weather permitting, but we had more cheerful news yesterday – just that she was no longer marooned [...]

My Mother goes to see Mr. Madden again tomorrow. I hope his findings will be satisfactory although I'm sure he won't say the operation won't be necessary. Mother is in quite good spirits but is not very comfortable and finds walking tiring and a drag. So we are anxious to know what the score will be after tomorrow.

Monday. Moira has returned from her travels & was really glad to see home again. She literally thought she never would at one point. She said parts of her holiday were really terrifying and she had first hand acquaintance with floods, landslides & avalanches. But in between all this there were apparently enjoyable moments. The climate in the Library is now up to its mid-winter, tropical temperature. Everyone is whacked with fatigue after the sudden contrast with the icy blasts which have been keeping us on our toes for the past few weeks [...]

Thanks for your card this a.m. No, I have not got any further with the periodicals memo, and there seems to be one hell of a lot of work to do before going away again. I have been spending a great deal of time with juniors lately, and on in-training in general, and they certainly need a lot of supervision – I mean one has to look over everything they've done and keep an ear cocked for questions all the time. I've talked to Peter about a replacement or replacements for Amber & he's not at all keen to release June Scott who appears to be everybody's treasure, but only too glad to let Janet go!

My parents have taken my aunt & uncle to the theatre-in-the-round at Scarborough so I haven't seen Mother yet since her visit to Mr. Madden. Apparently he has given her the option of having the job done in a month's time, but I don't know all the considerations involved yet. I suppose in view of this I oughtn't to be taking any further holiday, but I've a feeling this winter is going to be a hard one, so perhaps I'd better have a fling whilst I may [...]

Moira apparently had dreadful food whilst she was away and tells me she had bulls' ears and I thought she said wolves' ears, so she said it could equally well have been; the taste & appearance would be about the same. She also had fun & games with the jeweller who met her unexpectedly in London – when she was meeting someone else! So she has dismissed him – I really hope for good. No good can ever come of it. She grows more & more like Baba![11] [...]

[11] A character in *The Girl with Green Eyes* by Edna O'Brien.

Tell Monica, I don't suppose for one moment you will of course, that I'm on with the 8th out of the 9 novels which make up the complete *Forsyte Saga*. The last trilogy are not about the Forsytes really, but about one of their in-laws' family and so the emphasis shifts into a rather different society. These 3 novels, although every bit as enjoyable from the plot point of view, are far inferior in characterisation. The characters are just not mature, they're all simply very positive or very negative or very good or very bad, not a bit the mixture that people are. None-the-less I'm still enjoying reading them.

[...] I must finish now & lock all my valuables away in my cabinet and prepare the room in its work-a-day garb for tomorrow, when the surgery re-opens. I don't seem to have thrown in many terms of endearment in this letter, but I expect you can understand that I feel a bit 'annulled' towards you; not bitter, you understand, or cynical or cross, well I'm sure there's no need for me to go on. I still love you all the same, with a great wealth of altruistic affection. And love of this kind is worth having dear, so don't turn your nose up at it.

With love and a warm, but unadulterated kiss,

Maeve

x

[...]

❧

Dixcart Hotel
Sark
Via Guernsey, C.I.
16 September 1965

Maeve dear,

Very many thanks for your long letter, wch I thought *most* interesting & full of fascinating detail. I've just come in from the Sark Horse Show, an annual event I've never seen before because it's held in June, but this year the horses were coughing or something, & so it was postponed. It was held in a small field – or large one, perhaps – next to the Seignurie (where the Dame lives), and there were events for horses & equipage – carriage & so on – as well as more boisterous bareback items like the Sark Derby, Bobbing For Apples, & Musical Hats. The Dame presented the prizes. I tried to take a few photographs: for once the afternoon was reasonably sunny, though it had rained all morning. It really was a charming occasion: the main horse-owners are islanders – the Perrecs, the chap who keeps the Mermaid Inn – so most prizes went to a very few hands, but of course the one for Skilful Driving went to one of the old drivers who take the visitors round daily. Although many visitors were there, there was a strong sense of a simple small community, most refreshing. I hope the photographs I took come out, then you can see them – I don't suppose they're any good. Some may be.

The weather has been better Wednesday & today, but the season has ended, & the chef has gone. This makes the food take a nose dive & at times I could imagine I was subject to the ministrations of cher Maître Newlove again. Agreed the daily cost goes down 6/- but I'd sooner pay 6/- & be able to enjoy my food. Another bad thing is that a young layabout on the island has penetrated my anonymity and, being 'himself a poet', not to mention a drunken mannerless insolent swine, makes it nearly impossible for me to go into the bar at night. [...]

I'm glad your cabinet has come, & long to see it. Wine ought really to lie down if you are going to keep it long: this keeps the cork moist, wch otherwise wd shrink & let in air & the wine would go off. You of all people ought to have a 'mouse' cupboard, but I know you haven't. I don't mean a cupboard to keep mice in! Cupboard love.

I am hardly surprised to learn that ——, the Creeper of Cottingham has been climbing into your room – he is always on the job, isn't he! 'Lust As a Way of Life' – 6.30 Dr ——, B.Sc., PhD. Next week 'Lascivious Longings and How to Have Them'. Come Early. Silver Collection ... I'm glad he irritates you, though I shd prefer you to have no positive emotion towards him at all, unless it was to clobber [him] [...] with a volume of *Berichte*, or break a few of his fingers* [12] with a rattrap cunningly concealed under your skirt.

I must now wash & change for dinner. There's a Horse Show Dance tonight to wch, needless to say, I'm not going, but old layabout will, I hope, so the bar will be free for once. Goodnight, dear.

Friday Another wet day – rain or at least cloud until nearly 5. Do you know, we haven't as much as been to the beach yet, let alone bathe, & I don't suppose we shall. A pity, because I enjoy bathing. I beguiled the time by reading *The Collector*, a novel about a chap who keeps a girl in a cellar, & found it a good idea wasted by mediocre handling [...]

I did laugh about Moira & the bulls' – or wolves' – ears. Her holiday sounds all I imagine a foreign holiday to be, apart from fleas & dysentery

[12] Philip's own footnote: '*note my charity – not all'.

of course. There are no fleas here, touch wood, but of course there's no proper main drainage, and in consequence 'Sark tummy' is by no means unknown. I shd have thought that if the jeweller met her & a. n. other in London he wd dismiss *her* rather than *vice versa*. The food here isn't bad – the chef doesn't appear to have gone after all – but varies a good deal. Monica caught the sub chef in the bar last night & gave him a ferocious *viva voce* in the culinary arts. The breakfasts as often happens with continental staffs (the chefs are German) are not at all good – raw bacon, raw sausage, etc. Monica asked the chef what he had for breakfast & he said cake! Cake from choice! so you can see his heart isn't in it.

My postcard seems to have taken ages to reach you – I did write it as soon as I arrived, as far as I remember. No doubt you'll have my letter now: things aren't quite so bad as they were – it's not so *cold* – but I'm afraid there'll be no settled fine days here, now. No doubt you'll need your anorak. You have a host of clothes I never see – trousers, gaudy housecoats that I expect make you look quite a different mouse.

I was going to say that perhaps I ought to post this tomorrow – or even tonight – if you're to get it before you go away. There's no post on Sunday, so perhaps I'll bring it to an end, if you'll not think me too mean in not completely filling this sheet. I *did* think your letter amusing & interesting, & quite understand about the annulled feeling (doubt if this is quite the word, but still) – we can be affectionate friends as well as the somewhat reserved lovers that we are: I never tire of you & look forward to seeing you again. Send a line to PPk if you like. I'm not putting on weight as far as I know, but I'm not dieting *at all*. Have fun with your scales!

Much dear love
(and a kiss!)
Philip

Stratford
Easter Monday 1966
[11th April]

Maeve dear,

Not a specially cheerful day – cold, leaden sky, feel bored & fed up. There is really nothing to do: on Sunday the sun shone & we went to Charlcote, but there were so many people with the same idea we didn't feel inclined to go in & simply walked about the grounds. Coming back, a mere four-mile journey, we got involved in a hold-up for an hour – absolutely maddening – so that put me off going out today, even if the weather had been fine. How dreary my holidays are! I can't believe anyone is as incapable of enjoyment as I am. I just can't get on with mother either, really.

However, this isn't meant to be a groaning letter. I expect you are a good deal more comfortable at home and have been out on some visit or other. What does your father think of Bank Holidays? I expect he hates them, as I do: did you go to The Munster [13] on Saturday?

– Just at that point I rang you up, as I am in my room with a telephone, but no luck, I'm afraid. Pity, as I should love to have spoken to you for a few minutes. I ought to have thought of it sooner & forewarned you. Anyway, I had a few words with your mother. Now I think I shall go to the bar for a pre dinner drink & a further read at Boswell.

After dinner We are now sitting by a big coal fire on a sofa – not bad, really: it is rather cold outside. Dinner was turkey, pretty undistinguished as all the food is here.

I'd like to feel I was *resting*, but the bedroom is so hot I don't sleep very well. Did I say that I have the radiator switched off & *all* the windows *permanently* open, & am still too warm? I wake very early & can't get off again. The bed isn't very comfortable, either: it feels as if it's tipping over slightly.

The Charltons [14] came over last night, and we had a pleasant enough evening. Donald seems to be going up in the world – trips to America & all that. Thelma was an uncompromising brunette! & I thought looked a bit thinner. We just had drinks & dinner & coffee & more drinks (for

---

[13] An imaginary pub in York, invented by Larkin, playing on my father's Irish origin and York Minster.
[14] Former colleagues at Hull. Donald Charlton went from Hull to the University of Warwick, where he was Professor of French.

me at any rate) – they left about 11 pm, Donald sitting in the back for fear of being killed, as apparently is his wont! They seem quite immersed in Warwick.

I am so sorry about your not hearing from me. I really did make a point of writing, as I always do & wd, & *you* always do: it was just that I was a bit slow finishing it off and posting it on Wednesday. Still, it ought to have reached you – & I hope has now. It's being a long separation, isn't it? I felt so especially when I couldn't get you tonight, but of course I ought to warn you! I expect you'd like it here, though every time one goes out one encounters awful *crowds* that send one back into the relative peace of the hotel again. All the same I wish you were here, dear, and we could renew our brief Liverpool exchange – it was a sweet 35 minutes or however long it was. [...]

By the way, I was *very* shocked this morning to hear of the death of Evelyn Waugh. This is almost the first real writer born in this century to have died of natural causes. He was 62. *The Times* said he died after coming back from church on Easter Sunday. I expect this is an ideal way to die for one of your persuasion – and not a bad way for anyone. But what a shock nonetheless. Now he will never finish his autobiography. *The Times* gave him a long obituary, recalling that he had a notice on his gate saying 'No Admittance on Business'. It's very hard for me to imagine a world without Evelyn Waugh – he was one of the few really good living writers, & is a great loss. I went in the church again today, & thought that I shd have liked to pray for him if I'd known what to say & if he hadn't been a RC! Perhaps some strangled supplication escaped me & voyaged to the right destination.

One small comic touch – I found a suspiciously desirable place to leave the car in the yard last night, but omitted to notice it was under a telegraph pole. In the morning my car was buried, like Dr No, under a mound of bird crap. I've left it elsewhere tonight.

Tuesday Another grey day – I have just got the bill (£57) and packed my case. I can't really add much to this letter, but I am thinking of you affectionately and hoping you are in good spirits, even if you are back at work.

My own holiday seems inordinately long – and it's a trifle depressing. Mother brings out the depressing side, & my own worst side really, wch in turn depresses me further. This is being a gloomy year so far!

Hoovers are whining in the passages & I must get ready to do some shopping before we go. I'll write again from Loughb. & wd love to ring up, only of course I don't know when you'll be in. Thursday evening, about 7? Our number is 4958. Later in the evening isn't so convenient as the telephone is in the sitting room.

In the meantime a very loving & lingering kiss (& a few more adjectives beginning with l, I expect) – I look forward to seeing you. *Don't overwork.*

Much love & kisses

Philip

⁓

The University, Hull

30/8/66

My dear Philip,

I certainly am having my one short hour & sweet! Everyone has written in today wanting appointments from now until 13th Febr. 1967 and I've just spent half the morning in your room dictating replies and stalling notes! I've just realised, there was, of course, 3 days' post to deal with – Saturday's Monday's & today's. Let's hope A.C.W. will be in tomorrow, because I haven't thought of my own work yet.

Did I tell you that I wrote last week to the father of a student who had lost 6 books & their replacement cost, which the father in a rash moment had cheerfully offered to pay, was going to be in the region of £45 (there were 2 periodicals at £33.10.0. incl. binding)? I rather thought that the threat of a bill of such magnitude would induce someone to produce the books. A letter arrived this morning saying the books had been recovered & would be restored to us at the earliest opportunity. Obviously the way to deal with students who offend in this way!

The enclosed letter was the only item of interest to you personally – well perhaps even this isn't – but I thought I'd better not open it. If it is a business letter & you wish me to send a reply, send it back again & either Mr. Wood or I will deal with it.

Hope you are continuing to enjoy your holiday. This note is not intended to be very personal, since I'm writing in library time & am anxious to turn to my own work.

All for now,

With love from

Maeve

Hull

14th September 1967

My dear Philip,

I hope I can make my explanations briefly, so that this note is finished when my hair is dry.

You must have thought I was being very odd, capricious and illogical last night, when I had been quite prepared to go out with you even as late as 9.45 or 10 under one set of circumstances, and then not, when the circumstances had outwardly barely altered at all. There *was* a thread of logic running through my ravings, which you couldn't possibly be expected to detect. As soon as you explained what had happened, my immediate reaction, was, well couldn't you have post-poned the call until another evening? You had the perfect opportunity for doing so. But of course you wouldn't because that would have involved explaining what you were proposing to do, and this fundamentally is what saddens me so, rather than angers me. (I hope you got it that way). I thought what's the good of a friendship that can't declare itself openly? It is dishonest, valueless, degrading. And from there I progressed to thinking what a web of deceit this whole triangle is: each one of us deceiving ourselves at least, and 2 of the 3 of us deceiving *more* people than ourselves.

I really fail to understand why you can't be a little more open about me with M. I know full well you are not going to marry either of us. Monica must know it too. Consequently I cannot see the need for such silence on your part. I accept the fact that there is someone else in your life besides me, but increasingly I cannot accept the deception which seems to be the hall-mark of our friendship. I felt this very strongly when I returned from holiday in August and a month later I am setting off still with this impression uppermost. What is the point of it all? I am very depressed and saddened that you cannot see any other way than putting me in this position. Surely Monica cannot deny you all other contact with feminine company. She by no means denies herself male company. You have to take her relationship with Bill on trust. Why can't you get her to accept ours likewise? I think there is ample room for both women in this triangle, given you at its apex, but provided each one has some idea of the other's position in it.

Perhaps you can understand why I feel so utterly dejected. A month ago, on my return, you had no time for me; last night the same thing happened again. In between those 2 dates there was a month's absolute grind, which makes me feel that's the only thing I'm good for. And I mean grind, not intelligent organisation of work.

I do not expect to enjoy my holiday greatly. I shall be surprised if I get there without mishap (rail strikes which may cause me to miss plane connection etc.) But I don't really care. It will no doubt be exactly the same in a fortnight's time – Monica installed at P. Park and only a mountain of work to welcome me back.

A very saddened, disappointed Maeve

P.S. The very last straw! The hairdresser caught my pearl & chain with the cape as she was taking it off and the pearl broke away from its hook. What does this signify? The end of the affair, I can only suppose.

M

P.P.S. I do not accuse you of dishonesty with me, I think you are absolutely open *with* me, but not *about* me. I forgive you for the thought-less incident of last night, but that was only the straw which broke the camel's back.

If you really want to get in touch with me, doubtless your ingenuity will suggest a way of finding my address.

M

　　　　　　　　　　　　　　　　　　ᎶᕽᎨ

> 32 Pearson Park
> Hull
> 16 September 1967

My dear Maeve,

I was glad to have your letter, even though it didn't do much more than emphasise what you'd said the night before. You had sounded a *bit* angry, and you certainly were prepared to tell me off: I suppose I am 'weak', though whether I benefit from it I don't know. Truly, though, I was deeply ashamed of the way I had behaved: I can only say that like most really awful blunders it was unintentional. Otherwise I shouldn't have explained it all so cheerfully & innocently. I honestly thought you'd be glad of the extra time!

Once you'd made the point, however, I could see the ghastly offens-iveness of what I was saying. I hope I made *that* clear. I didn't think you were at all illogical. I could only think how obtuse I was being, and offensive: I felt awful. Thursday was a grim day.

I know, though, that your main objection is to my not telling Monica that I had planned to go out with you. It's ironic in a way that you should be blaming me for this: Monica was, the Friday after we returned here. I behave openly to you, why don't I behave so to her, etc. Sometimes I wonder if I should: I'm sure Monica imagines that we see much more of each other than in fact is the case. On the other hand, I shrink from doing so because of the pain it wd cause – you'll say, I don't seem to mind causing *you* pain, but this *isn't* a thing I do intentionally, and in any case M. is far from inclined to take a philosophical view of *you*: whatever you say, dear, we're not an innocent friendship no one could take exception to. It may be that she'd prefer me to have said I was going out with you, but to me it would sound more like either a deliberate slight or a deliberate challenge. (The telephone call, when it did take place, wasn't at all successful.)

At the same time, I hate to think of anything sounding like a deliberate slight or challenge to you – something you can't, in all self respect, swallow. I think Wednesday night was like that, accidentally, & I'm deeply sorry.

Anyway, *don't* let it spoil the holiday you need so much after all this work (it occurs to me I might have thanked you more for all you did on this AS&M stuff). The only 'ingenious' way I can think of to get this to you is to disguise it as a business letter & hope your people will forward it. I'm sorry about the pearl, but it can be mended.

Yours affectionately

Philip

☙

Dublin

16th Sept. 1967

My dear Philip,

I hardly dare write to you, and yet I long to more than usual. I kept thinking yesterday how hurt and upset you would be on reading my letter, and that pained me. But it wasn't written out of caprice or anger: you must understand that. I also was deeply hurt, but Wednesday's incident only brought a deep sore to the surface. Anyway, I don't want to pursue the subject throughout this letter. I know you try to act with the best intentions, but I can't always agree with you, though I do understand your motives, and that they are altruistic. Nonetheless I wish you would heed my point of view.

Enough on this painful topic my dear. Even now it makes me tearfully sad to think of the cause of our last conversation. On the other hand, when you upset me in this way, it usually has the reverse effect on me to you. I realise that I love you. Sometimes, often in fact, and especially at this time of year and onwards to about next May, we each get so very preoccupied with work, we haven't much time to enjoy one another's company unless we can get well away from the Library, that I often wonder if we're not keeping up appearances for form's sake. That was why it was so important to see you elsewhere than in my room on Wednesday.

Anyway I feel much brighter now and hope very, very much that you have found my address. I shall read your next letter like one of the first you ever sent me! Despite the blanket of depression in which I was enveloped when I came away, I am managing to enjoy myself very much. My aunt and her husband & her friend who lives with them, each in turn, as I met them, gave me such a warm, affectionate welcome that this helped greatly to melt the chill shroud in which I was cloaked. My queer aunt, whose eccentricity would get on my nerves to a frightful extent at home, is so genuinely delighted by my visit that I cannot be harshly critical. Moreover we seem to be getting on much better than I had expected we would. I thought her attitude would be one of constant raillery because I am too much like 'himself' (my Pa) 'too la-de-da' she always used to say! But time must have mellowed her, and although she accompanied me to the Abbey last night dressed like an eccentric pauper, I was very softened by her kindness & unselfishness in the programme she has arranged for me, which isn't really to her taste. She is the last person to appreciate the sort of entertainment the Abbey puts on – [for instance] this one, *The Invincibles* (Frank O'Connor & some. else) [...], the Invincibles being the lot who perpetrated the Phoenix Park murders. I was in the old Abbey only once: a week before it was burned down. They were 2 one-act plays I saw then, which were awful. The new theatre is the same style as Middleton Hall, in concrete, or possibly granite [...]

Today I'm expecting Mary —, who is staying at the Central with me overnight. They couldn't give her a single room, so I am moving into a double with her. No sleep tonight, I fear! The hotel is good. They go to quite a lot of trouble to get you what you want. And there is a quaint, old-fashioned flavour about it, lots of young Boots & Buttons about, wearing black aprons in the morning whilst polishing up the handles of the big front door. I haven't put my shoes out at night yet, but other people do, so presumably they do get cleaned. The first night I was awakened at about 4 am by a loud rapping on a door next to or opposite mine and a voice saying urgently 'it's me, Jim, may I come in?' and a very peremptory female voice answering 'No, you may not, let it be the last time I have to tell you and don't dare to come bothering me again'. I heartily echoed the last bit. Then there was a loud slamming of doors and all settled into silence once more but I didn't settle to sleep. I have a cold coming on by slow degrees, which probably was a contributory cause of my depression earlier in the week. The weather is very beautiful, just like I had in France last year, but on account of my cold I am not feeling the warmth overpowering! My hand is all right now, but still a bit numb in the middle.

Tomorrow, about mid-day I am going to visit cousins about 20 miles north of Dublin. I am staying with them overnight & returning on Mon. afternoon. There are several families round and about up there, so I expect I shall see more than one lot. I think it will be very enjoyable, but I haven't been in touch with any of them for years. They are not first cousins, but the youngest, who is a bit older than me used to be full of fun. She still sounds the same on the 'phone.

Tuesday I have booked on the train to go to Killarney £3.15.0 inclusive of lunch and dinner & morning coffee I think. I do hope this lovely weather holds out for the trip. The journey to Dublin was uneventful: no delay caused by strikes, but tiring because I had nothing from breakfast at 8 until after 3pm. Leeds airport at present is a dreadful dump, but new buildings are in course of construction. Anyway, it was impossible to get a drink of any kind (no buffet on the train either) and only spirits & soft drinks on the plane. I daren't risk the former because I had such a splitting head by this time. Had better think of finishing now. Once Mary arrives there'll be no chance of doing so until I'm on my own again, which won't be before Monday evening. I hope my letter didn't grieve you too much, darling, but I felt I had to explain what I felt. I long to know what you are thinking and doing, so please write to me. Hope you are missing me, but you're probably too busy.

Much love, my dear & a gentle kiss

Maeve

❧

32 Pearson Park
Hull
20 Sept. 1967

Maeve dear,

It was kind of you to write again & let me know you were feeling more cheerful. I shouldn't have liked to spoil your much-needed holiday. I wonder if you got my letter: I can imagine your family cawing over it suspiciously, putting it on the kitchen mantelpiece & going back occasionally to see if it's still there, and finally Scamp getting it.[15] You seem to be pretty sure I can think where your addresses will be: I asked the hopeful Lump with the Lamp if you'd left any addresses, but she said not. I'm afraid I'm too shy to ask anyone else. This will have to be fresh cawing-material.

I'm relieved you are charitable enough to – or rather, not to – pursue my blunder further for the moment. All I can say is that *I'm* often made unhappy by the situation. I'm *not* a philanderer, I'm *not* accustomed to keeping lots of girls on a string, I'm extremely faithful by nature. The trouble is there are lots of less laudable characteristics in me as well, I suppose.

Anyway, to other topics – Frank Harris-Jones has been made Deputy Registrar, much to his own pleasure. [...] I'm personally very glad: I don't think Frank is a great brain, but he seems efficient & pleasant, wch is all to the good. There isn't much news otherwise: I keep on at sort of half-cock, doing the small and medium-size jobs & dodging the big ones. There was a letter for me this morning bearing a House of Commons crest: I thought it was Mr. Wilson asking if I'd accept the Laureateship, but in fact it was Kevin MacNamara renewing his reader's ticket. I'm not in the best of tempers really – very apt to fly off into rages, at least where work is concerned. Probably the absence of your mollifying influence! Though I thought you seemed fairly glum yourself since the time we both came back from our first holiday. I think you do quite often find the return to work depressing, and so do I.

I laughed a lot at your story about the night wanderer Jim and his efforts to get into the room near yours. I hope he didn't transfer his attention to your door after a bit. Spending a night with Mary — would be gruelling – were you going to spend more than one night? I'm sure I've said before that she'd make a very good Scheherazade, who 'perceiving the approach of morning fell discreetly silent.' Only I don't suppose Mary would! Does she like the main library at Queen's any better than the medical library? How is she getting on with all these Irish poets?

[...] It seems strange without you here – you are so closely woven into my life here, and not seeing you about is a shock. Though of course it's more you as someone to touch or talk to that I miss, & as a 'personality'

---

[15] Philip sent this letter and that of 16 September to my home with a 'Please Forward' request.

– a knife & fork flourishing squander mouse. Familiar faces are beginning to reappear – Toad, looking like Greville Wynne before incarceration; new professors are flitting about – Pollard, Ramsden, Phillips – and I think I've even seen —— scuttling along by the wall, scaly tail dragging behind him. Tonight I am going to the pictures with Kenyon (& possible [*sic*] Angela), to see *Bonnie & Clyde*: this will probably be a queer evening – John says he wants to 'eat afterwards': I suppose he means drink afterwards, & this is the only way he can manage it. Berni's for 3 at 10.45 pm! I bet it keeps me awake all night.

I hope you enjoyed your day in Killarney, with morning coffee, lunch and tea, and I hope the tea was a good Irish bacon & egg variety. Beware putting on weight! How did Mary — get on in Greece? Well, I had better seal this, dear, & let it start its long & doubtful journey to you.

Much love & a kiss to remind you of home.

Philip

☙

Doncaster–London
10th June 1968

My dear Philip,

It seems silly to start a letter to you so soon, but I know what this trip will be like and Wed. evening will be here before I've managed to post anything to you. But by starting now I may get something in the post tomorrow evening.

I am sorry you are so worried by the student situation in Hull. It was obviously very much on your mind yesterday. I wish B.J. wd. take a tough line with them now. In the tone, we've conceded so much and if you don't like it you know the way out. And get the police in to shift them. If only they could see how stupid, irresponsible and ludicrous they look with their squalid encumbrances and unkempt appearances. How can anyone take them seriously? Anyway I hope the Administration foils them to the extent that they realise they are not able to paralyse the university and they'll pack up and go home – or be sent home. I hope for B.J.'s and your sake, and other serious-minded people like you that there are no dramatic developments on either side.

I enjoyed driving your car so much last night, which I find very heartening since I'm still somewhat apprehensive of cars. It's incredible that to me it is so much easier to drive than a mini! It gives me a great thrill to be sitting behind a (big) wheel, but of course it was all rather *too* big for me. I thought you were a bit nervous, as well you might be, wondering what I was going to do next. So even if you didn't enjoy it, I did, and am very grateful to you for letting me try. I don't expect anyone to surrender a car to anyone else's charge lightly, let alone such inexperienced charge as mine, and I'm very recognisant of this. Thank you very much for the dinner too. It was a lovely evening altogether, in full summer, with a full moon and so on: only a little marred by your worries about the students. Damn them!

[...] *Tues. evening.* I've had quite a hectic day but quite a profitable one. Everyone was extremely kind at the B.M. and I got exactly the kind of information I was hoping I would get. They let me work on their records, comparing them with mine, all afternoon, on my own which was most beneficial. I really *enjoyed* it. Tomorrow it has been arranged for me to visit the cultural attaché at the Malaysian Embassy (or rather I think it is a High Commission rather than an embassy) and the Singapore attaché too if I've time. Then the B.M. again in the afternoon. Then I was whisked into all the specialist booksellers in Gt. Russell St. all of whom seemed to be personally acquainted with Prof. Jaspan! You never saw such a pile of literature as has been thrust on me, including a tremendous stack from the BM itself. Dr Marrison is really very kind.

[...] Not much in the paper this morning about the sitters-in. I was pleased to read that they are not being joined as they had expected. How are you dear? I wish you had been able to arrange to come on Thursday. It would have been a nice finale. Anyway I look forward to a letter from you soon.

Wed. A beautiful morning which makes me want to sing! Nothing on the news about our stupid lot. Do hope you have cause to be less worried about it all now. [...] I haven't to see the cultural attaché until 11 (in Belgrade Sq.) so I am going to poke around Knightsbridge a bit first. So I'll finish this off now dear. Not a very interesting sort of letter, not in a personal way at any rate. It's a bit fragmentary on account of the way it's been written, but it doesn't mean to say I'm only thinking of you fragmentarily. See you Friday which will no doubt come all too soon.

With much love and a deep X

Maeve

[...]

32 Pearson Park,
Hull
11 June 1968

Maeve dear,

I expect you are concerned with far more exotic things in London than the sordid scene here. There has been one more day of sit in: it is the staff who are moving now, led by the Commies, & seemingly giving the students support. I believe there was a meeting yesterday that sent something to the Press; there was another one at lunch today, & BJ was going to address the LASA [16] tonight. Tempers are not as good as they were, & the gentlemen with degrees from foreign universities are well to the fore. The irritating thing is that it is they who get the publicity: Duffin's petition went to the Press, but only the *Yorkshire Post* mentioned it.

The students are trying to find out where the various admin. depts have gone, & to stage minor sit-ins when they find them. I don't know if it will end on Wednesday – there's a Union meeting & we hope so.

Are you having a nice time? Isn't the BM a dreary place to work in? Watch out for those SOAS turks. We didn't have dinner last night, in fact Brenda had nothing! The rest of us had beer. Much love dear [...]

X

Philip

☙❧

32 Pearson Park
Hull
Thursday
undated [?13 June 1968]

Maeve dear,

How kind of you to send me a proper letter! I thought it was just going to be a card, hence my brief note.

Well, this has been an ugly week you are lucky to have missed. Everybody connected with it is depressed, as you'll find. I'm very afraid the VC has sold out, or if he hasn't we may be in for more trouble. It seems clear that Kidron [17] & his friends have been acting as semi-professional agitators.

I'm glad you enjoyed the driving! You *must* keep your paws on the upper

[16] Lecturing and Administrative Staff Association.
[17] A lecturer in the Sociology Department.

196

half of the wheel, though, so as to have full control. Your friend —— has chaired a couple of difficult meetings over this business, & I reluctantly concede there *may* be some good in him, under all that wetness & lust.

I'm scribbling this before going off to G. Rees – he's invited me tonight as well as tomorrow, according to him; instead of, according to me. I'll drop it in on my way there, so that you'll have it when you get in.

Much love, dear – I look forward to seeing you X

Philip

⤫

Poul-ar-Feunteun,
Guipavas,
Finistère

19th July 1969

My dear,

I seem to be a long time getting around to writing to you, but apart from a short note home and a letter to Margaret Fowler, started on the journey and only finished this morning – a letter very long overdue, I haven't felt like committing my thoughts to paper. This letter will probably take days to write for I've much to tell in only a few days' sojourn here.

So here goes. The journey itself was fraught with excitement or boredom, whichever way you look at it. You may not have been up early enough on Wed. morning to know that there was quite a bit of fog about, which delayed take-off from Leconfield for 20 or 25 mins. (the plane comes down from Newcastle). However that delay turned out to be infinitesimal and didn't affect me as I had all the time in the world to put in at London airport. Apparently weather conditions on the Channel Islands that day were so bad that planes could neither land nor take off until late afternoon. So instead of getting to Jersey at 11.20, I got there at 4 pm [not knowing ...] how I was to make the next stage of the journey, Jersey-St. Brieuc. I was simply told at Heathrow that things were chaotic at Jersey and I shd. get there when I could and see the position on arrival there. 'They'll have to put you up in Jersey if you can't get to France' was all the comfort I could get. However I finally arrived in St. Brieuc 4 hours late, and Molly & her husband had waited (along with numerous others) 4 hours without being told the reason for the delay! I had sent a message by telex from London airport, but it either hadn't arrived or they hadn't passed it on. They thought the worst and that the plane was at the bottom of the sea. However all's well that ends well.

The weather is brilliant; sparkling like champagne; very clear, very bright, very hot but one can find a bit of breeze fortunately. I got rather sunburnt yesterday on the arms and shoulders so I'm trying to keep the top part of me in the shade today & my lower half in the sun in an effort to coax my legs to lose some of their ghastly pallor. I went swimming yesterday. I couldn't claim that the water was beautifully warm, but it was refreshing. I have had to buy a sun hat today.

[...] Molly has an American boy staying here for 3 weeks. A newly qualified graduate in psychology from Boston who wants to do a Ph.D. when he returns. He has come over with a group of 12 who are billeted in families all over Brest and district. One by one we keep meeting them at the house. Last night there was quite a party of jeunes gens for a *fondue bourguignonne* which is the same idea as a cheese fondue, but with cubes of best steak which one plunges into a pot of boiling oil in the centre of the table [...] There were 3 French, 3 English & 2 Americans in the gathering. The 2 French girls (Maurice was the third French person) were most striking in a very unusual way. Very Celtic, like something out of the Arthurian legends, with such attractive names, Gwenola and Gwenaëlle. I think you may have lost your head about them. I can't liken them to anyone we know.

I have wondered many times how you got on at the specialist's. What did he diagnose? What has he in store for you? Nothing alarming I hope. Don't forget to tell me all about it. Has anything startling happened in my absence? Not that I really care. It all seems 1000 miles away – and soon will be. There is a slight change of plan for departure for the Côte d'Azur. I had not realised how difficult it is to get from here to anywhere in France. We think Hull is isolated and on the edge of civilisation. Compared with Brest it is in the heart of England. The only way to go from Brest to Nice or Toulon or anywhere on that coast is via Paris: a distance of 400 miles from here, then another 600–700 from Paris. The only feasible way by public transport is by plane and that would cost £32.10.0. (My fare from Hull to St. Brieuc was £19!) So; the solution is that I shall accompany Molly & Maurice and Maurice's parents (who are all going on holiday together) as far as Paris, staying overnight somewhere on the way. Then I shall fly (on Thursday) from Paris to Nice. That means we are leaving here late afternoon on Wednesday.

[...] It is now 12.30 Mon. am. And everyone here is very excited about the landing on the moon. You would be if you'd digested the *International Herald Tribune* as we all have this weekend. Anyway I have come to bed for 1hr. 20 mins. since we hope to see the pictures of the first men on the moon at 2 am. It really is a fantastic feat of progress to have been able to listen earlier this evening to those men talking to earth from the moon and I could hear and understand what they said here in France! I do hope & pray all goes well for them. If it comes off, it will be like the mysteries of faith (theologically speaking): harder for me to comprehend than the Trinity or Transubstantiation. Anyway I should like to try for an hour's sleep if possible, so will finish for tonight dear. (I find we are becoming less & less affectionate in letters these days).

10.30 am. Mon. Well, we watched the first men step on to the moon, Armstrong at 03.50 and Aldrin at 04.15 approx. We had waited from 2 am and I took to bed again at 5. We had champagne and caviar & pâté de foie gras [...] All a bit mad and uncharacteristic of the Brennans, but not so much so of me. I believe in watching history in the making when possible. [...]

I'm sure I've told you of the wonderful view Molly's house has from the living room windows on a previous occasion but it bears repetition. The house, which stands in an acre of land on a hill-side, and is architect built in very modern, expensive-looking style, overlooks the Rade de Brest. This is a huge inlet, with many little bays and creeks within it, besides the very busy port of Brest (which one can't see from here – one looks beyond it) and little fishing harbours and oyster beds. The view extends far out to the Atlantic. We are well out in the country here of course. It is quite the most lovely view I've ever seen and Brittany is out of this world. You would love it. It is as peaceful and withdrawn as Spurn Head and much, much more picturesque in a thoroughly unassuming way.

By the way we have had quite a discussion about your poetry. A judge and his wife (more what we would call a magistrate or J.P. I think, altho' judge is the literal translation) came for dinner on Saturday and the wife is English. She knew your poetry quite well and had seen that little snippet on the T.V. when they read 'At Grass' last year. She quite raved about that. The world is small: no, that's the wrong thing to say. Your work is widely known. I had to educate the American boy however. He hadn't heard of you [...]

I do wish at times you were here dear to share some of these experiences I have abroad. A lot of it you wouldn't like of course: all the people, and the fact that most of them are French [...] But you'd be all right left at the bottom of the garden to your own devices for long hours and surveying the company from a distance!

This is really all my dear. Write soon. God bless.
Love and a deep, long kiss,

Macvc

32 Pearson Park,
Hull.

23 July 1969

Maeve dear,

Many thanks for your letter wch was brought to the University by Monica (!) at lunchtime today. I was glad to get it and interested to hear of how your travels had been turning out. The heat here has been unprecedented, and really unpleasant at nights – I can't remember when I last had a good night's sleep.

Well, the specialist, Williams, diagnosed polyps, sinuses & what not, & wanted me to go into the Nuffield for 10 days for a real good go of it. I said I couldn't really manage so long just now, so he compromised on taking out the biggest polyp on Monday – I'd be out by lunch, he said. So the day men landed on the moon I landed in the Nuffield, not in v. good spirits but supported by Monica who of course had arrived on Friday about an hour after I saw Williams. I had the operation about 10.15 (general anaesthetic) & spent the rest of the day bleeding & being sick. No question of being out by lunchtime! In fact I stayed in overnight, & was released during Tuesday morning with one nostril still blocked with dried blood (I hope you aren't reading this at breakfast!), which is still my condition – this will have to be removed by expert hands. The whole experience was rather more than I'd been led to expect, and the idea of the 10-day thing simply *terrifies* me – they must want to cut my head off or something.

Monica stayed, of course, & has been very helpful. I am still no better as regards breathing, but hope to be when the blood is done away with.

This isn't much of a reply to your nice long letter, dear! But in fact I'm writing it in my room at work, with Betty coming in every 2 or 3 minutes. You seem to be having a varied sort of time partly nice, partly not – how unhappy about the *crise de foie* (sounds like religious doubts), for instance. The journey you're starting today sounds long & tiring: I hadn't realised places in France were all so far from each other.

One result of my indisposition is that I missed the interviews on Tuesday! Arthur deputised!! So Pat was faced with him on the board! Anyway, they shifted her to cataloguing, & appointed *D. Dunn* in acquisitions. I find all this a bit staggering, but we shall see.

Jean Hartley is coming round tonight to try to persuade me to give evidence against George – ghastly thought. In the meantime, dear, enjoy yourself (not too much) & of course I'll write again.

Many kisses: I hope I'll be in better form next time I write.
X! Philip

×

Maeve dear,

I am much in your debt for post! I had your second letter at home yesterday, your postcard was waiting for me here & today your third letter arrived after lunch. Thank you *very* much for sending me such interesting accounts of things & people you have encountered. I fancy St Tropez would be rather too much for me, but it will sound very grand in the staff room.

I don't know that this will be much of a letter, not that I've lost my biro like you, but if you're to get it before you go – well, perhaps even tomorrow won't be soon enough. Also I'm not in very great spirits: Norwich is *ghastly*, & this hotel isn't all that grand. It's better today than yesterday, but really it's quite unsuitable for this particular holiday, being a sort of one-night expense-account place with nowhere quiet to sit. What we need is a country residential hotel, with gardens to sit in if it's fine, & good quiet lounges if it's wet. I must remember this. To hell with good food, wch isn't so good anyway. Mother finds walking far difficult, & some degree of mobility is essential unless one's going to sit in the hotel all day.

However! Your story about life among the rich bourgeoisie of France was interesting: I envy you all your bathing, as long as you didn't encounter any jellyfish etc. I hope you didn't shave your legs too drastically. Don't worry about your figure: you are heaps nicer than Michelle & other fugitives from Belsen.

I purposely didn't say what make the car was, in order to surprise you, but since Betty knows (I asked her to register it at the University) I'll tell you it's a Vanden Plas Princess, the kind I have always coveted. I feel like a v. gullible sucker who has been persuaded to buy the Queen Mary. I took a v. sentimental last trip in the Gazelle one beautiful evening, taking the first route I had driven alone, the first with you, & also to Cottingham & Beverley to all the spots it knew best. The mist was rising off the ground in that curious way it does in Hull. At the garage finally I made an excuse to go back & see if I had left anything in it, really for a last goodbye, very maudlin! Still, as you say, it has shared many associations, & I don't suppose I shall feel the same about any other car.

Send me your next address! I don't know where you are once you go off walking. Do you go on to Cheltenham or to Southport? I shall be rather restricted once I set off for Eire, but I'll do my best.

I hope you haven't found everything in too much of a mess at 'work'. Pat seemed to be in good spirits most of the time, but of course that doesn't mean anything. I too look forward to seeing you – when will it be? 18th? Well, take care of yourself, don't eat too much in the Pennines!!

Much love dear & many kisses

Philip

☙

578, Beverley High Road,
Hull
13th August 1969

My dear Philip,

Well, if I hurry, there is just about time to get a letter to you before you leave home for Hull. Since I returned home, I have as always been very, very busy. First of all there were many thank you letters to write to France and indeed I still have one more to do. Then followed the 2 days in the N.W. Riding with Ann Carter, meeting the Pennine Wayfarers. And today has been very gruelling. I had to attend an Appeal at the Guildhall concerning a proposal to convert the property adjoining our house into a grain & seeds-merchant's shop! The owner of the property was refused permission by the Hull Town Planing Dept. and so he appealed to the Ministry of Housing and Local Govt. So it was a case of S. Palmer v. the Town Planning Department with the man from the Ministry adjudicating.

Of course Father shd. really have gone but it never really occurred to him to do so although he was invited. However he did write to Whitehall objecting in very logical terms. I hadn't thought of going until late last night and decided it was the only sensible thing to do, since we were likely to be the strongest opponents after the Town Planning authorities. So it was all arranged at the eleventh hour [...] However the Town Planning people (a very personable young solicitor and a young man from the T. Planning Dept.) practically fell on my neck, and actually I was quite brave and made some very relevant observations and asked pertinent questions which caused a good deal of fluttering in the dove-cotes. Then at the end of the hearing I had to put forward an exposition of our views and objections which I did fairly competently! [...] But oh dear, the time it took. The hearing started at 10 (and I was there at 9.30 – I like to be in good time for this sort of appointment) and we adjourned for lunch at 12.45 till 2: but it was only the summing up and my evidence afterwards which took until 3. I had thought about 10 minutes, or if there were several appeals and ours happened to be one of the last to be heard, I thought we might be there an hour at the most! I couldn't find a parking place except at a meter and so I had to get someone to go out at 11.30 and move it [my car]. I eventually got to work about 3.40 and then worked until 8 to try and make up for lost time. With the result that I'm completely shagged out. I suppose the concentration required at this morning's proceedings was quite intense & therefore very tiring. Anyway I think I acted worthily enough of Miss Bianca,[18] but I wasn't wearing my chain of office!

All this is by way of explanation why I haven't written for over a week. And just in case you calculate that even with this programme I must have had *some* free time, don't forget WORK, which I'm so passionately fond of, and which I bring home to keep under my pillow; and a bit of social entertainment, just to keep me going when I might have sat back & brooded! With the result that I'm too tired to write more tonight my dear, other than to say that I *shall* be glad to see you darling because I miss you an awful lot when I'm here and you're not. No-one to tell all these exciting happenings to; no-one else who is willing to listen to the boring details. How nice it will be to see you next Monday, but you'll need so long to get over this holiday & so long to prepare for the next, which starts very soon, doesn't it, that I suppose all we'll manage will be a late & hurried drink about mid-week[...]

Sorry the car is giving trouble. Mine had an oil-leak when I bought it (still has in fact.) I must compare notes because I'm a bit worried although the garage doesn't seem to be. Had to have 2 new tyres this week, £12-17-7, paid my LA sub, bought Estelle's fridge. Thus went the extremely welcome £60 extra I got in my last month's salary! [...]

Am looking forward to seeing you on Monday. I hope you won't have to pay too many visits to the garage next week, and that there'll be some chance to see you.

With much love

from

Maeve

[18] See Chapter 3.

Set 3
Beechwood House,
Iffley Turn,
Oxford
24 September 1970

Maeve dear,

Here are four fellows of All Souls to wish you a happy birthday. They assure me that the college never serves mice and that they wouldn't hurt the little creatures for anything. The one on the right has been at the port.

It does seem strange to think that as I write you will all be getting ready for this plaque business – 6.30 pm sherry & sophisticated canapés, as Newlove said. I hope it goes all right: Brenda will dine with the select ones. I bet she's going round in circles – not that I mean to disparage her, but she'll be very hard pressed. The thought of BJ's fatuous speeches reconciles me to missing it. But I expect it will be quite an impressive occasion really.

Well, I've been here a week now, and have more or less settled into a routine. I go in by bus, & try to get into the stacks by about 10.30, where I stay for 2 hours. Then a pint at the King's Arms, & lunch at All Souls. To the Upper Reading Room at 2 pm till 4 pm, and then tea at AS & return to Iffley by about 5 or so. Then I play records, & change, & get back to AS for dinner at 7.30, having a little drink in my own room first. Dinner & dessert lasts till about 9, & then I read or work in my own room until I drive (having brought the car in) back to Iffley about 10 or 10.30. It sounds a lonely life, & indeed is. I miss your company badly!

However, I ran into Toad on Tuesday, so I had to have dinner with him & Mike & 2 of his students last night: they seem just the same, & not showing signs of marital disharmony, or no more than usual. Today I encountered Barbara Jones (used to be Barbara Everett) in the Upper R Rm, & had tea at her flat with husband, visitor (and two children!). In general I seem to have been away for weeks: I ring up the Library occasionally, but only on business, or mainly on business. I wonder how you are – half the poems I read seem to be about Queen Maeve, as I have been concerned with Austin Clarke, Seumas O Sullivan & sundry Irishry, no doubt all drinking pals of your father. Actually the work side of things is fine, although I haven't started the hard part yet, the actual selection. That will begin soon: as it is (as I suspect) going to be the hard part, I want to grapple with it as soon as I can. Anyway, I fear you will have lots of work of your own without me talking about mine, though when I think of the Library as distinct from the people in it I shudder rather. I did hate it towards the end, finding it worrying and boring as I'm sure you gathered: perhaps I got things out of proportion, but I doubt it.

I shall be going home tomorrow, & then to Hull on Monday, arriving – I don't know – probably at lunch time. It will feel odd! I hope I can see you either Monday or Tuesday evening – I'm not sure if I shall get drawn into the SCONUL course at all, but I don't much want to be. Will you be free one night or other? I do hope so. I expect I shall come into the Library on Monday afternoon – I ought to plan what I am going to say on Tuesday.

Later. Had dinner now. If I can find it, I'll enclose an order form for a new periodical [19] I think we might take – it's local history, apart from being literary. The first number has a poem of mine in – a v. modest one. Jean Hartley is acting as 'business manager'. I saw her before I went off – I think I told you. It does seem monstrous – George never pays her, & she really can't do anything about it. The law is *useless.* George ought to [be] loaded with chains & flung into the deepest dungeon in the length and breadth of Merry England.

I wonder what you'll do on your birthday – at least, having it on Sunday, you'll be able to indulge yourself a bit. Have a good day – I hope the weather is as fine and warm as it has been all this week. I have the vaguest idea of what you wanted for a present – shall have to devote time to getting it tomorrow. Oxford shops don't seem all that good, insofar as I've seen them.

Before long I shall be able to wish you all happiness in person. In the meantime, I hope you have a very happy day – don't 'go in'! An affectionate hug and many kisses –

Philip

ᏭᎯᎤ

Set 3,
Beechwood House,
Iffley Turn,
Oxford
5 October 1970

Maeve dear,

It seems a long time ago since we parted quietly after seeing the architects at Cottingham, and yet it's less than a week – and of course I saw you

[19] *Wave*, ed. Ted Tarling (Hull), nos. 1–8, 1970 74.

on Wednesday morning, but I hardly count that. Well, as you may imagine, Wednesday was mostly devoted to getting back here, where nothing much had happened. I collected the Library record player & paid £6.5s.0d in respect of a new speaker & a new needle, so Hull isn't losing by my borrowing it. Only wish I had some records to play on it!

Of course your nice card of rabbits was waiting here: rum-looking rabbits they are too, more like deer some of them. Still, very pretty: thank you. There are some squirrels here: one usually sees them in the morning, scuttling up the trees. I found a hedgehog on the lawn one night – I didn't exactly stroke it, but I patted it gingerly.

Social life has been hotting up since I got back. On one night – Thursday – I went to *Juno & the Paycock* at the Playhouse, & having a small meal in the King's Arms beforehand saw Iris Murdoch & her husband, & they invited me to lunch on Saturday. Charles M went too, & there was Jacquetta Hawkes & another woman. On Sunday I went to lunch with Warden Sparrow, and didn't get away till nearly five. Ian Fleming's widow and son were there, & Anthony Eden's wife. All this takes up a good deal of time and nervous energy!

Juno was a terrible waste of an evening: I couldn't hear a word. I just about gathered that it took place in Dublin. Really, I must read it one day to find out what it was all about. However, it was quite pleasant sitting in a theatre for a change: better than sitting next to that paranoiac pest Rowse, who has gone to America for a month now thank God. He really is a hazard.

I'm working fairly hard, social life permitting, and have started to paste up my xerox copies – an awful slow job, involving much scissorwork. I wish I was more certain of my choices. Some of them seem very strange to me now – I showed my Auden selection to Charles, but he didn't say anything.

Isn't today the first day of Hull term? My heart goes out to you all in sympathy – really, I've stood it in the past and no doubt I shall stand it in the future, but just at present I don't feel as if I could. By now I expect you'll have had your first staff meeting – at least, you'll have *started* it! Hope it doesn't go on more than a day or two. Of course, term starts here *next* Monday. Certain aspects of life will deteriorate, I expect: harder to park, pubs all full, no seats in the Bodleian, people pestering me. Ruth's[20] boss, a chap called Simmons,[21] is a fellow here & has already

[20] Ruth Cannell, a former colleague at Hull.
[21] Librarian at the Ashmolean Museum.

relayed greetings to me from her [...] I expect I'll have to look in on her one day.

Warden Sparrow is what you might call a collector. He has little paintings by Constable on his desk, and books inscribed 'To Maud Gonne from WB Yeats' (or the other way round) – he's invited me to come & see them some time, so if I'm apprehended at Dover with a large suitcase you'll know what temptation I have fallen to.

Another man has turned up here – a Dane called Laessoe – and Connell from Belfast is due any day now. I like L. on about 3 days' acquaintance. The breakfasts are *fair*: I said I wanted an apple, and they are producing terrible sour things that set my teeth on edge. I also said I wanted grapefruit juice, but this they ignore, persisting with the horrible orange juice that tastes of cardboard. No doubt everything will get worse when term starts: more people in the house, for one thing.

Tuesday a.m. – before breakfast Again a fine looking morning, after being wettish yesterday. I'll finish it off and send it on its way, to carry my loving remembrances. I've just finished *The tree in the garden*, by this Edward Booth chap – all about a girl deserted in Holderness who goes on the streets in Hull – very harrowing. Don't you go to such measures! I shall be back before long. Should we try to fix a weekend for you to come here, & work towards it? Say the middle of November? I can see weekends may get filled up well in advance the way things are going at present. I think I shall go home on 31 Oct, & 21 Nov is Guest night – what about 14 Nov or thereabouts? I mean, 13–16 Nov or whatever you can manage.

Must descend into the murky depths of Bodley now. Do write when you have time – I miss you. Love as ever

P.

X

⚬✗⚬

578, Beverley High Road,
Hull
16th October 1970

My dear Philip,

The choice of materials at Carmichaels' was very poor, but the girl who sent you the estimate was very obliging and has given me samples to send you. The big piece is a whole sample from a book of patterns, since a snippet would not have given you any idea of the material. Would you therefore please return it as soon as possible? It costs 71/- per yard; the plain one 45/-. In the estimate they quoted from the cheapest range (40/-?) which were all like patterned rexine binders' cloths. Ghastly. There was nothing in biscuit colour or pink and all the patterns (apart from the rexine styles) are big. I think the expensive one is very nice, but I'm not sure whether it will go with your curtains. It would certainly fit in with the studio couch and the other chair. The plain one is Balmoral Lincoln. The other is a Sanderson fabric. I do hope one of them will be suitable, as I didn't like anything else I was shown – and I'm sure you wouldn't.

I have put in an order for a copy of *Encounter* for you, but I don't know whether I'll be lucky enough to get it. I ordered one for myself whilst I was about it. I'll send one as soon as I get it, if I do.

I am just beginning to unwind a bit after having had the afternoon off and done nothing this evening. It has been a tough week and I got to screaming pitch yesterday. I have not been very well and have been very, very tired. I suppose it will pass, except that the weekend won't be very relaxing with all the entertaining that's to be crammed into it. At least I managed to get the shopping for it done, which would not have been possible had York not put off yet another meeting re this co-operative scheme for newspapers, and again at the 11th hour. I'm getting rather fed up with them … Glad you are enjoying Oxford: how lucky you are and how grateful you should be to be out of the rat-race for once. Had a nice letter from John Brown today, inviting me to stay should I be visiting you at Oxford! So I'll have to call on them after all I think. Let me know about the chair covering in due course, and I'll go ahead as advised.

Love Maeve

xxx

P.S. This is when I miss you, when I'm fed up & worn out & you're not around to take me out of myself!

M.

Beechwood House
Set 3
Iffley Turn
Oxford
19 October 1970

Maeve dear,

Your letter turned up *second* post today, wch means that I didn't get it till I got in about 10.15 pm. *Many* thanks, dear, for taking so much trouble when you were so hard pressed. It's *most* kind of you, and eloquent of that kindness and efficiency of wch you are such a luscious blend. I quite agree that the big sample is suitable & accept it. I had better write to Carmichael & say that I understand it is 71/- a yard, not 40/- !! In fact I might as well write direct to them, & save you trouble. I think the big sample very nice – wish I'd had it for the bigger chair. Good mouse!

I am getting [on] well with my anthology – it's *terrific* having all one's time free to devote to a single interesting project. Really, I wonder if I shall ever grapple with 'work' again.

As regards your visit, there's an AA 2-star hotel on Iffley Road – would this do? It'll be in the AA book. Probably all 'reps'! Still, you won't be in it much. 'Melville', it's called. It *will* be nice to see you here. Take it easier, dear, & much love

Philip

578, Beverley High Road,
Hull

17th November 1970

My dear dear Philip,

I did enjoy my weekend and hope you did too, and that it wasn't too much like time-wasting! The journey back was uneventful except that I didn't make King's X in anything like the good time you did – had to wait about 20 mins. for a train at Paddington. Then the Pullman was 20 mins. or so late into Hull, but it wasn't a bad journey all told. I have spent today re-adjusting myself to work, more normal eating habits and far less drink! The scales touched 10 stone tonight. Terrible! It's a good job Advent is nigh. I'll have to pretend it's Lent!

Work was a nasty shock; hadn't been in the place half an hour when I had to be reminded about a meeting that was waiting for my presence before it could start. Having got there and endured it for 2 hrs plus, I had to break away at 12 as I had a poetry room duty at 1pm. And so it goes on. Always having to be elsewhere. However, I mustn't go on. It doesn't really interest you. That's one of the pains of being parted: one can no longer share the everyday things to the same extent.

Anyway dear I loved everything about the weekend and will feast on its memories for a long time to come. Thank you very much for your hospitality and for all the sumptuous treats. Thank you for taking me to so many places and for letting me have a glimpse of your life behind those holy cloisters. It's a strange seclusion, rich and yet almost monastic. I wonder if you could stand it indefinitely? It seems to me very thrilling and fascinating for a short period, but I'm sure one would very quickly lose touch with reality. Too much mind and soul (especially where you are); not enough flesh and blood. Not that I want to complain about that!

I can picture your life so much better now so that when you next ring me I'll know just what your surroundings are and I can trace your daily routine. When have you re-arranged the lunch with Elizabeth Jennings? I see she is 45. What does she look like? At one time that would have seemed quite old to me, but of course it's only 4 years older than me. What did you do after seeing me off? I forgot to ask if you were going back to Beechwood or the College? [...]

I haven't had a chance to speak to Brenda about Sunday yet. However I will give you supper at whatever time you want it. I can also provide bread, butter, milk etc. in quantities sufficient for your breakfast on Monday so that you needn't buy anything or waste much. Do you want me to do anything else? Remember to bring some tea with you if you haven't got any at Pearson Park. I don't undertake to buy your favourite brand of china tea.

Well there's not much news since yesterday. I wish I could express myself eloquently about the weekend, but all I can do is to say quite simply that I loved it all because of you and through you. Thank you very much for having me. I look forward to seeing you again my dear. Take care; safe journey.

Very much love,

Maeve.

P.S. Even the rain and the darkness of Saturday had a cosiness about it; a something associated with you.

ᘓᕽᘙ

> Beechwood House,
> Set 3,
> Iffley Turn,
> Oxford
>
> 6 January 1971

Maeve dear,

Well, back again yesterday, a nasty drive in mist entailing much crawling behind lorries that sprayed much mud. It seemed nice to be back at first, but I had rather a bad night – couldn't sleep – & today I felt much less cheerful. It's an unreal kind of place: no work, no disease, no age, no unrequited love (or requited for that matter). I broke my washbowl on arrival by dropping a hairbrush in it. Hope they don't send me the bill!

I didn't mean to interrupt you the other evening (though I'm glad I caught you), nor to suggest that you 'ought to have written'. You sent me such a nice long letter after Christmas that I'm probably in your debt in that respect. I looked for a postcard to send in Haydon Bridge but couldn't see any, not that it's much to look at. They've finished the motor bridge, & the old one's just being used as a footbridge. There was snow on all the surrounding hills all the time I was there, and in general the temperature was icy.

Plenty of Brenda-post on my return! I've been poring over good old quinq[ennial] estimates most of today. But one of her letters mentioned disturbing cases of illness – Nita (again?), Barbara G and jaundice, and Arthur and *heart* trouble: this all sounds upsetting. Can you tell me anything more about it? I wonder if I ought to write to Arthur: probably not yet. [...]

This reminds me of another thing that I mention with some embarrassment: Monica maintains still that she is getting things I've said to *you* reported maliciously to *her*. I've always said that this was impossible, and since she's not prepared to say who her immediate informant is I tended to dismiss it all, but this time the charge was rather more convincing. I'm inclined to think the link is ——, but is anyone at Hull in close touch with him? I didn't think so. Anyway, I do feel rather embarrassed about it all, from several points of view, and perhaps we can talk about it some time. M thinks it is *your* fault, but I don't believe this: fault, I mean, in passing things on. If they're things I shouldn't have said, the real fault is mine, of course. Perhaps I shouldn't have raised this in a letter, where one can't 'discuss' things, but please don't be cross: I'm not making any accusations, I just thought you should know &, if you did, you might be able to solve the mystery, or help solve it.

It's Mother's 85th birthday on Sunday. I suppose I might go home for an hour or two, but I'm fearfully busy here, and one doesn't know what the travelling conditions will be like. She seems very courageous when I visit her for a short time, but I go on being worried about her: she fell down again recently, through tripping over something. She throws her feet about in an odd way. Kitty & co will go there for tea. I expect I shall ring up.

You'll be slaving away now, I expect, with full term approaching. I hope the good effects of your holiday are longlasting, and that you're getting proper support from those very illness-prone staff members who work for you. I must say I shall dread returning, from the work angle that is.

I've brought both the ginger & the dustbug here, but the latter doesn't fit (I thought it wouldn't) so it'll have to wait till I'm back at Hull again. The ginger won't! Preserved mice. Now I'm back here I can carry on with the rebel countess,[22] wch is interesting me very much. Have you seen the Irish number of *Punch*? The one of the chap confessing that he'd nobbled the favourite in the 3.30 at Leopardstown made me laugh.

Must end now, & think about changing for dinner. A happy 1971, dear, and plenty of kisses for your beautiful face.

Philip

[22] *The Rebel Countess*, by Anne Marreco (London: Weidenfeld and Nicolson, 1967), which I had given Philip for Christmas.

The University,
Hull

8.1.71

My dear Philip,

Of course I am distressed by your latest letter, and angered too, although anger is slowly giving way to less base sentiments. I realise you have put the matter extremely tactfully and that you are anxious that I shouldn't be unduly upset. But I am, and more than anything, I'm completely baffled.

After you mentioned it the last/first? time, I completely put further thought of it out of my head – a proof of innocence, because quite honestly the suspicion was so preposterous I was completely unconcerned about it. But obviously something is going on, so it isn't so preposterous as I at first thought. But I'm at a complete loss for an explanation. I hope you know me well enough to be sure I'm not a gossip. On the contrary I pride myself on being discreet. Furthermore I am very proud and flattered that I have your confidence and wouldn't dream of betraying it [...] I don't think I have ever passed on anything private or confidential to anyone; I wouldn't dream of it. So what is happening? What am I supposed to be leaking to Leicester in a steady trickle? I cannot even be said to be in touch with ——, except through Christmas cards. I haven't seen him for 15 months and neither then nor at any other time have I had any conversation with him that could have any bearing on this matter.

I am appalled that someone is trying to undermine our trust in each other, if indeed it is as deliberate a process as this. Without knowing what kind of things Monica is hearing, it is hard for me to even defend myself on any ground. Presumably they are things you've only told me and no-one else, and they could therefore only have come from me? Are you *sure* they are not things that are fairly general knowledge, but confined to our lives here, and that observers could have passed on? Is M. herself magnifying or misinterpreting things she hears or is even told? —— would not be the only link. There must be plenty of contact between Leicester and Hull English departments generally and you once said Monica had a very malicious colleague who drew her attention to 'Broadcast' under very unfavourable circumstances. [...]

I must confess my first reaction was to write to Monica direct, but this I know would upset you very much, and I don't suppose I would get any satisfaction. I do feel angry with her because I think she wants to undermine your trust in me. Still, she undoubtedly seems to have grounds for some kind of complaint. The whole thing seems as fantastic to me as saying a fly on the wall must be responsible for the whole thing. I know I would have grounds for concern if I were a gossip or malicious, but unless I just don't know myself or I've gone mad and honestly don't know I'm repeating confidential information (of course I know what *is* confidential information) – sorry I've been interrupted & lost the thread of my train of thought, and in any case I feel quite speechless and helpless. It would be fairer if you were to say what this 'rather more convincing charge' is.

I am very upset and feel there is nothing more I can say, or want to say. In great haste.

Maeve

Hull

9.1.71

My dear, dear Philip,

I was very happy to hear your voice this morning and somewhat relieved after we'd talked. It was very kind and loving of you to reach me so quickly and I appreciated that beyond all measure. I hope that for my part I was able to convince you of my innocence in this matter and my complete inability to recall the remark which upset you most. Mind you it is a common enough remark, although one I never use (even in quoting any one else!), so the only possible explanation is that of idle conjecture, misinterpreted or exaggerated (understandably) into the bargain. I have never said such a thing, never heard you say it – so much for my memory – and if I had, would never have repeated it because I know full well it's just not true. Please try to convey to M. that I'm neither malicious, an idle gossip, nor conceited, so could only have said these things under the influence of drugs or hypnosis – not drink; I don't drink that much! If she still remains unconvinced by what I say, I must be schizophrenic and unaware of it, so I may as well give up. Thank you dear for believing me and trying to put things right – I was very touched by your anxiety to do this.

Actually it is very late and I'm dead tired. I have been to the Rumbles for the evening. I ate and drank a good deal (delicious meal of coq au vin), but resisted strong drink at the end of the evening. There was some discussion about 'High Windows' (not directly with me), and a bit quoted I don't remember. Where can I see it? In what did it appear? Did I tell you about my mishap on New Year's Eve after the Boatman's party when I came out to a flat battery on a bitter snowy evening? Yes perhaps I did, but I didn't tell you I bought something very uncharacteristic to wear at it, a trouser suit, in 2 shades of grey jersey. Quite smart & very warm. My Mother's comment is: 'It makes you look fat!' My Father is speechless! Fact is I've put on almost half a stone over Christmas; so it's little wonder. It will be a good job when Lent comes along for me to go on voluntary starvation!

[...] Oh my dear, I do hope I haven't to go through more than 2 months yet without seeing you although I don't want to moan about this. You know what absence does to the heart. I am longing to get into bed. I've had terribly late nights all this Christmas-tide and very, very few free ones for a month now. I bought a very pretty floral bra today which I hope you'll see before too long. How is your work going? When will you get on to the final selection? Please write soon.

My love,

Maeve

Sunday

P.S. I'm so glad you like *The Rebel Countess*. I thought it had all the right elements for you!

P.P.S. I suppose I should like to know what M's further observations are. I would like to know who and what is at the bottom of all this. It is very worrying and I'm very sorry M. most of all has been caused pain and bitterness by it. If things have been reported to her just as you say, it's horrible. If, as you think, things have been said in a more kindly-meant spirit, well, it's pretty interfering of whoever it is. Mind you people used to give me all kinds of well-meant advice about Philip C. which I was quite capable of interpreting (and even taking) far more seriously than was probably intended.

I wonder what news your next letter will contain. I'm still worried though convinced that I'm guiltless – unless as I've said before I'm mad and don't realise it.

It's a beautiful day here and so mild, really springlike. How different from last week. I'm in a very hard-working mood, cleaning, baking, car polishing & cleaning etc. Must go dear. Hope you get this tomorrow. You're never far away from my thoughts.

Fondest love,

Maeve

Beechwood House
Set 3,
Iffley Turn,
Oxford
10 January 1971

Maeve dear,

I'm sorry it's only quite late in the evening that I'm writing this: quite a lot of today was spent in listening to records, & getting my v. flimsy piece in type form. The weather has been extremely mild & pleasant, & I took a stroll out into the University Parks after lunch, staring rather blankly at the leafless willows & the river. I woke up with the feeling that I ought to go home & be present at my mother's birthday tea, but I rang her up and tried to express my congratulations in that way. I hope they had a good day (my sister & co was [sic] due to go to tea). I certainly had a good dinner with pâté maison, duck & cheese soufflé. Rather reminiscent of mouse meals in Hull!

This is a good time in Oxford in that it's vacation and College life is cosy & on a small scale. We dine in the Common Room because there are so few of us. Tonight I sat next to an old boy who'd known T. E. Lawrence, & who kept mixing up the wars. He must have thought I was about 80! Still, he was remarkably spry.

I must say that I'm sorry for raising this mysterious charge of Monica's, when you clearly had nothing to do with it: I did so for two reasons – one, that she'd said it before, and you might as well know what's being thought or said; two, that I was shaken by that one sentence I quoted, & I suppose I thought there was some chance that you might have heard someone repeating it inside the Library. Well, there we are: sooner or later I'll put it back to M. that someone is playing a very odd game. Friend Dick has just been to a conference – we'll see if anything is added to the score. It's all very curious.

I'm pushing on with the rebel countess – fancy marrying a beastly Polish art student! She sounds as if she was anxious for bit of excitement, from no matter what source. I liked that story about trying to get Yeats to fight a duel with someone on behalf of her & her sister, and not succeeding.

It won't be long now before I have to pack up & come back: Sept 15–March 15: I'm 2/3 through. Of course I shan't enjoy the work – in fact I really can't imagine how I shall do it – but I look forward to the Beverley Arms & Beverley Market, and of course to you. Keep some stockings for me! When I get back I shall have to give up eating, if not drinking.

Keep me posted about ACW[23] and other news.

In the meantime, several big affectionate kisses,

Philip

᠂᠂

Duke's Head Hotel,
King's Lynn,
Norfolk
15 July 1971

Maeve dear,

It was a new sort of parting, seeing you speed away down the M1 when I was diverging towards Loughborough, one that made me feel curiously helpless; but *true*, very like life, I thought. Of course I wondered how you were getting on, whether you followed all the turns to Oxford, and whether Ruth's plan really did lead you to her house (I suspected it left out too much to be really accurate). And of course by the time you get this you'll have had the Oxford-Cardiff run to contend with. I do hope it wasn't too nerve-wracking, and that you accomplished it successfully. Very Miss Bianca-like of you to undertake it! Much more difficult than the diplomatic bag.

We, as you see, are here. We set out about 11.30 am, lunched at The George at Stamford, and rested a while, then came on here (by an unintended short cut) to arrive about 4.30 in time for tea. Quite a reasonable journey except for the *extreme* heat! It's a wonder we weren't boiled alive.

The hotel is hot too – I honestly believe they have the heating on. Our rooms are side by side, overlooking carpark and *ballroom*. They have rather miniature bathrooms. Dinner was quite all right: melon & cold salmon. Like most hotels nowadays there is nowhere to sit except the compulsory moron's twilight of the TV lounge, the public drinking lounge, or one's own room. What has happened to the deep flowered armchairs of the residents' lounge, with its pile of tattered copies of *The Field, Country Life, The Lady*, and so on? Gone with everything else good.

I feel our parting keenly – that sort of breathless pain so associated with you, too silly and complicated to explain. It was kind of you to say

---

[23] Arthur Wood, co-deputy librarian with Brenda Moon. His health suddenly deteriorated in January 1971, and he died early in February.

you value our friendship. Sometimes I think I do nothing for you but entangle you in my own hopeless life, to your loss. I only hope I do cheer you up sometimes. You are very kind to me. I sound like my idea of D——, don't I!

Friday, before breakfast A patchy night, but reasonably comfortable. I wonder if it's going to be hot again. I took a quick walk round the town between 5 & 6 yesterday & didn't think it looked very good for its purpose (our holiday), though rather fascinating, like Wincolmlea (is it?) with shops.[24] The Ouse very muddy and smells rather. I expect we shall spend the morning at any rate looking at such shops as there are.

I do hope you have a successful day, pursuing your intrepid path down into Wales. Send me a little word as soon as you can, so that I'll know you're safe. I hope too that the car goes well and there are no mechanical worries. In the meantime I send love and a *loving* kiss, and hope you are having a good holiday once you settle down.

XXX

Philip

PS *After breakfast* – how lovely to have your card & hear from you so quickly! Thank you so much. I'm delighted to hear you got to Oxford safely – isn't the Towcester-Oxford road slow! especially if you get behind a lorry – and found your way to Ruth. Not so pleased with the young man: *curse to Hell* every young (*and middle-aged*) swine who wants to get his hands on you. I'm not surprised though: in addition to being *smashingly* beautiful, you *radiate* charm, kindness & friendliness.

After breakfast I asked at Reception '*If* by any chance there *were* any post for us, *where* would it be? After some thought the girl said 'Here', & withdrew a battered cardboard box from under the desk – the sort of box you keep records of subscriptions discontinued in Miss Cuming's[25] time in – and lethargically sorted through the accumulation of post for people who *hadn't* asked ... I don't think this place is designed for long stayers.

Well, dearest, I must escort Mother out on her usual postcard hunt. I'll write again before long. Pray all goes well on the road today.

Much love, dear,

Philip

---

[24] Wincolmlee is an industrial area on the banks of the River Hull.
[25] Larkin's predecessor as Librarian at Hull.

578, Beverley High Road,
Hull.

7th May 1974

My very dear Philip,

I want to be one of the first to congratulate you on the appearance of
High Windows.

I read all except one or two of the longer poems late last night, and
was delighted to find several which had given me much pleasure in the
past, have done so now, and will do so again.

But my greatest pleasure was in receiving one of the first six copies of
the book. And the inscription means a very great deal to me, as only you
will know! I hope the book will receive as happy a reception with your
reading public as its presentation means to me. Thank you very much.

With love from

Maeve

⟨∞⟩

St John's College
Oxford

St George's Day 1975

Maeve dear,

I've just had my B. Pym lunch, in the Randolph Hotel – ghastly food,
Trust House at its worst – and hurry to send a word in addition to the
postcard. The day has turned into a really pleasant one as far as the sun
is concerned – very warm & friendly. B. Pym was a bit like Joyce Grenfell,
but very pleasant and accommodating.

She is still under care after her mastectomy (is it?) and of course she
did have a sort of stroke recently, but she seemed quite normal.

How are you, dear? I hope the disagreeable impact of returning to
work has worn off, and Brenda C. has come back. I dread the start of
term, & reading all the replies to rude letters I sent just before I went
away – but I look forward to seeing you.

Much love,

Philip

105 Newland Park
Hull HU5 2DT
7 August 1975

Maeve dear,

It's rather early to be writing to you, but I mistrust the GPO and Irish hotels and indeed the whole business of getting a letter to you in the wilds of incompetent Ireland. I hope you got away safely with a well Moira, and arrived equally safely, and find the hotel expecting you and generally all right.

When I rang my sister tonight to say I should like to come to lunch on Sunday she said Walter was 'in hospital' with 'food poisoning'. I expect it's no more than Moira had: Walter's a fearful hypochondriac. Funny they should both have been to the same part of the world. I believe there's a similar bug roving about this country anyway. Hope it doesn't come my way.

Thanks for your annual report, wch I read with great interest. Parts of it ought to be set to music, preferably by Wagner. Overture: High, Medium and Low. The Ride of the Working Parties. The Met Deadline: an Idyll. Death Song of Cancellations (duet: Blackwell and a Subscription). No, seriously, I am glad to have such a coherent and in parts funny account of what went on. I am shaping up to draft my own report now. I don't know whether to do the short one first, in the hope that it'll inspire me to do the long one, or the long one in the hope that it'll make the short one easier. Whichever I choose will be wrong, I expect.

I wish you hadn't gone away just when you did: I miss you. A fearful boiling night was diversified by two dreams about you, both 'losing' dreams – you going off with someone else – wch was all very silly, for how can one lose what one doesn't possess? I hope it will be cooler tonight.

Cards from Brenda have begun to arrive, recounting the flowering of waterlilies on the lochans (whatever they are) and other exciting (her word) events. The Library is beautifully peaceful, as is the whole university: sometime I must write a poem about the academic year. It's like the farmer's year: sowing, storms, snow, spring, sun, harvest & so on. Mrs S. & a colleague are busily engaged in bookshop business in the catalogue hall. I spoke to them & she began to grumble about aspects of life in the bookshop! [...]

The visit to Devon is still unsettled. I wrote to Bruce today saying that

I really didn't think 20–22 Aug was on: 19–22, or 18–21, yes, but where's the sense in travelling all that way for one day? He may say, come 19th, of course. I don't know. It sounds an awful fag.

John Brown rang up today, offering a run of the Oxford U. *Gazette* for carriage – carriage being a trip to Hull *for him*. I'm torn between accepting an Oxford item & filling our shelves with junk.

Well, I must see if my room is fit to sleep in. Have a good holiday, dear. I look forward to your return.

Lots of kisses in all sorts of places
Philip

＠

3rd November 1975

My dearest Philip,

I am so sorry I missed you today, and I don't even know whether or not you got the hastily scribbled message I left with Sally B. If you didn't, you will not know that I made several attempts to contact you by phone, and personally, but without success. I daren't stay any longer because I had a very long agenda for the Division Meeting, and I hate to arrive back just on time, with no opportunity to compose myself [...]

I wanted to know if you were feeling better from the cardial [*sic*] [26] condition, and if your cold had developed. And of course I had wanted to wish you well for tomorrow's proceedings and to assure you that you are bound to carry off the occasion with grace and great dignity.[27] Finally I should have wished that you would enjoy it, and that it will be an occasion with pleasant memories for you.

I loved our weekend and all its thrilling associations. It's funny how it was almost a repetition of the same weekend last year, with equally beautiful weather. It is very hard for me to believe that after all this time I have not grown stale for you. Needless to say, it is also the most wonderful thing that ever happened to me. It wouldn't be like that with any marriage partner after 14/15 years, so look what we have gained!

I shall look forward to hearing all about your visit to London, to see the Queen! But I don't look quite so forward to opening the evening

[26] 'cardiac' is the obvious word, but not one I would be likely to get wrong; 'cardialgia' = heartburn; 'cardia' = upper opening of the stomach which lies immediately behind the heart.

[27] In June 1975 Larkin was awarded the CBE, which he went to collect in November, accompanied by Monica Jones.

paper tomorrow night, nor the Wednesday morning editions! My only reason is that I may have to counter awkward remarks from my family. I don't care about anyone else.

With much love,

Maeve
And extra special xxx

☙✠❧

105 Newland Park
Hull HU5 2DT
25 May 1977

Maeve dear,

'No letters' needn't stop me writing to you,[28] I hope, as of course you're much in my mind and I should like to keep in touch, however tenuously.

I'm sure that the present days are as unhappy as the earlier ones – perhaps more so in a way – but at least one is dealing with certainty rather than uncertainty, and there are practical matters to be coped with. I hope you're finding the strength to deal with them all, one by one – don't try to face more than one thing at a time. But you will already be better schooled in this kind of ordeal than I.

It's being a wretched time: as if the week has taken its tone from your distress. I am deeply at war with the Staffing Committee: all this upsets me fearfully. I've just 'had lunch' for the first time at 'the Club': I asked for two sandwiches & when they arrived they were about a quarter of a loaf each. I had to pass one on to some other character. All this to avoid the hog-faces at the bar!

There isn't much news at the Library as far as I know. I hope *one day* we can have a quiet drink together. I will look in at 6 pm on either Thursday or Friday – perhaps Friday might be better. Much love, dear, and all sympathy –

Philip

---

[28] Following my mother's death on 22 May.

105 Newland Park
Hull HU5 2DT
3 Aug '77 Tuesday

Maeve dear,

This is just to say you will be constantly in my mind in the next few days, and perhaps this may count as a sort of prayers. [sic]

I shall ask for news, and hope to see you as soon as is welcome.

Much love,

Philip

೧✕೨

Wed. 3rd Aug. 1 am 1977

Dear Philip,

As you can imagine, our manner of parting upset me grievously. Your note went some way to assuaging the hurt, and I was thankful to get it.

Could you please come and see me this evening,[29] Wednesday, 6–6.30 ish, I suppose, but try to ascertain when Brenda intends to visit (as she does, after work) and prevent her if it means clashing. It is very important that I see you alone if at all possible.

I shall not refer to our disagreement, but beg you to think of some way of breaking this six-week parting from 24th. August–3rd October in the next three weeks. Please don't fail me at this time.

I long for the comfort I didn't get from you yesterday.

Maeve

೧✕೨

The Inn for All Seasons,
Great Barrington,
Nr. Burford,
Oxon.

21st Sept. 1977

My dear Philip,

I realise that if I do not write to you again soon, you will not receive a letter before you set off for London or Oxford. It's a pity we don't yet know whether we are extending our visit down here beyond 27th or not.

---

[29] In hospital, where I was due to undergo surgery the following day.

If so, perhaps you would have driven out for a drink one evening. My guess is that we probably will by a day or two but the weather is not at all encouraging; very cold and grey at best; wet and cold at worst. However the holiday is relaxing us both and we are very comfortable at the Inn. It is very cosy in the evenings up by the log fires either in the buttery or the bar. We retire to bed – or rather to our bedrooms quite early – soon after ten. It sounds very dull, but reading in bed is enjoyable and very therapeutic. My appetite has returned and my sleep pattern is coming back, enabling me to cut down on the sleeping dope gradually. In fact I feel much more restored and more like my former self, although I still cringe mentally at the long haul ahead, and the many problems yet to be faced. Still, following the advice of the hymn, 'Lord for tomorrow and its needs, I do not pray'.

My G.P. doesn't want to see me again until 17th October. I imagine he will let me return then or just after, but said he believed women should have 3 months off after this operation. We'll see. I couldn't stand another long spell at home.

I have more or less arranged with Frances to go to her for 8 or 9 days around 5th October but no-one except her is exactly encouraging me to go. I still feel I need a break from all the mental strain of the last few months, in company completely disassociated with events causing the strain.

I am taking the opportunity of this break to do pretty well all of my Christmas shopping. I am getting on quite well with it! We went to the N.T. shop at Hidcote Manor today but it wasn't nice enough to go round the gardens, so I just did a lot of shopping there. Cavendish House of course is a mouse's dream of heaven. We are going to a matineé performance of *A Lion in Winter* in Cheltenham tomorrow. I'm pretty sure Katherine Hepburn was Queen Eleanor in the film version and Peter O'Toole (whom I don't like) was Henry II. We don't plan to go to Stratford this time unless we remain until the end of the month when we might try for a matineé of *As You Like It.*

Brenda came and had dinner with us last night. She was full of enthusiasm for her various research plans which she had been pursuing at Oxford and hoped to continue at Bristol [...]

By the time you receive this you will be thinking about the Booker meeting, followed by Sconul. I have your Oxford address so had better send my next communication, if any, there. I feel I have almost forgotten what you look like and it seems like a millennium since we spent an evening together. I suppose life will never be the same again. My Mother's associations with Cheltenham and this area make memories of her very keen and very sad. I can't bear to go into the restaurant she frequented in Cavendish House; fortunately there's another, a little coffee bar which holds no memories of her. I don't know when I shall see you – the separation just seems to go on and on.

All for now. I shall probably only send a notelet to Brasenose. I have written so many cards this holiday, my pen needs a rest!

With very much love dear,

Maeve

P.S. I am enjoying M. C. Wedderburn's autobiography, and the car is much easier to drive.

M

☞☜

Cottingham

19th November 1977

My dearest,

My thoughts have been much with you ever since Betty 'phoned me on Wed. afternoon to say you had been called by the nursing home. We agreed it would be better not to try and 'phone you at Newland Park as it would cause delay which would probably be vital. Freda brought me the news of your Mother's death on Thursday, during the final stages of the removal from 578. I am glad you got to her bedside in time, although she probably wasn't conscious. I know you will take it hardly, because, despite the frustration and helplessness you often felt in regard to her various circumstances in the last 20 years, you were nevertheless deeply attached to her. Your extreme sensitivity will not help you and for you, as for me, it will mean a terrific emotional re-adjustment. I am very, very sorry for you.

However, as you yourself said after your last visit to the nursing home, your Mother's life was not really worth living. You cannot, must not, wish for the prolongation of her slow dying which was all her life had been in the last 12 months.

I am very anxious to get this off by today's post and am writing at the hairdresser's, and therefore cannot send you a little prayer card which someone sent to me on the same sad occasion. However I can remember more appropriate parts of it which is probably better, since you can't believe the Christian outlook on life and death. Nevertheless this little bit of it is comforting and helps one to cope with the death of a loved one a little ... 'Life is eternal and love is immortal. Death is only a horizon and a horizon is only the limit of our sight' ...

You know full well that I know exactly what you are going through, having experienced it all so recently myself. Is this the most important bond we shall ever have between us, the incidence of both our Mothers' deaths within 6 months, in 1977? My darling, please accept this very inadequate expression of my sympathy, and be glad that your Mother doesn't have to go on living in the twilight world which was her existence for so long.

It hardly seems appropriate to refer to my own affairs, but I know you will want to know how the move went. Well enough, I suppose; but it was quite the most ghastly experience I have yet had. I think you said the dismantling of 578 was like the fall of the House of Ussher [*sic*]. It was terrible; but Dermot & Moira have been wonderful for weeks past, and Peter & Jan. Crowther were both enormously helpful on Thurs. evening. They at least got us to bed, by clearing the mountains of books left on each bed, by the removal men, and actually made up our beds for us. I fear I have undone all the good which my long convalescence did me and feel I have done myself internal damage. It is very timely that I have an appointment to see Mr. Madden on Monday. I fear/hope he will order complete rest for a week.

I hope this letter will reach you before too long, but don't know where else to contact you in the Midlands. No doubt there will be much to-ing and fro-ing from York Road. I shall be thinking of you and all the sadness and worry which faces you. I am only too recently familiar with it. Then you have the Booker Prize Award on Wednesday. I hope it goes well; at least you haven't time to dwell on it before it is on you. Try to have courage; and just go with the tide of life; it is all you can do just now.

All my sympathy, love, and good wishes for 23rd, dearest.

Maeve

❧

Leicester

22 Nov 1977

Maeve dear,

Many thanks for your letter, wch my sister picked up and was able to give me yesterday. I knew you would be thinking of me, but it was very comforting to hear in reality. Yes, it is odd our mothers should die in the same year, & that mine shd die on the day you left your old home.

The funeral was yesterday, a cold & wet day. My sister & I then went to the solicitor and put the legal side in hand. There is a good deal to be done yet! I'll tell you more about it when I see you.

I went to All Souls in the end, and went to chapel on the Sunday. Strangely enough they read Ps. 39 wch is part of the burial service and was read at my father's funeral in 1948.

Now, dear, I am very sorry to hear of the awfulness of the move and of the possible set-back in your convalescence. I sincerely hope you do have a further period of rest. How kind of those who helped you! I'm afraid I did very little – did those electric things work? By the way, there are two kinds of kitchen timer – 1 hour and 5 hours – wch do you want?

I'll be back Thursday evening & give you a ring. Meanwhile many thanks for your sympathy & love. It is all v. sudden when it comes, even in this case.

Much love, dear

Philip

☙

105 Newland Park
HULL HU5 2DT
17 March 1978

Dear Maeve,

I write none the less, to repeat my regret at Thursday's debacle and to apologise for it. It was all so different from what I had imagined, yet looking back I now see how very improbable that was and how silly it was of me to think it could have been achieved. The whole thing was a fitting climax to a day of – a week of – increasing discomfort about it all. I'm deeply sorry that you should have suffered through it. Please believe me when I say that none of it was intentional. Not that that excuses me.

I realise that you are very hurt, and that this explains the angry home truths, as last August. I know most of these are justified (not quite all), but they leave their sting. Perhaps when we feel better we can meet again. I don't say this vindictively: I am extremely sad about it all.

Philip

[This short letter signalled the end of our eighteen-year intimacy. As recorded in my memoir, we had been to a performance of *Larkinland* at the University the previous evening. It ended in a serious misunderstanding and I considered Philip had gravely misled me about the subsequent reception. We parted company but before making my way home, I left a hastily written note at 105 Newland Park, indicating that I felt our relationship had reached the end of the road.

We did not meet the following day but a bitter quarrel took place on the 'phone that evening. I, in particular, vented some painful home truths which merely widened the rift between us. Philip's letter (above), written later that evening, did little to reassure me that the breach could easily be healed.

By contrast, my letter two days later was a heartfelt admission of blame and self-reproach. At the same time I tried to vindicate my earlier outburst over the 'phone as a cry of desperation, prompted by the ever-present threat which Monica posed to our relationship, and the severe depression I had suffered for many months, brought about by illness and my mother's death. The letter survives but for personal reasons I do not wish to reproduce it here.

After a weekend of profound soul-searching, Philip came to see me at home, in effect to end our affair. He presented his case gently, but rationally. He accepted full responsibility for allowing the situation between Monica, himself and me to continue unchecked for so long. My position in particular, he conceded, was untenable. He blamed himself for being indecisive and weak. He felt that Monica's health would break down before his and when that time came, he would want to take care of her. Our quarrel, he said, had profoundly shaken him but it nevertheless provided the catalyst which spurred him to make the ultimate choice between Monica and me. He felt he had no alternative. I was shattered but admitted the logic of his resolution.

After an initial distance, we resumed a close, but Platonic friendship which was not always easy to sustain on this level. I believe I remained just as much a confidante as Monica or Betty to the end of his life, and as the final exchanges which follow show, our relationship, if somewhat restrained, had regained much of its earlier sensitivity and warmth.]

105 Newland Park

Hull HU5 2DT

14 November 1985

My dear Maeve,

I am deeply sorry to say that I shan't be able to be present on the 21 November.[30] On Tuesday I developed some new alarming (though they don't seem to alarm Richardson) symptoms wch. are now being analysised [sic] & all that by the Health Laboratories. He has therefore signed me off for the week (next week).

I have written to Eddie asking him to officiate. Despite your feelings & mine, the show must go on. It will be a very big occasion.

I shall also miss the LC on Monday & seeing the VC on Tuesday about the dep'ship. It is all very 'uncharacteristic'.

Two things: I really do feel wretched and incapable. Second, although as you know I was rather dreading this occasion I knew it had to be [me] who did it, for all the reasons we both know. But this is one of life's little ironies.

V. affectionately,

Philip

☙❦☙

Cottingham

First Sunday of Advent 1985

[This letter, written a few hours before Philip's death, was never posted]

My dear Philip,

I had written to you last night but the news that you are now in the Nuffield again meant re-writing my letter. I am so sorry you are feeling no better and know how low and wretched you must be feeling. Perhaps you need anti-depressants which are stronger than tranquilisers. I had to have the former in December 1981 for several months and again in September 1983 for another spell. I hope, at any rate, that you will be given something to pick you up and raise your spirits quickly. I am sure you are in the best place since you were making no progress at home.

I had tentatively asked in my first letter if it had occurred to you to

[30] The date of my retirement party.

229

consult Aber [31] again. You were very impressed by his thoroughness and accurate diagnosis even though it was not what you wanted to hear. However, I suppose you will have to let events take their course for the time being, but it might be worth bearing in mind.

I don't know if you even want letters, let alone visitors, so I will close now. If there is anything I can do, I should be only too pleased to do it, as you well know.

I look forward to hearing better reports soon. In the meantime you are much in thought.

Affectionately,

Maeve

[31] Dr Clive Aber, cardiologist: the first consultant Philip saw at the beginning of his illness.

Index

Markievicz, Constance 8, 10
  see also Marreco, Anne, *The Rebel Countess*
Marks and Spencer 56–7
Marreco, Anne, *The Rebel Countess* 212n.22, 215, 216
Marshall, Alan 30, 31, 122, 123, 160
Marshall, Thomas Falcon 44
Marvell Press 22, 23, 103, 104
McGough, Roger 85
McKeown, Ann 99
'MCMXIV' 131, 134
McNally, Margaret (Peg) 116–18
Merriman, John 96
Milton, John 80
Miss Bianca books (Sharp) 50, 203, 217
Modern Academic Library, The: Essays in memory of Philip Larkin (Brian Dyson, ed.) (*MAL*) 3, 106, 125
'Moment of Ecstasy' letter 5–6, 43, 73–4, 79, 80–2, 146
Monitor: Down Cemetery Road (BBC) 23, 54, 60–2
Monteith, Charles 96, 98, 101, 102, 206
Montgomery, Bruce 135, 220–1
Moon, Brenda 29–30, 94, 96, 97, 100, 101, 106, 125, 127, 129, 166, 176, 196, 204, 210, 211, 220, 223–4
'Morning at last: there in the snow' 66, 67
Morris, John 124–5
Morrison, Blake 103
Motion, Andrew 67–8, 70, 85, 98
  Philip Larkin: A Writer's Life (*Life*) 51, 67, 68, 69, 72, 78, 79, 85, 102, 109, 115–21, 119, 120, 131, 133
  'Philip Larkin: Sex and Political Correctness' 110

Mottuel, Michèle *see* Roullet, Michèle (*later* Michèle Mottuel)
Mowat, Ian 3
'Mower, The' 64–5
'Mr. Bleaney' 25
Murdoch, Iris 206
Murphy, Patsy (*formerly* Strang) 25, 135
Murphy, Richard 86
music 30, 31, 43, 51–4
  classical 52–3
  Gregorian chant 53
  jazz 51–3, 62, 70, 101–3, 124
Myers, Angela 46

National Heritage Memorial Fund 3
National Lending Library *later* British Library Document Supply Collections (BLDSC) 27
National Manuscript Collection of Contemporary Writers 85
'Neglected Responsibility, A' 85
  see also manuscripts, preservation of
New English Bible with the Apocrypha 75–6
'New Larkins for Old' (first international conference) 108–9, 112
  see also Philip Larkin Society
New Statesman 62
New York Review of Books 60
Newland Park 64–5, 87, 97
Newman, John Henry, Cardinal, *Dream of Gerontius* 64
nicknames 49–50, 144
'North Ship, The' 134
North Ship, The 56
Nowell, Hilary 113–14

Oakes, Philip 62
obituaries 100, 109